A SCANDAL AT FEL

C000043686

BOSWORTH

www.ascandalatfelbrigg.co.uk

A Scandal at Felbrigg

The true story of the notorious
Miss Willoughby and 'Mad' Windham

TREVOR HEATON

BOSWORTH

www.ascandalatfelbrigg.co.uk

First published 2012
Reprinted 2013, 2014
ISBN 978-0-9551153-4-1

Published by Bosworth Books, Rose End, Whissonsett, Dereham NR20 5AP

Cover design and production by 4plus2 Design (07834 736817)

Typeset in 11 on 14pt Garamond

Printed by Lightning Source

cover picture: Agnes 'Willoughby' (nee Rogers). (*Mary Evans Picture Library*)

'From the moment [they] met... *she* was his evil genius'

Norwich Argus,
17 February 1866

Acknowledgements

MANY PEOPLE have helped me with this project. I am particularly grateful to Helen Denney, who has enabled me to understand Agnes' context within the family. The novelist, broadcaster, and critic D J Taylor has taken a personal interest in the project and I am immensely appreciative of his sound advice and constant encouragement. My wife Velma has been supportive throughout and has helped with research.

My special thanks are due, too, to Sue Giddings (London Borough of Sutton Local Studies Section), Rosemary Dixon (Librarian, Archant Norfolk), Ruth Battersby Tooke (Norfolk Museums and Archaeology Service), Caitlín Browne (Co. Roscommon Library Service, Ireland), and the always-helpful staff of the Norfolk and Norwich Millennium Library, Norfolk Record Office, General Register Office, British Library, British Library Newspapers (Colindale), The National Archives, the General Cemetery Company, Her Majesty's Courts Service (York Probate Sub Registry), Dorset History Centre, Surrey History Centre, West Suffolk Record Office, National Trust staff and volunteers at Ickworth and Felbrigg. Julie Dicks and Sylvia Roberts helped read the manuscript and provided important comments. Michelle Grigg helped with information about Agnes Rogers' family background. My thanks, too, to photographer Bill Smith for his painstaking work in providing illustrations. Any mistakes, of course, are my own.

I am grateful too to Peter Stibbons of Poppyland Publishing, Jan Mayor of 4plus2 Design and my former colleagues Ian Collins, Steve Snelling and Mark Nicholls.

A note on modern monetary equivalents: these are notoriously fraught with difficulty, as comparing a price from a previous era with the modern day is not simply a question of a formula, as the relative values of goods, services, wages and land have fluctuated. For simplicity's sake I have followed the converter provided by The National Archives at www.nationalarchives.gov.uk/currency/.

Introduction

IT IS a fine day for a funeral.

The carriages are all here now. The great and the good of the county and beyond have come to pay their respects to one of their own. Horses' bridles jangle, and frosty-breathed coach drivers huddle and stamp their feet in a vain effort to keep warm. They get no help from the January sun, which seems to have barely made the effort to make its daily appearance. As they look from the great house of Felbrigg to its wide acres, and then across to the estate church marooned a few hundred yards away, it is a scene which seems almost devoid of colour, as if painted by the hand of a divine but desultory watercolourist.

In this landscape, it is black which is the starkest colour. In the distance, the handsome trees of the estate are in their gaunt winter guises. Closer, the carriages are dark-liveried, enlivened only by the occasional faded gilding of a coat of arms. The mourners gradually emerge into the thin daylight. There are almost two hundred of them, great-coated and top-hatted, or bonneted and crinolined, and all of them in black.

They all know each other, of course. Not just through the ties of family, but through connections made at school and club, regiment and office, parlour and dinner table. The nods they make to each other convey a world of meaning; they all know the code. 'You here too? - bad business, this - never knew him too well, of course - something of a reputation, if you get my drift...'

Their attention is suddenly taken by a strange youth approaching from the front of the house. At first they take him for one of the rougher sorts of servant, then realise, almost exactly at the same instant, that this is *him*. The boy; the heir to all these vast acres; William Frederick Windham. He is - they quickly work out the passing of the years as the youth approaches - what, 14 years old? Big for his age, with his clothes barely enough to contain his ungainly body, as if his arms and legs have been flung out through centripetal force. As he comes closer they see his heavy, clumsy gait and the curious drawing-up of his top lip to expose his front teeth.

And he is smiling. No, *laughing*. A braying, discordant laugh. 'So good to see you - glad you could come - would you like to see the coffin?' For the distant Hervey and Windham relatives this is the first time they have seen the boy. Of course there have been hints at the dinner table, scribbled postscripts to family letters, that sort of thing - but nothing has prepared them for this.

Time crawls. The mourners are seated now in the boxed pews of St Margaret's Church. A church door opens and there is a shuffling of feet as the estate workers carry the oak coffin to the front of the building. Behind the coffin walks the widow, Lady Sophia, nervous and slight, and with her - still smiling, and looking round the church as if looking for a favourite playmate - is her son.

Soon, as the rector begins the lesson, a low keening sound is heard from the front pew. It grows in intensity, louder and louder until it drowns out the priest's words, then rises in pitch still further until it is transformed into an almost animal-like cry of pain and despair. In the pews, the mourners shift uncomfortably. Some, iron-willed, keep their eyes on the rector, but most of the others dart glances behind their orders of service.

In their embarrassed state they are not to know what the author of that unearthly sound will soon bring to these ancient acres. They are not to know that in a few short years both his name, and that of Felbrigg, will become famous - or rather, infamous - the length and breadth of the land, and beyond. They are not to know that scandal will scorch across the path of public life like a meteor, illuminating some of the darkest corners of the secret lives of the land-owning classes.

That is for the future. For now, at this moment, in this lonely Norfolk church it is a matter of shocked whispers, or of thoughts barely articulated. And they are all saying, or thinking, the same thing: 'The boy - my God - the boy!'

1

1840-1854:
A Tale of Two Childhoods

Azure a chevron between three lions erased or; family motto 'Au Bon Droit': 'With Good Right'
The arms of the Windham family

A FAMILY does not own a house for 400 years without shaping it with the quirks and enthusiasms of its more active and richer members. And so it is with the Norfolk estate of Felbrigg. The long carriage driveway, flanked on the north by woodland and to the south by pasture and parkland, soon leaves behind the throb of the Norwich-Cromer holiday traffic.

As you draw near the first impressions are of a jumble of buildings, a stable block and a service wing. But move to the south, and the classical Jacobean frontage of the hall is opened up. Work on it began around 1620, with Norfolk flint, brick and pebble inlaid with Ketton limestone and a layer of rendering to protect it from the relentless Norfolk coastal weather. Around the corner of the house is another surprise, a 1680s West Front built at right angles to its Jacobean predecessor. Its restrained elegance is in contrast to the oldest part of the house. Here the rendering is, in places, beginning to erode, leaving a palimpsest of repairs made over centuries, exposed flintwork and plaster.

Felbrigg endures. But the Windhams did not.

William Howe Windham: An energetic and far-sighted landowner, but also a man whose argumentative and domineering personality won him few friends or admirers.

(©National Trust Images/John McLean)

IN 1833 it was a very different story. William Howe Windham came into the property at the age of 31 on the death of his father, Vice-Admiral William (Lukin) Windham. The new owner of Felbrigg set about combining an active political career with a determination to build, improve, and expand the estate. Felbrigg seemed on the threshold of a new golden age. And yet, only 23 years earlier, it had looked as if the tenure of the Windhams was drawing to a close.

The family had first come into absolute ownership of the estate in 1461. It passed down the generations, but not without the occasional dynastic mishap (including a beheading). The Norfolk Windhams gradually died out in the 16th century, leaving Sir John Wyndham of the family's Somerset branch to inherit in 1608. The existing medieval and Tudor houses were largely swept away for the grand 1620 house, made grander still by the 1680 extension under the patronage of William Windham I, who also planted hundreds of trees. His son Ashe had a calamitous falling-out with his wife in 1720, but luckily only after she had produced an heir, William.

When he was older William Windham II duly went on the Grand Tour, regarded as an essential part of the education of every well-to-do young man. He accumulated the usual plethora of paintings - which still cluster round the walls of the room at Felbrigg known as The Cabinet - but also a complicated love life involving a betrothal (expensively untangled) in Switzerland and a pair of mistresses in London.

He eventually married one of those mistresses, Mrs Lukin, and fathered a son who became the first member of the family to achieve national fame. The Rt Hon William Windham III served as Secretary at War from 1794-1801, and from 1806-7 as Secretary for War and the Colonies. The Felbrigg estate then passed to a distant

12

relative, Vice-Admiral William Lukin, who kept the now-celebrated Windham name alive by the simply expedient of changing his own. In the subsequent events, much was made of young William Frederick Windham's links - and his poor contrast with - his famous forebear, but the truth was it was Lukin and not Windham blood which flowed in his veins.

Felbrigg: Pictured in the mid-nineteenth century, when it had largely acquired the appearance it would maintain until the present day. *(NRO ref: MC580/1, 780x1)*

WILLIAM Howe Windham proceeded to run the estate with as much energy as any of his namesakes. His father had remodelled the house, and now his son continued the process, ensuring the farms on the estate were modernised and adding two new sets of lodges, among much else. William Howe Windham was a passionate supporter of the Whig cause, serving briefly as an MP for Norfolk, an attachment which would often bring him into heated argument with his neighbours.

That argumentative side to his character was often commented upon, and rarely favourably. He was quick to grow angry and swear out loud - and did not give a damn who heard it, whether local worthies or his servants and estate workers. Charles Meering, his head gamekeeper, recalled how Windham used to swear a great deal

Lady Sophia Hervey: A member of an unconventional aristocratic family, her fey and nervous nature would lead her to be dominated by her future husband and, latterly, her son. *(©National Trust Images)*

when 'hot and passionate', while Mrs Martin, who as Felbrigg's cook and housekeeper for almost 30 years had an intimate knowledge of the family, chose her words rather more carefully, describing him as 'quick, hasty, and passionate at times'. Sir William Foster, a Norwich solicitor who had stewardship of the Windham estates for 40 years, said he had been 'hasty and choleric'.

One similarity between William Howe and William Frederick was the loudness of their voices. Time and again, even young Windham's supporters in later life conceded that his habit of shouting created a bad impression in polite circles. In 1835 William Howe Windham married Lady Sophia Hervey, youngest daughter of the first Marquis of Bristol. The family seat of Ickworth, a few miles from Bury St Edmunds, is now - like Felbrigg - in the care of the National Trust. Much was made in subsequent years of the effects of William Howe Windham's forceful personality on his son's character. But of equal significance, and arguably more, was that of his mother. There is a portrait in the Museum Room at Ickworth of the young Lady Sophia, probably painted in the early 1830s (she was born in 1811) which shows her in a standard, though rather unconvincing, pose on horseback. She has a certain conventional early nineteenth century prettiness, with dark-brown ringlets spilling out from under her elaborate riding hat, a girlishness which had matured - but only slightly - by the time of her post-marriage portrait which can be seen at Felbrigg.

Lady Sophia was the sixth child of Frederick William, 5th Earl of Bristol and first Marquis. The Hervey family had a well-known streak of unconventionality, with previous members including the flamboyantly ambiguously-sexual John, Lord Hervey and the eccentric Earl-Bishop (Lady Sophia's grandfather). From the first, Lady Sophia was in the considerable shadow of her new husband; daughter of a marquis she might be, but this was no question of a marriage of equals. She was nervous and uncertain, 'a person of excitable temper', as one lawyer later described her.

THIS, THEN, was the world into which William Frederick Windham was born on 9 August 1840. Unlike other members of the Hervey family (Lady Sophia was one of nine siblings, her grandfather one of eight, her great-grandfather one of 17), Lady Sophia was not blessed with fecundity; William Frederick was to be her only child Young William Frederick was given the family nickname of 'Gla' at an early age, with obvious (to modern eyes at least) learning disabilities soon becoming apparent. Young Gla exhibited a tendency for strangeness which concerned his father and mother. But it took until 1844 or 1845 for William Howe Windham to consult a Norwich doctor, Dr William Nicholls. He considered him well-placed to give an expert verdict: Dr Nicholls was the owner of Heigham Hall, a large private asylum, and also chief medical officer at the Bethel Hospital for the insane in the Norfolk city. Dr Nicholls visited Felbrigg and observed the young William over several days. His verdict was not reassuring. The doctor believed that Gla's 'deficiency of intellect', which showed itself in his inability to speak, would only increase with age. He was a child of 'defective mental organisation' which would most likely turn itself into fully-fledged idiocy later in life. Gla's father, shocked, did not consult Dr Nicholls on the subject again, but did remain in touch with him over the coming years.

One of the signs claimed for this apparent lack of intellect was young Gla's habit of slobbering, which for those sharing a dinner table with him could be a trying experience. Throughout his life this was taken as the most obvious physical sign of his idiocy. But the truth had probably more to do with genetics, not intellect. Young Windham's had a peculiarly-shaped mouth with a narrow upper jaw, something which had been seen in at least three members of Lady Sophia's family. This was to cause him huge problems in eating in later life, and was even blamed for the way he laughed. The top of his mouth was drawn to a narrow point, which had the effect of pulling up his top lip, a feature which Windham tried - unsuccessfully - to disguise in his early 20s by growing a moustache.

That problem was bad enough, but Lady Sophia also put her young son through the ordeal of 1840s orthodontic techniques between the ages of eight and ten. The surgeon extracted several teeth, then inserted a plate with pegs or wedges into his mouth to stretch the upper jaw. The operation was a complete, and painful, failure. It was the second time he had been let down by a medical procedure: while still an infant, Windham had been operated on for being tongue-tied, a condition in which the frenulum - the thin connection under the bottom of the tongue to the lower jaw - is abnormally short. Lady Sophia blamed her son's later slavering on the failure of this operation.

PERHAPS William Howe Windham was profoundly disappointed in his son and heir. Certainly Dr Nicholls' verdict had shocked him, but at the same time he showed a high level of indulgence towards his son. And here was the root of another of young William's problems. There was no evidence his parents ever agreed on a consistent approach to their son's behaviour. Merlin Waterson, in his 2011 book A Noble Thing, has suggested that Windham's condition could best be described as 'disinhibited', with suggestions of ADHD (attention deficit hyperactivity disorder) or perhaps Tourette's Syndrome. But Tourette's was not described until 1885; in these early Victorian times doctors reached for the terms they understood: idiotic, high-spirited, passionate, choleric - and, naturally, 'mad'.

A family friend, Norwich surgeon Dr Donald Dalrymple, said: 'He was not what I should call a petted child. He was often restrained by one parent for a fault, which the other passed over... he was an only child, and a spoilt child.' And Mrs Martin, once again with her privileged position at the heart of the Felbrigg household, confirmed that the Windhams had been inconsistent, veering wildly from indulgence to severity. His uncle Lord Alfred Hervey, too, said: 'He was a spoilt boy, and very badly managed at home. His father was very passionate, and he was very unequally treated. Sometimes he was indulged and sometimes he was rebuked.' At first Lord Alfred could use Gla's affection for his mother as a way of controlling his behaviour.

But as Windham grew older, invoking her feelings grew less and less effective.

The first attempt to educate the young heir began early in 1844 when he was aged three. Miss Rauschen served as nursery-governess for young Gla until August 1846. She later recalled him being 'very high-spirited' - governess-speak for badly behaved - who required a great deal of telling-off before he would attend to his lessons. But she insisted he was also 'sharp and intelligent'. It was a view not shared by many.

Solicitor William Henry Scott acted for Gla's father on several occasions, and had known the boy since the age of five. 'I early formed the opinion that he was of weak intellect,' he said later, basing his opinion on young Windham being over-excited in play, being prone to 'unreasonable fits of passion' and with a peculiarly vacant expression.

From his early years, young Gla must have been a trial to take into polite company, so much so that on a family visit to Brighton aged seven or eight, his mother resorted to carrying a small whip to discipline him. The Windhams took more notice of their son when he reached the age of seven and was able to follow his father around the estate on his pony, and also to take part in games of whist (Mrs Martin making a fourth) which became an almost-nightly ritual.

Life was undeniably lonely for young Gla at Felbrigg. His father was out and about his estate at every opportunity, leaving his young son to his own devices. And when William Howe Windham returned back to the hall after another long day in the saddle or on foot, he often fell asleep straight after his dinner. The boy craved companionship in vain in the dark and chilly rooms of Felbrigg Hall, with its rows of Grand Tour paintings and portraits of patrician ancestors staring down disapprovingly. He had found some fellowship in

William Frederick Windham: The portrait of the young heir which still hangs in the Morning Room at Felbrigg. A lonely childhood was combined with learning and behavioural issues. (©*National Trust Images/John McLean*)

the rough-and-ready company of the servant boys, but the vast social gulf between them meant that there was little chance of any lasting friendships being made.

Enjoying the company of the servants, what was subsequently to be described as 'very low company and low pursuits', was even claimed by his later critics as another manifestation of his lack of intellect. That it might be only natural for a lonely little boy to seek company in the warmth and noise of the neighbouring servants' quarters was not taken into account; what mattered to Gla's relations was that here was a young gentleman associating with people clearly far below his natural station in life.

To humour him, but compounding the sin in other eyes, William Howe Windham even bought his son a suit of footman's livery so that he could wait on table. The suit was made in the family colours of blue coat, red waistcoat, red plush breeches and dress buttons. Gla loved it, only abandoning it when he grew too large to fit into the outfit.

But he continued to wait at table until he was 14. Gla's friendships with the 'lower orders' also left him able to converse both in the polite English of his land-owning social circle and the broad Norfolk accent, still rich in dialect in the 19th century and almost impenetrable to (and therefore, inevitably, ridiculed by) many non-East Anglians. This, too, was to be taken later as yet another example of his lack of intellect, despite the fact that his father, and for that matter many a Norfolk landlord before and since, was able to converse in both the genteel speech of parlour and public school and 'broad Norfolk' when occasion demanded.

IN 1847 the butler James Nolls remembered seeing Gla marching around pretending to be a soldier, and a love of all things military, along with later passions for fast carriage-driving and women, was to be one of the abiding themes of his life. Another was for the railways. From an early age Windham was fascinated by this still-novel technology, opening and shutting railway carriage doors and calling out the names of the stations. It was a fascination which was to continue for most of his life, with many unexpected consequences.

When Gla turned eight, his father asked the Rev Frederick Askew Bickmore to take him as a pupil at his school at Eaton, just outside Norwich. Windham was with him from September 1848 to Christmas 1850. While he was there he had the dental procedure, and also suffered from a bout of whooping cough. The illness meant he had to take some 'unpleasant medicine' (although not, one hopes, the traditional Norfolk country cure: fried mouse). Dr Dalrymple was the witness to one of Gla's 'outbreaks of passion' (as he was later to describe them) around 1848, when the boy, in front of 'company', threw himself down on the floor when chastised and 'shrieked and bit the carpet'. When he was an adult William Frederick Windham admitted he had inherited some of his father's personality: 'I am very passionate; my father was passionate; and I am very sorry for it.'

But young William was capable of tenderness too. In February 1849 he sent his father a Valentine greeting with a coloured print in return for a small gift his father had sent. 'My dear mamma,' he wrote, 'I am very much pleased with what papa has given me, and I hope he will received this simple present in return for his great one; and, as I have told him, I am so thankful to him I cannot really express myself for his kindness to me and I hope that you are stronger than you were.... Dear mamma, I shall soon be home now; it is only a week now... 'Good by (*sic*), dear mamma, your most affectionate son, GLA'

18

It was some indication, incidentally, of the oppression Lady Sophia felt in her husband's presence that when he was safely away on business, she used to bring the servants up to the dining room to 'romp and play about' with young Gla while she played the piano. Friendships might have been expected with the sons and daughters of Norfolk's other landed gentry, but Gla's misbehaviour and tantrums meant it was usually easier for his parents to simply avoid public contacts.

AFTER THE Rev Bickmore's establishment, the nine-year-old Gla went to the school of one Dr Buck. It was later claimed that while there he exhibited a combination of 'peculiarly childish' manners, at the same time showing 'particularly dirty or nasty habits with regard to his person' and swearing. In autumn 1854 he followed his father by going to Eton. The rough-and-tumble and enforced social contact of public school life must have been quite a shock to the awkward 14-year-old. The decision to send him to the school was made not just in an attempt to raise his intellect but also to improve his sometimes lamentable social skills. And also, naturally, to remove him from the influence of the servants' quarters - or so his parents thought.

In August the Rev Dr Henry Cheales was engaged as Gla's tutor, with the aim of given him greater guidance while at school and as his companion during the holidays. Cheales was the first of what was to be a steady stream of largely ineffectual supervisors over the next six and a half years. Almost immediately Cheales found Gla hard to deal with, citing his tendency to tell ridiculous lies and his inability to learn. Of equal concern were his allegedly dirty personal habits and gluttony. Windham's slavering was, once again, hard to accept.

And it was at Eton that Gla first attracted the nickname which would create much discussion in the years ahead. Already the largest boy in class, Windham's excitability and distinctive laughter (once described as a 'donkey laugh') made it inevitable he would become known as the class joker - and provide the epithet which would come to haunt him later. His mathematics teacher (and another some-time tutor) the Rev Edward Hale recalled: 'He was a buffoon in the school. The other boys used to get him to make noises, and they called him "Mad Windham".'

THE PRIVILEGE of Felbrigg and Eton was a world away from the life being led by Ann Agnes Rogers. She was born a few months after Gla, on 19 December 1840 in the village of Rotherwick, some miles north of Hook in Hampshire. She was the second child of William and Ann (*née* Grigg) - an elder brother George was born in 1838 soon after the marriage, and her parents would go on to have two more children, Thirza (born 1846) and Emma (born 1850).

Unlike the well-documented Windham, Agnes' early years are a series of snapshots through a few official sources - birth records, census returns and the like. But they are still eloquent about the family's circumstances, and especially its peripatetic lifestyle. Agnes' father, William, was born in 1816 (or perhaps 1814) in Basingstoke, a few miles to the west of Rotherwick, and also close to the village of Greywell, from where his wife Ann (born 1817 or 1818) originated. Agnes, in her urgency to escape from her humble background, was to claim later that her father was a clergyman. The truth was more prosaic: he was a sawyer. The close-knit Grigg family produced many a canal worker and sawyer, so it was no surprise that Ann married one of the latter herself.

The Industrial and Agricultural Revolutions, far from causing the traditional rural woodland industries to wither, had led to exactly the opposite: a massively increased demand for every kind of product from carts to containers. For much of the century many landowners, especially in the southern counties of England, exploited the ancient coppiced woods on their estates to feed this voracious appetite. William Rogers would probably have been part of the 'underwood' economy - the name given to these coppicing activities - which was strong in Hampshire and Dorset.

It is an economy which is vividly brought to life in Thomas Hardy's 1887 novel The Woodlanders. Drawing on his considerable experience of rural life in 'Wessex', Hardy paints a picture of a community where wood harvesting was mostly carried out in winter and spring. Rogers would have worked as either a top or bottom sawyer, in a saw-pit operating the two-man saw blades. This was heavy and demanding work, with sawdust a constant irritant to eyes and lungs.

The workers tended to operate by contract, part of the labour force of underwood dealers who bought lots of standing wood at auction or by arrangement with the estate owners. Away from the peak winter and spring months, Rogers would have had to find other employment. John Creasey (1982) quotes the example of the workers of Tadley in Hampshire, who became general farm labourers in summer and early autumn, helping with harvests or hop-picking.

It was no surprise, therefore, that William's trade meant the family was rarely in one place for very long. George had been born in London, while sometime in the 1840s the family moved to Dorset: Thirza was born in Poole, Emma at Weymouth, and by the time of the 1851 Census the family was living at Terrace Court, Melcombe Regis, technically the eastern twin town to Weymouth's west but now effectively subsumed by the latter.

In 1851 young Agnes was still being described as a 'scholar', but the world of work would not have been far away; the family finances would have demanded it. George, at 13, was already apprenticed as a carpenter. The family's life must have been one of constant upheaval, short-term job succeeding short-term job, William Rogers forever chasing opportunities where work might last more than a few weeks or months. There is a tradition, passed down through the Grigg family, that Rogers was a heavy drinker who frequently beat Ann. Impossible to verify at this remove, of course, but the situation was an all-too-common one in many households. Whatever the truth of the situation, Agnes would have had to develop an inner toughness to deal with the constant changes, and her family's intermittent poverty also gave her an ambition - which she was to maintain until the end of her life - to ensure that her sisters and mother were given something their father had never enjoyed: financial security. Such single-mindedness would later lead to her being criticised as mercenary; those doing the criticising, however, already had an assured place in polite society.

In late 1851 or early 1852 disaster struck. William Rogers developed the symptoms of one of the nineteenth century's most feared killers, 'consumption' or, as we know it today, pulmonary tuberculosis. His disease was formally diagnosed in January 1852. It must have been a devastating financial as well as emotional blow for the Rogers family, coming as it did at his very peak earning months of the year. The disease continued to make inroads over the next few months until by the summer William would have had the classic final stages of the disease: bouts of sweating and chills, helpless coughing and, naturally, the dramatic wasting away which gave rise to the disease's common name.

On 24 August, William's racked body could take no more. He died in the family's current home, at Steward's Court, Melcombe Regis. The court - swept away in the 1960s - was one of many put up in a rush of speculative Victorian building as land was reclaimed in the Dorset town. Ann Green, an illiterate fellow resident of the court, was there at the death. Where William's wife Ann was, and what was so important as to take her from her dying husband's last hours, remains a mystery. Opera and melodramatic fiction has romanticised the illness (especially in the persona of the consumptive heroine, a literary staple) but there was nothing romantic about it, and Rogers' death would have been as appalling as any of them. It took eight years for his estate of less than £20 to be settled. Her father's death and the family's desperate need for money was the catalyst for Agnes to tread a path worn familiar by thousands of other young Victorian girls: she went to work in London. She probably went as a domestic servant - country girls, especially West Country ones, being in the most demand - later that year or in 1853. It was inevitable that the petite, pretty and strikingly blonde Agnes would soon attract male attention. That male attention was to change her life, and begin an unpredictable rollercoaster of fame, riches, public fascination, and disapproval. With no advantage of birth, Agnes would have to live on her looks - and her wits.

A SCANDAL AT FELBRIGG

BY CONTRAST young Gla seemed sure of a prosperous future. William Howe Windham, by dint of shrewd estate management, had gradually increased the size of the already-handsome Felbrigg estate to what was to prove its zenith. He took out a £160,000 mortgage to buy the neighbouring 1,500-acre Hanworth estate in December 1845, money which was to be largely paid back by 1869, with the income of £7,000 per year leaving a healthy rental surplus.

The estate now extended to more than 10,000 acres - five times its present-day size - comprising a huge swathe of north east Norfolk. Young Gla would be able to look forward to an eventual gross income of about £9,000 a year, or perhaps £4,000 to £5,000 after outgoings - equivalent to around £215,000 in today's money. It was a sound, forward-thinking plan from an active and ambitious Norfolk landowner. But at the end of 1854 something happened which was to shake Gla's world to the core: His vibrant and domineering father suddenly died.

2

1854-1859:
The Hero and the Boy

'You must try and cure him.'
Lady Sophia Windham's instructions to her son's tutor, 1857

THE DEATH of Gla's father - from inflammation and ulceration of the bladder - was a desperate blow to the Windhams. The family had gathered at the St James' Square, London, home of Lady Sophia's father, for Christmas, only for William Howe Windham's sudden death on 22 December when, in the words of the Norwich Mercury, he had 'scarcely passed beyond the age of ripe and vigorous mankind'.

Despite William Howe Windham's standing as an important member of the landed classes, the newspaper's obituary has a curious and inescapable feeling of going through the motions. Admittedly, the paper was obsessed with the Crimean War siege of Sevastapol - then, again, so was the whole country - but the relative brevity of its report, and lack of any subsequent comment or reaction tell their own story. 'Mr Windham possessed considerable talent,' it said, 'but he was not gifted with that popular engaging manner to which success in the search after public support is very often far more attributable than to superiority of intellect.'

A frank assessment, then, and significant, too, is its description of the heir of Felbrigg. 'There is only one son and heir, who we believe is about 14 years of age'. Not named, hardly known; a poignant indication of the family's success in keeping young Gla away from polite Norfolk society.

The funeral in St Margaret's Church on the Felbrigg estate was a rare chance for the curious among the mourners to observe this obscure young heir at close quarters. For many of the extended Windham and Hervey family, it was the first time most of

St Margaret's Church, Felbrigg: William Howe Windham's funeral in the estate's ancient church in early January 1855 was the first opportunity for many to see the young heir at close quarters.

them had seen him for years. They were not impressed. Scott, the solicitor from the nearby market town of Aylsham, later recalled how young Windham went 'among the people, welcoming them almost in a joyous manner, and asking them with a delighted expression of countenance whether they would like to see the coffin'. Gla gave a 'cry like an animal in distress' during the reading of the lesson, which Scott later explained as a 'manifestation of grief uncontrolled by reason'. William also stared around at the other people in the church, which many of the two hundred or so there found disconcerting. And yet back at the hall, Scott added, the young squire was 'as cheerful and careless as ever'. Dalrymple, too, spotted the change of mood, being 'painfully shocked' by Gla's lack of emotion. Many began to draw the conclusion that there was something not quite right about the heir of Felbrigg.

When William Howe Windham died, it was not only a parent the young Windham had lost, but the dominating presence in his life and his moral compass. In retrospect, the eventual fates of Windham and Felbrigg seem to stem from this moment. But several other factors were to turn this terrible setback into a fatal weakness. The death left the Felbrigg estates in the care of his two trustees: his father's brother Charles Ashe Windham and his mother. The estate brought in an income of about £3,100 a year, less the £1,500 willed to Lady Sophia for her use and around £350 for unavoidable outgoings of the estate. The most important male personality in young Gla's life had now shifted to be his uncle, an enormously complex character whose mercurial nature was shaped by extraordinary highs and lows of fortune.

Charles was born in the same year as William Windham III died, one of the sons of

Vice-Admiral Windham (né Lukin). He began his military career in approved officer style - Sandhurst, the Coldstream Guards - but the Purchase System of promotions then still in operation meant his progress up the career ladder was painfully slow, as even the owner of a landed estate had a finite amount to spend on the career of a junior son. Charles was commissioned as ensign and lieutenant in 1826, and served with the Guards as captain of the 2nd Battalion in Canada in 1838-42 during a rebellion, becoming a lieutenant-colonel in 1846. He retired on half-pay three years later, frustrated by his lack of progress, and married Marianne Catherine Emily Beresford. Uncle Charles was a good choice as a role

Charles Ashe Windham: Pictured with his daughter. 'Redan' Windham became a national hero for his dashing exploits during the Crimean War, but was later to experience the harsher whims of public opinion. *(NRO ref: MC580/1, 780x1)*

model in many ways: he had been very close to his eldest brother, and young Gla admired him immensely. But his military career was to result in some lengthy absences at key parts of his young charge's life. And, as fate would have it, one of those periods was at the very time of William Howe Windham's final illness.

It was the outbreak of the muddled, often disastrous, Crimean War in 1854 which brought Charles back from half-pay retirement into the army, and was to propel him from obscure career soldier to national celebrity. Promoted to colonel, he landed with the 4th Division of the Army of the East in September 1854, taking command of the division when his senior officers were killed at the battle of Inkerman. The harsh winter which followed began to cruelly expose the army's appallingly-inadequate supply chain, and Windham found himself forced to make frequent trips to the Balaklava base to try to secure adequate food and equipment for his troops and to protest bitterly about the lack of basic care for the soldiery. He even survived an attack of cholera, one of the lucky ones who did.

The Crimean War was not the first modern war, but it was arguably the first modern media war. The electric telegraph meant war correspondents could, and did, file vivid and damning accounts of the bloody shambles back to London. And their disturbing accounts of the war's mismanagement were augmented by the journals of serving soldiers, among them Windham. His diaries are full of attacks on his senior officers, the army's inefficiency and even the Cabinet itself - Prime Minister Lord Palmerston being singled out as 'that old petrified dandy' - plus his continued bitterness at being passed over for promotion. Windham's accounts were passed round those in high places and helped motivate public opinion, but also made him many enemies in the Establishment. Those enemies would bide their time and counter-attack to devastating effect.

GLA, MEANWHILE, had resumed his studies at Eton, still accompanied by Cheales. In April 1855, it was decided that Cheales should be with his young charge full-time, and he remained in this position as tutor-companion until just before Easter 1857. But by his own admission, his attempts to reform Windham's behaviour were a complete failure. Cheales asked Lady Sophia what he should do about the young heir's dirty habits, and she merely replied: 'You must try and cure him'.

Mrs Voysey kept a boarding house at Eton, where Windham was a guest from the Easter quarter of 1855 to July 1856. She remembered him as a 'decidedly noisy boy' but said there was no significance in his being called 'mad', as boys at Eton often were. Her view is supported by a letter from Henry Sidgwick to E M Young, written on 28 January 1862 , which poured scorn on claims that Windham was a lunatic while at the school. Sidgwick wrote to Young - a contemporary of Gla's at Eton - that 'Wilson is convinced he is a lunatic' but every other Eton man he had seen thought the idea was simply unbelievable.

There was some progress in Windham's learning - 'He could do school work: Latin and Greek, arithmetic, and other things when he left me that he could not have done a year before', Cheales was to later observe - but it had been a frustrating situation for him. His attempts at telling off Windham were simply met with a grin. Cheales resorted to beating him on occasions, also with absolutely no apparent effect. While at Eton, and under Cheales' watchful eye, Windham protested to his mother that he was 'being kept like a prisoner', being beaten if he went to another boy's room. While he languished alone, he complained, Cheales was out all day. Gla also continued to mix with the servants, particularly enjoying - as he had at Felbrigg - the warmth, companionship (and, no doubt, food-purloining opportunities) it offered. Cheales complained later: 'One one occasion when I saw him in the kitchen he was laughing and screaming and jumping about among the servants.'

It was also at Eton that Windham started to turn his love of trains into a fully-fledged obsession. It was easy to understand his fascination: the new mode of transport was still barely into its third decade and had already changed British life irrevocably, with its previously-impossible speeds and cutting-edge technology. Windham took to going to Eton station with a railway whistle and opening the doors for passengers. He even talked about having the railway brought to his park gates, twenty or so miles from Norwich, once he had inherited his estate, an idea, incidentally, which would have bankrupted him if carried out. Windham's railway fixation continued during the times he was back in Norfolk, where he became a familiar face on the platforms of Thorpe, one of the Norwich stations, from around 1854.

One of the contradictions about life at Eton at this time was its policy towards discipline. Naturally, beatings were commonplace, with Windham, the biggest boy in his class and therefore the hardest to miss, earning his share - but Old Etonian E D Stone in his memoirs also talks about boys being allowed to drink beer freely. For an impressionable boy such as Windham, setting the parameters of what was considered civilised behaviour was thus made all the more difficult. At Eton, too, Windham picked up another habit which was to be a constant source of frustration to his family, but of delight to his friends and drinking companions (frequently the same thing): a lack of financial acumen. He managed to run through his allowance of two to three shillings per week with ease, running up debts of 'several pounds' with local traders. Small change for the heir of a wealthy Norfolk estate; but a foretaste of which was to follow. Windham's letters to his mother from Eton were full of the usual cares of a young boy away from home, mainly revolving around the amount of his allowance. In one letter written in 1855, he mentions spending 'his last two shillings' on seeing a lecture by the celebrated author of Vanity Fair, William Makepeace Thackeray.

IN THE CRIMEA, meanwhile, Charles was steadily rising through the chain of command. In July he was made a companion in the Order of the Bath, which was followed in August by command of the 2nd Brigade of the 2nd Division. At home, the British public's initial patriotic fervour was fast becoming tempered by disquieting reports of the numbers of battle casualties and those dying from illness. A famous - and damning - leader in The Times of 22 December 1854 had soured the public mood.

The country desperately needed a hero, and in September the following year, Charles Ashe Windham provided one.

It is difficult, at this remove, to appreciate the popular fervour which the Crimean campaign stirred. Two shattering world conflicts and the passage of more than 150 years have reduced the war in most people's minds to a mere mid-century footnote: images of Florence Nightingale, Mary Seacole and, of course, the Charge of the Light Brigade. At the time it was a different matter, with the campaign the first time Britain had been involved in a European war since Waterloo. The French and British armies were seen as mounting a noble campaign to stop the territorial aims of the Russians, and thus protecting routes to India and the waters of the Mediterranean. Battles such as Alma, Sevastapol and Balaklava burned themselves into the public's consciousness and were commemorated with the naming of terraces and roads all over the country.

But who, now, remembers the Redan, apart from military historians? And yet this bloody action propelled Windham to dizzying heights of national fervour not seen since Duke of Wellington's victory at Waterloo in 1815. The long and bloody siege of Sevastapol, on the south-western corner of the Crimea, was the pivotal action of the war and cost the lives of 100,000 Russians alone. The Redan was one of its most formidable batteries. The Allied troops had already failed in several times when, in early September, Windham led the assault, constantly urging his troops on while strolling through the bloodiest part of the fight with astonishing *sang froid*. His efforts were, ultimately, as unsuccessful as the other attacks, but his heroism was immediately lauded by both the army and the war correspondents.

It was an act of incredible bravery, typical of the 'up and at 'em' approach beloved of another famous Norfolk warrior, Admiral Lord Nelson, and typical too of a daring (or reckless) streak in the General's character. Within weeks he had been made a Major-General, and - though he did not know it - the Cabinet even considered making him the commander-in-chief of the British forces, but he lost out by three votes. Although he was undoubtedly brave, the Cabinet decided there were doubts about his foresight and his ability to be cool-headed. The British newspapers, meanwhile, dubbed him the 'Hero of the Redan' or, simply, 'Redan Windham'. Charles Ashe Windham was now, de facto, the most famous soldier in the Empire. To his credit, Charles treated the acclaim with ironic detachment. He wrote to his friend Charles Greville that 'the newspapers... seem to make me the greatest hero that ever was, which is purely and simply ridiculous'. He added, presciently, that he was well aware the public could have him in their 'black books' within a fortnight.

By February 1856 both sides in the war had had enough and an armistice was signed, which meant Windham could join the rest of the weary army in returning home. Windham had entered the war as just another half-pay officer, but had ended it as a major-general, chief of staff to the British commander and a national hero. He landed in July, when he was feted by everyone, including Queen Victoria herself. 'I assure you that since I landed in England,' he told the crowds in Norwich on 1 August, 'from the Queen downwards, I have met with such a reception as many bad half-hours in the Redan would have been well spent to serve.'

The reception in his home city was to be the pinnacle of his acclaim. In a city of 70,000 people, an astonishing 50,000 were estimated to have turned out to see him. Blessed by glorious summer weather, the cheers started as soon as the General disembarked at the city's Victoria Station and hardly stopped for the rest of the day. The bells of the city's beautiful civic church, St Peter Mancroft, rang out, mingling with a salute fired by a detachment of artillery on the nearby meadow dominated by the brooding bulk of Norwich Castle. The Norwich Mercury, devoting the best part of two pages to its description of events, reported 'Never was the feeling "Honour the brave" more truly and enthusiastically displayed - never more deservedly won... we doubt if ever there was so great a day of excitement and feeling as today, August 1st, in Norwich.' The paper's support for the General was never to waver over the coming years. When the 'slings and arrows' were flying, the newspaper remained his staunchest supporter.

But no-one could have foreseen any such difficulties from the perspective of that summer's day in 1856. Cheers erupted wherever he was seen, accompanied by vigorous waving of banners, handkerchiefs, hats, anything. At one point someone even managed to place a Roman-style laurel wreath on his head. At the elegant Guildhall on the city's market place, the General was addressed by the city mayor. 'May you receive the rewards of a grateful country and may you live to enjoy all the happiness which a man can enjoy through the medium of a happy and virtuous family,' he told Charles.

If the mention of his family made the General's mind stray, momentarily, to his nephew we cannot know. But there is no doubt that the heir of Felbrigg was deliberately kept as far away from his uncle as possible. There was no place for him on the triumphal dais outside St Andrew's Hall on which the rest of the Windhams and Herveys had gathered. There was to be no chance of Gla causing any distraction on the greatest day in the General's life; or at least that was the plan. Being Gla, however, he managed to do so. Riding a pony, he tried to force his way through the crowd until Lord Suffield pulled him back. And while travelling to the reception with his mother he began shrieking at the top of his voice, and was only quietened with difficulty.

Around 3pm the General arrived at the official civic banquet. Six hundred guests sat down for a meal and a long (very long) series of speeches which lasted more than four hours. If he was tired, then his speeches did not show it, mentioning everything from Nelson to his pride in being a Norfolkman (which, naturally, received the biggest cheers of the night).

Unfortunately William, by now the worse for drink, was by now jumping on tables and chairs and trying to shout and interrupt proceedings. He was drowned out by the frequent cheering from the hundreds of guests, but many people, including the Windham and Hervey families, noted his behaviour. One witness was Lt-Col Hugh Fitzroy, a deputy lieutenant of Norfolk, who sat opposite the 15-year-old Gla. For the first half-hour Windham was well behaved, but after he had grown drunk 'on a quantity of bad champagne' - something which was to become a recurrent theme in his life - he become excitable and loud, especially when his uncle was speaking. But then, again, so did many others on that day.

If Fate lifted the General high, then it was also to cast him down. But for now, this, truly, was his moment.

THE GENERAL remained in England for another year, turning down various postings. The reason seems to have been pressure from his beloved wife Marianne to stay with her and their young family. While Charles was enjoying family life for the first time in years, his nephew continued his travels. Back at Christmas 1855 it had been decided that Gla needed to take another step on his faltering journey into polite society: that of dealing with the company of young ladies. Gla travelled with Cheales to Torquay, a resort they revisited the following Easter and Christmas. The trips were not a success. During one, it was later alleged, the boisterous Windham seized Signor Campana, an Italian music teacher, by the whiskers and pushed him against the wall, which Campana himself later down-played as a well-intentioned joke. The ladies he was meant to impress were instead repelled by his rudeness.

Windham's Eton career petered out to an unsatisfactory close in the fifth form. Another clergyman, mathematics master the Rev Edward Hale, was his private tutor from Easter to Christmas 1856, when Windham left the school. Hale's appointment was another unsuccessful one with he, too, admitting that his young charge failed to make any progress under his guidance. Windham had an unwelcome reminder of his stay at Eton: during one of his frequent trips to the town's railway station he decided to see what would happen if he stuck his hand into the cogs of one of the lifting machines. The result: the top of one of his fingers was cut off.

There are hints that Windham's behaviour at Eton included rather more than misbehaviour, boisterousness and accident. Towards the end of his time there he wrote a rather abject letter to his mother about causing 'offence' by the 'wicked way

I have been going on for the fortnight I was in town'. Windham travelled to London by train, and around this time it was apparently common - as mentioned by Windham himself when recalling his Eton days - for a 'great number of women of the town [to be] waiting for them at the station'. Only those boys travelling on in other trains escaped their attentions. Windham, as the most mature physically of the boys in his class, would have been an obvious target. Certainly it is a fact that by the time Windham was 17 he was no stranger to venereal disease, admitting in later years having had such an illness at Torquay in 1858. This was taken as simply another element in Windham's moral turpitude. But it is possible that its significance played a far more central role in the subsequent path of his life.

AN EXCHANGE with his tailor Tom Bingham in November 1861 shows a degree of bitterness from Windham about his education, or rather the lack of it. When Bingham commented that Windham could 'read a [rail] timetable pretty well', Windham replied, 'Yes, I can, considering that my education was neglected. I have nothing to thank my family for.'

But in the late 1850s there was still hope for Windham. Suitable companions, who ideally would have combined a flair for communicating knowledge and a framework for morals and behaviour with an empathy for their charge, might yet have turned William into a competent squire-to-be. A suitably no-nonsense female companion could have given Windham valuable lessons on the correct ways of talking to and behaving in the presence of the opposite sex, and curbed his forays into boorishness. Instead Windham was given a succession of dry, crusty, and disapproving middle-aged clergymen and soldiers. As one expert was later to say, surely with much truth, 'I think that Mr Windham would have been very much improved by care and kindness.' Only perhaps with his final tutor, Mr Peatfield, was there, briefly at least, any sort of warmth. But by then it was a case of too little, too late, and being a paid companion of Windham had become all about trying to keep him out of as much trouble as possible.

It is not clear what Windham's guardians (and, later, the Court of Chancery, who took a close interest in his case) were trying to achieve with this succession of uninspired companions. It is tempting, and perhaps inevitable, to draw the conclusion that they, in effect, had given up on him. The steward of the Windham estates, Sir William Foster, certainly thought so. In a damning verdict, he said: 'He had no education at all, nobody to teach him, no opportunity of learning the value of his timber, or how to manage the estate.' Other male members of his family wanted as little as possible to do with the odd youth, and it was a mutual feeling, as an undated letter from Windham reveals. In it he protests to his mother about his uncle Henry

Captain (John) Henry Windham RN: Receiver of the Felbrigg estate's rents, and Gla's uncle; their dislike was mutual.
(NRO ref: MC580/1, 780x1)

being the receiver of the estate's rents. It was not simply the matter of Captain Windham's blindness, he claims. The captain had been 'very drunk' at a social event, 'rolling about, swearing, and bellowing like a mad bull' and all the tenants wished rid of him.

The dominant female presence was his mother; but Lady Sophia remained a fey and nervous creature, and events were to prove that her love for her son was not an unconditional one. Although Windham's affection for her is clear from his letters, the fact remains that she joined the General, as co-guardians, in court proceedings from 1857 in trying to stop Gla gaining full possession of the contents of Felbrigg and Hanworth halls, the 'household furniture, paintings, books, plate, and plated goods, wine and jewellery'. She was already fearful of the effects of her son gaining control.

THE GENERAL, meanwhile, had seen his Redan popularity transferred into political capital when he was returned as one of two Liberal MPs for East Norfolk in 1857. But his political career was destined to last only months. Later that year the Indian Mutiny erupted, and Windham immediately offered his services. He still found time, however, to write home of his concern for his nephew. To try to fill the gap it was agreed to appoint one of Lady Sophia's brothers, Lord Alfred Hervey, as a guardian, along with another distant relative, a Mr ffolkes.

During a 1857 visit to Torquay, yet another cleric - the Rev Thomas Goodwin - was engaged to look after the 16-year-old Windham. Although his task was only for two to three weeks, young Gla left an abiding impression on the clergyman. He went to Lady Sophia's house every day to try to instruct him but was left frustrated and bemused by Windham's antics, which even included, he claimed (although this has something of the hallmark of exaggeration given their relative sizes) Gla trying to jump on his mother's shoulders and ride her like a horse. It is clear that Lady Sophia, at least, had effectively given up any hope of educating her son. It was now, to use a phrase from the next century, all about damage limitation. Goodwin later recalled how Lady Sophia asked him to be with her son from 10am to 1pm every day, but not to study. 'All she wished was that I should keep him from excessive mischief,' he said.

During 1857 Windham had got to know the Andrews family from Rimpton in Somerset well, sometimes travelling out with Mrs Andrews and her daughters. Despite Windham's well-attested faults, the family had grown fond of him and realised what many others in his life had signally failed to do so: that if you looked past the 'high animal spirits' and dealt kindly with him, then he would be kind in return. When Windham was about to leave in the latter part of 1858 he made a proposal of marriage to one of the Andrews' daughters. The Andrews and Lady Sophia had to reject the offer on the grounds that both Windham and his intended were under age. One cannot but help but wonder what different path his life would have taken had they met only two years later.

WHILE GLA continued his merry-go-round of visits round various resorts, his uncle had more serious things on his mind. While defending the town of Cawnpore for several days in late November 1857, incompetence by one of his officers led to the British force of around 1,300 infantry, gunners and troopers being driven out of the town and, humiliatingly, losing most of its equipment. His furious commander Sir Colin Campbell left out all reference of Windham and his troops in his despatch, a damning snub.

By the time Sir Colin had become aware of the real story behind the incident, it was too late. Windham, hailed a hero in 1855 by the British press, was now savaged by an element of that same press only two years later. His letter to his friend Charles Grenville had proved only too prescient. The Daily News, in particular, was scornful of the 'incompetence, ignorance and breach of orders' it claimed Windham had shown, its scathing editorials backed on 18 February by a letter from an anonymous 'old KCB' alleging that Windham had only achieved promotion through his family connections.

On the same day Prime Minister Palmerston insisted in the Commons that 'explanations had been given which completely acquitted General Windham from any blame connected with the operations at Cawnpore which had resulted in the loss of baggage and the camp'. Windham, he added - to cries of 'hear, hear' - had displayed the 'qualities for which he was so distinguished'. Even the Royal Family rallied to his side: in the Lords, the Duke of Cambridge, Queen Victoria's uncle, spoke in his support. But the damage had been done. The General still had many allies, but there were also many in high places who now whispered that there was something not quite sound about the Norfolkman; that he was reckless, headstrong, a loose cannon. His reputation took years to recover from the affair. Although he eventually resumed his rise up the army career ladder, he was never again given command of an army in the field. It did not help that Charles was still far away in India and had little chance to defend his own reputation. But as he served his country in the sub-continent, he still found time to receive reports of his nephew's doings.

WITH YOUNG Windham's formal education already over, his life now consisted of years of travelling. In late July 1858 Windham was introduced to the Rev Devere, and the party travelled through North Wales, the Lake District, Scotland, then back to Felbrigg via Durham and York. Their travels (described as 'very unsuccessful' at a subsequent court hearing) took around five weeks, and apart from the clergyman being struck by Windham's 'boisterous and rather blustering' manner, he had little trouble with his new companion. During the Scottish leg of their travels in August, they met Mr Murray, a Glasgow ironmaster and (ironically in view of later events) a director of the Gartnavel Lunatic Asylum, who was travelling round the Highlands with two of his daughters. Murray remembered Windham as a 'rollicking, thoughtless and free-and-easy young man'.

Later that year Dr Nicholls, the medical man Gla's father had consulted all those years before, met up with the now-teenaged Windham for the first time since at a ball. He was not impressed. Windham's strange braying laughter, occasional incoherence, obsession with his militia uniform (at this time he was toying with a military career) and apparent forgetfulness created such a disturbing impression in his mind that he communicated his fears to the family's solicitor, Peter Hansell.

The ostensible reason for Windham's succession of companions was to complete, or at least continue, his education and instruction in the social niceties. But Windham himself had another theory: that Lady Sophia now simply wanted him out of the way. The reason? She had fallen in love with an Italian, Theodore Maine Giubilei. In April 1858 Windham met Lady Sophia's young fiancé for the first time, and the marriage took place on 10 May. Lady Sophia's marriage to her young Italian beau, then aged around 25, took her family by surprise. It was not a popular choice. There was a 22-year age gap between them, and her decision to marry out of her class, and to a foreigner of no breeding to boot, caused a breach in the Hervey family. The future 2nd Marquis, for example, pointedly did not attend the wedding, spoke to his sister only once after it and even three years later had still not met his brother-in-law. Another brother, Lord Alfred, later (1861) said: 'That marriage was very distasteful to the whole family, and has caused a great rupture in it.'

Shortly after the marriage, Lord Alfred was appointed one of Windham's guardians. He allowed him £5 a month spending money, but Windham often managed to get through it in a single day without having much to show for it.

Lady Sophia's marriage did, in fact, mean that she began to step away from the burden of responsibility for her son. It was perhaps understandable that she wanted to devote time to her new husband, but for Windham the move was another step on the road to chaos. In a private court hearing in January 1860 she was to concede that her influence had always been 'of the utmost service' in helping both her son cope with his 'peculiar disposition' and to give support to his tutors. Without her, things began to unravel.

In September 1858 William returned to his latest companion (a Mr Hawtrey) but then ran away to London. He eventually turned up at his mother's house in Grosvenor Street, when she was shocked to discover her callow 17-year-old son was living, utterly unsupervised, at the British Hotel. Lady Sophia managed to get him to stay with her for a few weeks before persuading him to go to Wokingham to join tutor Mr H W Burr, who specialised in helping young gentlemen reaching the required educational standard for an army commission.

Windham took steps to begin a military career, the acclaim for the 'Hero of the Redan' having made a lasting impression, and proved himself more than capable of drill at Shorncliffe on the South Coast. Windham stayed with Burr until February the following year, studying such subjects as geography and fortifications. He left, not from academic reasons but because he had run up debts of £70 (settled by an exasperated Lord Alfred) for a new dog cart among other items.

He turned up again at Lady Sophia's house early in 1859 on the death of his grandfather, the 1st Marquis. Once again, she was shocked to discover he was not under 'proper supervision or control' so agreed to have him stay with her for a few weeks. She was due to travel to Paris, and tried to place her son with another member of the family.

It was a futile mission. 'No-one would take him,' she explained later, with devastating simplicity. After the succession of clergy had failed to instil a sense of moral decorum in the fast-growing and ever-wilder youth, the family turned to a taste of military discipline, in the form of an ex-Coldstream Guards officer and militia commander, Colonel James Bathurst.

He was a constant companion for Windham in the seemingly ceaseless travels round the Continent and English holiday resorts, in return for a 'very handsome remuneration'. Windham's family (and Vice-Chancellor Sir William Page Wood, of the Court of Chancery, who took a particular interest in his case) were putting their faith in the power of travel to somehow educate the young heir, in the same way that the 'Grand Tour' had once been considered an essential part of any young nobleman's cultural armoury. Instead of paintings and an appreciation of high culture, however, Windham merely collected more strange looks and tales of impropriety.

From 19 June to September Windham and Bathurst travelled to Plymouth, Brussels, Spa, Frankfurt, Baden-Baden, Switzerland and then back to Spa once more, before returning to England. They were joined by London visitor Mr Bruce at Baden Baden, and they travelled together for around ten days or a fortnight through the Black Forest. Bruce had ample time to observe Windham's coarse language and also the clear mutual dislike between the young heir and his companion. He even saw a fight between them, when the colonel - maddened at Windham's imitation of his manner of walking - had expressed his displeasure.

Windham had countered that he was a '---------- aristocratic humbug', then repeated the insult. This was too much for Bathurst, who punched Windham to the ground, where he sat and 'blubbered like a child', according to Bruce.

In August Windham was with the Colonel in Lucerne, Switzerland, when he bumped into a former Eton schoolmate, Whiteside, and asked to join his travelling party. Out of politeness, Whiteside agreed. He soon came to regret it, with Windham 'very dirty' in his habits, swearing in the presence of the two ladies of the party and - in the time-honoured manner of the English boor overseas - pointing at foreigners and making loud and abusive remarks about them. At dinner, when there would be perhaps 100 people at their tables, Windham would shout loudly and let food fall from his lips onto the tablecloth while he was laughing - only to pick it up again and stuff it back into his mouth. The sound of cutlery being dropped as appetites evaporated on surrounding tables can only be imagined.

Something which did not emerge publicly at the time was that the young Windham also found time to become engaged to a 'young lady he met during his travels at one of the Watering Places'. The private 1860 court hearing which heard this claim summed up the previous year's trip thus: 'It seems the minor's time was spent in idleness - seeking pleasure and occasionally at the Gambling tables. He did not study and on his return her Ladyship found he had lost in a general degree what he had before acquired.' The colonel might have been able to command a detachment of militia with ease, but trying to dictate orders to a gangling and ill-behaved 18-year-old proved a far more difficult task. In the end it was too much. Bathurst gave up, and returned to England early. And no more was heard, too, of the mysterious Continental fiancée.

VICE-CHANCELLOR Wood then appointed the delightfully-named Mr Edgeworth Horrocks as Windham's next companion in October or November 1859. Like Bathurst he came with a military background (he had served in two Scottish militias);

like Bathurst, he found his 19-year-old charge hard to deal with. He stayed with Windham until June the following year, but found him slow to learn and obstinate. And by now there was another growing distraction for Windham: women. They were already rivalling or even overhauling his long-standing love of trains. 'His great subject was ladies,' Horrocks said later, adding that Gla would propose to all of them within a few weeks of a meeting - 'sometimes within a few days'. Worse, he was fond of 'associating with ladies of doubtful character'.

Vice-Chancellor Sir William Page Wood: His Court of Chancery role led him to take a particular interest in young Windham's upbringing.
(NRO ref: MC580/1, 780x1)

Earlier, at Spa, Windham found himself the centre of attention of a Mrs Wilkinson, who called him by his first name and 'seemed to take a considerable interest in him' according to one witness, who had also seen them driving around together, although this was later said to be because the older woman was interested in pairing off Gla with her daughter.

Back again in Spa in October, Windham's peculiarities included staring at the women in the gaming rooms. He annoyed fellow hotel guests but his manners were accepted as eccentricities by the staff, who no doubt had considerable experience of the quirks of the English. In England that autumn, at the Norwich Sessions Ball, Windham again caused a disturbance, running backwards, tearing ladies' dresses and being 'very uncouth' to them. None of them, naturally, were inclined to dance with the strange youth.

Like Bathurst, Horrocks ended up having fisticuffs with Windham. And like the colonel, it was to no effect. Two letters from Windham to his mother in late September 1859 show the battle of wills going on between the 19-year-old and his latest companion. One, dated the 25th and written from St Leonard's, states:

'DEAR MAMMA - I have had a hard battle, but I stood my ground against going abroad in spite of Lord Alfred's threats, which he sent to me through Horrocks, saying that if I did not go abroad I should not be allowed to go to Felbrigg in the autumn; but I was more determined than ever not to go. When I received these messages from Horrocks, I told him simply I might perhaps have yielded and gone; but now, since I have been threatened and intimidated, I will not leave England, in spite of any threats. This morning, at Folkestone, he went, with a friend of his, who was going to London, to the ticket office and asked me to come down to the station. Well, I walked down, and I saw him go to take two tickets, so I said, "Where is the luggage, and where are we going?" He said, "It's on board; here is your ticket for Boulogne." I said simply, "Then the luggage may go without me, and so may you. I shall not touch that ticket, or get my boot on the boat." He then commenced blackguarding me before all the porters and people, called me a lunatic, and said I was mad and insane, and never should come to the property, &c, and said to his friend, "Oh, he has had a letter from his dear mother," with a sneer...'

The letter shows that the supposedly backward Windham was perfectly capable of drafting such a communication and, equally, perfectly capable of rational argument. It shows, too, the level of dislike which existed by now between Horrocks and himself. The comment which the angry Horrocks made about having him declared insane is an even more significant one, as it echoed events from two years later. Horrocks, perhaps, had been party to family discussions to do exactly this, a suggestion which - in the heat of the moment - he had blurted out in his contempt for his young companion.

Three days later Windham was writing to his mother from the Grand Parade, Hastings, expressing his desire to join a regiment 'and then Alfred cannot help my being with them and allowing me a good sum of money... I think it might be managed that we should be embodied [= formed together] and stationed in some jolly place like Shorncliffe or Plymouth.' This vague plan to join the military was the closest Windham got to making any sort of firm plans for the near future.

Lack of ambition was not, however, a charge which could be made against Agnes. By the end of 1859 she had already transformed herself with a society-defying determination.

3

1854-1861:
'These delightful dashing creatures':
Agnes and the Démi-Monde

'Hunting young ladies are very popular in the hunting field. I know of no place in which girls receive more worship and attention...'
Anthony Trollope, Orley Farm (1861-2)

THERE WAS plenty, as usual, to amuse the readers of Punch in the issue of 13 July 1861. One of the choicest moments was a cartoon headlined 'GROUNDLESS ALARM'. A silk top-hatted matron-like rider is pictured alongside her younger - and altogether comelier - riding partner. The 'Stout Equestrian' turns to her companion, saying: 'Do you know, love, I'm rather sorry I got this hat, for I suppose I should be taken for a "pretty horsebreaker".' Her companion is smiling to herself, as well she might.

For the pretty horsebreakers - or 'fair equestrians' as they were also known - were renowned for their fashion sense, their beauty, and for being the most notorious courtesans in London. And by now Agnes was at the very heart of their world.

In her 1839 book Women of England, Sarah Ellis had written that in dealings with men, it was 'impossible but that a woman should feel her own inferiority; and it is right that it should be so'. The image of Victorian society as strictly patriarchal, with the gentleman of the house concerning himself with business and other weighty affairs while his dutiful wife supervised the servants and equally dutifully produced 'heirs and spares' at regular intervals, is an abiding one. But Agnes was one of those who defied convention. Agnes, and her contemporaries 'Skittles' (Catherine Walters), along with the likes of Louisa Turner, 'Sweet Nelly' Fowler and Ellen Clarke dared to turn on their heads these contemporary mores about men and sexuality - and win.

IT WAS a well-worn path from the virtuous domestic servant girl to the seduced version. Not for nothing was it one of the stock themes of Victorian novels - as, incidentally, was the scarcely less shocking theme for the 'better sort' of reader, that of the '*mésalliance*' between classes. Contemporary newspapers portray the all-too frequent outcome of such dalliances, with grim accounts of the aftermath of concealed births. In some London hotels, indeed, the availability of the servants for sexual amusement of the visitors was fully accepted - and expected. Limmer's in Conduit Street, for example (a few minutes' walk from the Haymarket) catered admirably for the racegoing 'swell' who was seeking readily-available women too.

Agnes was different from the rest of the country girls. Whether that was because she had already been picked out as a potential mistress while still in Dorset or Hampshire, or whether she had followed the frequently-travelled route of country girl, to London servant, to partner in sexual dalliance, is unclear. Agnes herself was vague on the subject. A possible explanation comes, curiously, from a newspaper in Canada from 1884. The Newfoundlander of January 25 that year, quoting an anonymous 'London letter' claimed that Agnes 'began life as a bar-maid at Highbury barn but quickly graduated to the Haymarket' [ie, prostitution]

Agnes' own story at the time - for those who would listen - was that she was a clergyman's daughter who had been left £600 a year, in addition to money to bring up her two younger sisters. She called herself 'Agnes Willoughby' on and off for years, because, she said, she had been seduced by Lord Willoughby de Broke. When the claim was mentioned in court in 1861 it was immediately rebuffed as having 'not the slightest foundation'. But the damage, of course, had been done as far as wider publicity was concerned.

Robert John Barnard Peyto-Verney was the 17th Baron Willoughby de Broke, who lived at a magnificent mansion in Compton Verney, near Warwick. Agnes could have known Lord Willoughby de Broke, at least by repute, as the family were closely linked to foxhunting circles - indeed his son Henry and grandson Robert Greville Verney, the 18th and 19th barons respectively, both wrote books on the subject. Competition for the prettiest mistress was as intense as that for the gamest quarry on the hunting field, so perhaps the 17th baron was secretly rather flattered. True or not, she was calling herself by this name as least as early as 1856 - when she was just 15 - and already living in some style in Orchard Street, including having the use of a carriage. She had a manservant (John Foyle) who acted as her coachman. He later said she was living 'under the protection of a gentleman' at the time, whom he hinted was not (if indeed, of course, it ever had been) the baron.

We next have a window into Agnes' life through a court hearing in July 1857, reported in Reynold's News, a newspaper with a keen ear for scandal. As 'Agnes Willoughby' she had been taken to Bloomsbury County Court by an upholsterer for a £15 10s debt - perhaps her first hearing for debt, but certainly not her last. She was living at 1 Eccleston Terrace, Pimlico, and the court case turned on whether the summons had been properly served on her. The court's officer said that he had left it with a female servant, but Agnes' sister Thirza (incorrectly reported as 'Theresa'), described as 'a young and beautiful girl' (she was by now no older than 12), insisted that she had received the summons but had not passed it to her sister. She said she had then given it to someone the paper described, in ironic quotation marks, as 'the butler' John Burden.

But the paper (and the judge) reserved most of their ire for Agnes' mother Ann - 'a woman dressed in the height of fashion' - who then went into the witness box. 'I am the mother of the defendant,' she told the court. 'I act as her housekeeper. I am, in fact, her servant and receive wages from her... Agnes has not had the summons.'

When cross-examined, Ann Rogers said 'with great effrontery' that her daughter 'sees gentlemen'. She continued: 'I can't tell you how many. She lives that way, and has no other mode of supporting herself.' She went on to explain how she had a perfectly adequate income of her own (perhaps hinting at Agnes' property portfolio) but that she also received wages from her daughter. And she was not the only one: the court heard Agnes was supporting a brougham carriage, the butler (on a reported £50 a year), her 'secretary' - and her sister Thirza.

Agnes' house was described, with acute though inaccurate moral umbrage, as a 'brothel', but the judge was more concerned with the conduct of Ann Rogers. 'Woman,' he told her, 'your conduct is most truly degrading.' Looking at Thirza, he went on: 'You are bringing up a young and beautiful child to a career of vice and infamy... the disclosures made in this case are disgusting.' If Ann had felt chastised, she certainly did not show it: leaving the court, she 'gaily stepped inside' the waiting brougham, and the debt was paid off shortly after that.

The report shows not only the full complicity of Ann in her daughter's way of life but - and this was what stuck so much in the craw of society - her utter indifference to any moral niceties. Significant, too, was the clearly implied wealth which Agnes was

Ann Rogers, later Ann Burden: Agnes'
mother was a willing and unashamed
supporter of her young daughter's chosen
profession, that of 'seeing gentlemen'.
(Michelle Grigg)

already accumulating, and her dominance in her relationship with her mother. She was already operating as a highly-successful and high-class courtesan. And all this, and she was not yet 17.

Agnes' unrepentant attitude to her chosen profession was not unique. An anonymous correspondent (known only as 'Unfortunate') wrote to The Times in February 1858 to explain, in detail over two solid columns of type, how - far from being a victim of the 'Social Evil' - that she had decided to become a prostitute from her own free will. It was a decision, 'Unfortunate' said, that she had not regretted, as it had given her a good living (like Agnes), allowed her to educate herself (like Agnes) and to support her family (like Agnes).

She also insisted - and this is where the analogy to Agnes broke down - that she always paid her debts. 'Unfortunate' also highlighted the hypocrisy at large in society. 'You, the pious, the moral, the respectable... why stand you on your eminence shouting that we should be ashamed of ourselves?'.

The anonymous correspondent even piqued the interest of Charles Dickens who - in a letter revealed during researches at The Times for the writer's bicentenary in early 2012 - wrote on behalf of social reformer Angela Burdett-Coutts trying to track down 'Unfortunate' to offer her help. Dickens almost immediately sent off a second letter until he realised, belatedly, that the correspondent had no regrets about her

OPPOSITE PAGE: Agnes the 'pretty horsebreaker': Probably photographed around 1860, this image is taken from a gentleman's album (with the initials 'S. N. P.') of cartes de visites photographs featuring noted courtesans of mid-Victorian England, including Trotty Stuart, 'The Kid', Cora Pearl, and Catherine Walters. *(Mary Evans Picture Library)*.

chosen path through life, and the offer of help was quickly - and quietly - dropped.

Meanwhile it was not just in London that Agnes was well known. Whether it was Lord Willoughby de Broke or not, at some early stage one of her wealthy gentleman protectors introduced her to the hunting field where, like her contemporary Skittles, she became an expert rider.

Combined with her striking blonde hair and expertly-tailored riding gear, she was the object of great attention. Agnes' riding ability - commented upon almost as much as her looks - must have been an innate skill, as a village sawyer's daughter would scarcely have had many opportunities to ride thoroughbreds. Perhaps (as seems likely to have been the case with Skittles) she taught herself to ride through helping out in an inn where a local hunt gathered. Her future solicitor James Bowen May later recalled meeting the 18-year-old Agnes in 1859: 'She rode remarkably well and was a woman of great personal attractions'.

Agnes never seemed to lack invitations to join the hunting field, at various times riding with Mr Young's hounds in Hertfordshire, Her Majesty's Staghounds in Buckinghamshire, and with hunts in Leicestershire and many other places.

Her very presence added the spice of novelty, as by 1860 there were still only perhaps two or three women in each hunt. But what they lacked in numbers they generally more than made up for in expertise - and daring. Riding fearlessly to jump one of the notorious 'bullfinches' (prickly newly-planted quickthorn hedging) was something many male riders would baulk at, but as R S Surtees put it in his novel Mr Sponge's Sporting Tour in 1853: 'When women do ride they generally ride like the very devil. There is no medium with them. They either "go" to beat the men or they don't "go" at all.'

Fortunately we do not have to rely on portraits or words or photographs to guess how striking Agnes must have looked. As part of its impressive and important collection of clothing and textiles, the Norfolk Museums and Archaeology Service has one of Agnes' riding habits from the years 1858-1860. Its opulence is immediately, and impressively, apparent. Made from scarlet material and trimmed with black lozenge-shaped 'slashes' of velvet, it would have been worn over a longer skirt as a riding apron. There is nothing subdued here; everything about it says high fashion, self-confidence, and the desire to be the centre of attention.

Even the pocket on the back of the habit is beautifully, and strikingly, stitched - clearly designed to attract admiring glances after its It is easy to picture Agnes, riding her sleek thoroughbred with graceful ease, the nipped-in waist of her outfit (the item shows this was no more than 26 inches) showing off her superb figure, her blonde hair a beacon over the already-striking vivid scarlet of her riding apron. Almost 150 years on, it is still stunning.

Stylish rider: Seen from two angles, one of Agnes' riding habits from 1858-60, now in the Costume and Textiles Collection of the Norfolk Museums and Archaeology Service. In striking scarlet material and black velvet, it would have been worn over a longer skirt. It also reveals Agnes had a 26-inch waist.

Everything about it says: 'Look at me, everybody.' And, naturally, everybody did.

Others had ridden the same path through society before Catherine Walters and Agnes. Laura Bell, dubbed 'the Queen of London Whoredom' by William Hardman during the 1850s, was the daughter of an Antrim bailiff who went with dizzying speed from shop-girl to attracting admiring glances in Hyde Park and even having an affair with the Nepalese ambassador. Laura was described as having a 'pretty doll-like face', and both Skittles and Agnes were noted for their petite figures. Agnes had much in common with Catherine, in figure, hair colour, humble background (Skittles' father was a Liverpool customs man) feistiness, skill on a horse (Skittles hunted with the Quorn) - and sense of fashion. And their shop-window was Hyde Park.

45

FRANCIS WEY, writing in his 1856 book Les Anglais Chez Eux, told of the crowds of people, carriages and riders which thronged Hyde Park. 'Sometimes a squadron of amazons, their skirts trailing to the ground, cantered past us, dazzling us with the beauty of their horses and with the vision of such grace and charm, such suppleness, ease and daring.' Hyde Park and Kensington Gardens often attracted enormous crowds of 40,000 plus, their presence mingling with the sight and noise of flocks of sheep and cattle still grazed in the city by London butchers.

The term 'pretty horsebreaker' originated in the practice of the owners of livery stables in employing pretty girls who were excellent riders to ride their finest horses in the Park to advertise the owners' wares. Rotten Row was flanked by a magnificent avenue of trees, wide enough for four carriages to pass abreast with ease. It had a railing and wide pavement, ideal for those wishing to stop and stare at the early-evening parade - and there were always plenty who did. On at least two occasions (and probably many, many more) in 1861, Windham was one of them.

The Row ran from the western edge of Kensington Gardens through to Hyde Park Corner. It was, and remains, perhaps the best known of the riders' thoroughfares, but not the only one: the Ladies' Mile ran from the Serpentine and was known for its mix of elegant carriages, superb riders and the highest echelons of society in charge of both. From May to July, the 'Season', hundreds came to see and be seen, and thousands came to watch, and admire. Rotten Row represented one of the few places in Victorian England where, if you were beautiful enough, fashionable enough, and a good enough horsewoman, then no-one, frankly, gave a damn about class, background or anything else. Here was the battleground in which the most beautiful courtesans competed with each other - and respectable maidens - for the security that only marriage could truly bring. Here, and only here, could a village sawyer's daughter such as Agnes compete with the most eligible ladies in the land.

For make no mistake, it was a wealthy marriage that was seen as the glittering prize for the mistresses and 'prima donnas'. W Acton, in his 1870 work Prostitution, wrote of 'the better inclined class of prostitutes [becoming] the wedded wives of men in every grade of society, from the peerage to the stable'. Marriage equalled security. Looks inevitably faded; with careful management, wealth would not. And the potential prizes could be glittering indeed. Louisa Turner competed with Ellen Clarke for the affections of the Duke of Brunswick, Louisa fought a winning battle for the affections of Lord Yarmouth, while Catherine was mistress to Lord Hartington.

But making that advantageous match called for a large degree of cool-headed judgement on the part of the women. The reason was the long-held common law principle of 'coverture', which held that everything a woman owned became the property of her husband on marriage.

It was a situation which was not to be legally addressed until the Married Women's Property Acts of 1870 and 1882. Therefore, for a mistress to consider giving up her lucrative financial independence in this way was a matter not to be considered lightly.

Punch of 13 July 1861, in two brilliantly observed cartoons ('Ways and Means') had its own view. The left hand page shows a bored courtesan, her 'pretty horsebreaker' riding habit draped casually alongside, contemplating her new carriage, while her maid attends to her elaborate hair (which happens, incidentally, to be blonde). Everywhere is luxury, from her vast crinoline dress to the pearl-stuffed jewellery box, while on the wall she has pictures of thoroughbred horses - and houses - to contemplate.

Pleased as Punch: This cartoon from the satirical magazine from July 1861 illustrates the moral ambiguity many felt towards the 'pretty horsebreakers'.

And how does she afford all this? The 'means' is pictured opposite: a louche, rich provider takes his self-satisfied ease in his club, flunkey at hand. 'Why They Don't Marry' says the caption: 'They don't have to' being the unspoken comment.

The term 'pretty horsebreakers' had been in circulation for some time, but a famous letter in The Times thrust it on everyone's lips. On 27 June 1861, under the heading 'The Slump in Marriage', a 'Sorrowing Mother' wrote on behalf of seven others ('with one exception, noblewomen') to complain how their carefully brought-up daughters were still at home, unmarried. 'However unpleasant, indelicate the truth, all dreadful as it is to us to write it, marriage in our set is voted a bore - is repudiated. And why? Because what our simple-minded daughters call "the pretty horse-breakers" occupy naughtily and temporarily where we should occupy en permanence.' The letter (which was read by Windham, among many others) sparked a reply, purporting to be from the first-born son of a noble family (under the pseudonym 'Primogenitus'), who said the "heir-hunters" of Belgravia were as much to blame as the fair equestrians for their daughters being unmarried. 'I firmly intend to marry some day - not yet; but when I do marry I intend to try and pick out a wife for myself, and not to have one forced upon me by scheming old women.

'Take a chair in Rotten-row tomorrow, Sir; look about you, and then tell us what you see there... Who rides the best horse in the row? Who drives the most rampageous (*sic*) ponies? Whom do all the best girls ape in dress and deportment, and in equipage if they can; aye, and in talk too? Who first set the fashion of the "pork pie" hat? Who restored the ancient chimney pot [ie silk top hat]? Why, one of our "pretty horsebreakers".'

They soon became the stuff of catch-phrase, cartoon and more. By the end of July they were the subject of a skit at the Adelphi Theatre 'on the question of Belgravian Mammas vs Pretty Horsebreakers'. They (and especially Skittles) caught the attention of poet (and future Poet Laureate) Alfred Austin who wrote in his 1861 satirical work The Season: 'Though scowling matrons champing steeds restrain/She flaunts Propriety with flapping mane.' The phrase was still in use as late as 1864 when it was used - to laughter - in a Parliamentary debate about parks and pleasure-grounds. But 1861-3 was its high-water mark, and that of its two leading exponents. Polite society was left in a confused and unresolved state of moral ambiguity over Agnes and her kind.

Another Punch cartoon of 20 July 1861 shows something of this confusion. Two pretty top-hatted horse riders are seen leaning over Mr Punch with, in the background a poster advertising a meeting concerning a new ride in Kensington Gardens. 'Now, don't be a cross old Punch,' one of the 'fair equestrians' (that euphemism again) is saying, 'We really won't spoil the beauty of the gardens'. Mr Punch is looking, well, as pleased as punch with their attentions; he was just as hopelessly intrigued as everyone else.

George Augustus Sala, too, writing at this time, was equally ambiguous. He gushed 'The Danae! The Amazons! The Lady Cavaliers! The horse-women!', adding excitedly: 'Can any scene in the world equal Rotten Row at four in the afternoon and in the full time of the season?', continuing in similar besotted vein for several sentences. It is only at the end that he sounds an unconvincing moral note: 'Some of these delightful dashing creatures have covered themselves with shame, and their mothers with grief, and have brought their fathers' grey hair with sorrow to the grave. All is not gold that glitters, my son.'

BUT THERE was plenty which glittered for Agnes. Thanks to her personal magnetism, attractiveness and determination, by 1861 she had thrust herself into the highest echelons of the démi-monde, those women considered to be outside the bounds of respectable society. There was talk of several properties by now - including a pied-à-terre in Paris. Her mother and sisters were living at 36 Queen's Road West, Chelsea, by 1860, which naturally would have been due to Agnes. By now she was the mistress of one Jack Garton, known as 'handsome Jack', who could afford to lavish £2,000 per year on an allowance for her.

By coincidence, this was exactly 100 times the wealth her father had accumulated in his whole life; that was the measure of how far Agnes had already travelled. The centre for kept women such as Agnes was St John's Wood - known as 'the Wicked Wood' for just this reason until at least the 1890s. Along with Brompton, it was the suburb of choice for courtesans by the 1860s. As Lesley Blanch has observed, these villas commonly provided 'high-walled gardens and roofed-in carriageways' perfect for rendering discreet the visits of admirers.

How many other lovers had Agnes had by 1861? There was a mention in later court proceedings of an unnamed 'young dragoons officer', which seems perfectly possible, and David Llewellyn (a future landlord of Windham's) was to claim that Agnes had been 'on the town for years, and had ruined many a man', and, of course, there were the unnamed 'gentlemen' which her mother had alluded to in the 1857 court hearing. But the best-documented of Agnes' lovers was not one of her protectors, but an Italian opera singer.

Agnes' cool and business-like detachment vanished with the man who was, if not the love of her life, undoubtedly a source of fierce passion for several years. Decades after the relationship had cooled, Agnes still kept a drawing of him. Born in 1827, by the late 1850s Antonio Giuglini was one of the greatest stars on the London operatic scene, a figure of enormous public regard. Making his debut around 1849, he quickly built up a reputation through appearances in Venice, Rome and Milan. Giuglini arrived on the London scene at Her Majesty's Theatre in 1857, and if the evidence of Agnes' coachman John Foyle is anything to go by, Agnes lost no time in becoming his lover, with Foyle frequently taking her from Orchard Street to Giuglini's house in Somers Terrace, Brompton.

Agnes was passionate about the opera, having her own box at the Lyceum by 1861, and attending at least two to three times a week. In 1858 Giuglini came under the orbit of 'Colonel' J H Mapleson, whose lively autobiography The Mapleson Memoirs gives a vivid portrait of the frequent crises, precarious finances and double-dealing which were a feature of an impresario's life. The singers may have performed in roles which showed them as the models of heroic stature, but off-stage it was a very different picture.

'Ways and Means': Punch readers in the summer of 1861 would have picked up the

subtle messages being expressed in this superb pair of cartoons.

Mapleson wrote of his frustration at being unable to enforce contracts (the unsympathetic Lords Justices having told him in 1859 he might as well try to 'restrain the birds from singing on the trees'), his despair at the mercurial financial demands of his stars, and their tendency to fall prey to a hard-to-define malady known as 'grippe', which owed little to medical cause and more to hysteria and petulance. And Giuglini was just as hysterical and petulant as the rest of them.

Mapleson's company, led by Giuglini and the equally well-regarded Thérèse Tietjens, put on a triumphant - though loss-making season - which began on 8 June 1861, despite competition (for the operatic crowd) from Covent Garden and (for the general public) from a huge fire in Bermondsey. An Illustrated London News profile and flattering engraving of Giuglini in his prime shows him as handsome and serious, with dark, brooding Italian looks. Sadly, the reality was altogether more prosaic. A carte-de-visite photograph taken in April 1861 by Hyman Davis and now in the National Portrait Gallery collections, shows him as short and tending to portliness, while affecting a - frankly - absurd heroic pose. When the diarists Ellen Hall and Louisa Shore went to see him in concert their appreciation of his singing was tempered by the fact that 'he looked like a great fat fiend frowning over his music'.

So what did the hard-headed Agnes see in him? There is no doubt that, although no great actor, Giuglini had an undeniable stage presence and, naturally, a winning voice. The Punch critic wrote approvingly in 27 April 1861 of Giuglini's ability to sustain notes, while on 6 July he added: 'Titiens [Tietjens] and Giuglini were both in glorious voice and have rarely pleased me more'. One can imagine Agnes, on the arm of her current protector, leaning forward in her box in rapt concentration to catch every nuance of the dashing tenor. There is no doubt, too, that being Italian had a huge cachet with the public at this time because of the young country's heroic efforts to shake off the Austrian yoke. Patriots such as Garibaldi were mobbed by adoring crowds whenever they came to Britain. Giuglini, naturally, was fully aware of this, even writing a cantata in 1862 during which he insisted 120 Italian flags should be waved as the Orchestra struck up the 'Garibaldi hymn'.

But off-stage he could be absurdly petulant. Mapleson went further: 'Giuglini was in many things a child,' he wrote. Famously, he was obsessed with flying kites - to the extent of risking life and limb on the Brompton Road - and with letting off fireworks. That did not mean he could not be hard-headed and extremely demanding when he came to money, as Mapleson was to discover to his cost. Giuglini also had a curious platonic relationship with Madame Puzzi, a former opera singer then in her mid-50s, whom the tenor came to rely upon to extricate him from the clutches of a long line of 'enterprising young women' who attempted to woo him. Agnes, typically, succeeded where the others had failed, a measure yet again of her single-mindedness.

There was another figure in Agnes' life by 1861, another colourful character - although of a very different ilk - who was destined to play a key part in ensuing events: James 'Mahogany' Roberts, Piccadilly resident, former bankrupt, timber merchant, and reputed owner of several high-class brothels. Agnes' relationship with him was more complex, there being no particular evidence that he was her lover, at least at this stage.

By now Agnes was famous enough to be mentioned in weighty tomes of social commentary. In the fourth volume of Henry Mayhew's survey, London Labour and the London Poor, published the following year, Bracebridge Hemyng contributed a chapter on prostitution which divided the capital's prostitutes into three classes. At the top were the ones kept by men of independent means (in effect, the mistresses). Hemyng wrote, unusually for Victorian social commentators, with both perception and sympathy

Antonio Giuglini: The Italian opera singer with whom Agnes quickly became besotted. *(National Portrait Gallery, London)*

when he described the women of the highest class of prostitution as in 'the nearest approximation to the holy state of marriage and [which] finds numerous defenders and supporters.' He continued: 'These have their suburban villas, their carriages, horses and sometimes a box at the opera'. He could have been writing about Agnes. He was. She was being described in the text in the most flimsy of disguises as 'AW'.

We have a description of Agnes in that box at the opera from exactly this time. In an article in The Morning Chronicle of February 1862, 'Agnes Willoughby at The Lyceum', the writer looked back to the previous June, when Agnes' passion for Giuglini was in full flower. She was there every night during Giuglini's engagement, 'a charming tableau of the status certain of the Sociable Evil [ie, higher class of prostitutes] have attained... amongst us'. Agnes, the writer continued, was to be seen in her 'neat little box' and generally in a pink dress. She 'was always alone, save for one of her sisters, a mere child [Thirza]. Dressed in a quiet and unostentatious manner, her conduct... was in corresponding style, in no way calculated to draw attention. No bouquet; nothing in the Dame aux Camellias fashion; and only a few diamonds in the hair, of which there is a profusion.'

'Seated at the back of the box, she had no eyes for the audience, only for the stage; and only for one individual thereon,' the report said. Turning to Agnes' physical appearance, it continued: 'Her countenance is more pleasing than picturesque; - more Saxon than classic; neither spirituelle nor sensuous; rather matter of fact than romantic. Middle-sized, her figure is singularly graceful' - which the paper put down to the physical exercise involved in hunting.

BY 1861 Agnes had much to be thankful for. She had made an astonishing journey from poor village girl to glittering mistress-about-Town, breaking through barriers of class and social convention. But she was shrewd enough to know that the life of the courtesan was inevitably limited. Perhaps she knew something of the fate of her famous predecessor, Harriet Walters, the Regency courtesan admired and sought by a large section of the British aristocracy from the Duke of Wellington downwards. Walters had narrowly missed out on an aristocratic marriage and had ended her days instead lonely, embittered and a hopeless drunk, her famous memoirs sparking the equally-famous riposte from the Duke to 'publish and be damned'. In June Agnes prepared to travel with Jack Garton to the Ascot meeting, then, as now, immensely fashionable.

What happened in the next few hours was to change the course of her life for ever.

4

1859-1861:
The Meeting

'London, then, was a monster of desire.'
J White, London in the Nineteenth Century (2007)

'There is, perhaps, more shouting in the Haymarket than elsewhere.'
PC Charles Brown, 1862

IN THE latter part of 1859, visitors to London's Haymarket began to hear strange tales of an odd and boorish youth who was fast becoming a figure of fun to be pointed out and commented on. The young man - some said he was the heir to a country estate - attracted attention through his screeching in the streets, and persistent 'shouting and halloaing'. The youth, of course, was Windham. And he was rapidly being drawn into an area of London which was proverbial throughout the land as a sink-hole of sin.

A world away from the faux-gentility of St John's Wood were Bracebridge Hemyng's lowest class of prostitutes - those who plied their trade through the brothels, centred round the Haymarket, as they been had for generations. The area's notoriety extended far beyond London as a byword for moral and social degradation.

The Saturday Review of April 1858 summed up the prevailing belief that moral laxity in the shires could set a woman on the path to total decline with the phrase 'the cottage bedroom is the first step to the Haymarket'.

For most Londoners, of course, this area was just another part of the wallpaper of city life. It took a visiting novelist's powers of description to conjure up a vivid picture of its day-to-day realities for those outside the capital. Fyodor Dostoevsky, writing in 1862, claimed that sooner or later every London visitor was irresistibly drawn there. Dostoevsky wrote of 'thousands' of prostitutes gathering in the gas-lit streets, with the 'all gilt and glass' cafes the only safe place to escape their attentions. 'They are all thirsty of prey and recruit the first-comer with complete cynicism. Grand clothes rub shoulders with rags; the same contrast in age; everything is mixed up,' he said. The novelist wrote, too, of consumptive women and mothers putting their little daughters up for sale. 'I remember,' he added, 'seeing in the crowd a little girl of barely six, in rags, dirty, barefoot, haggard and bruised... no-one noticed her. Her face had an expression of utter despair.'

Promenading prostitutes handed out business cards to their would-be clientele until at least 1870. And woe betide any respectable woman who went into the area alone. In the Haymarket all women were liable to be propositioned, a state of affairs which had existed since at least 1808. Into this swirling, noisy, colourful mass of humanity - which typically kept going in full flow until four in the morning in the night-houses [all-night pubs] - came the sons of lords and country squires, eager to s ow their wild oats before the 'old man' insisted on their settling down to run the estate or join the regiment.

Two of the most familiar characters in popular culture in the early- to mid-Victorian period were 'Tom and Jerry', fun-seeking gentlemen out on the town, and firmly in the public imagination since the 1830s. Punch cartoonist John Leech, who chronicled the images of contemporary society in almost 3,000 cartoons for the magazine between 1841 and his death in 1864, superbly captured the essence of this type of 'young gentleman'. His absurd 'swell', with monocle, extravagant facial hair and affected speech appears time and again in its pages of this period. It was a role which the already-dissolute young Windham was doing his best to fill in his own way.

WINDHAM certainly cut a strange figure. He pretended to be a policeman and threatened to lock people up if they loitered, and was often heard shouting in the streets. The Haymarket was hardly one of London's quieter areas - Metropolitan police inspector William Holden said there was 'not a noisier place in London at night than the Haymarket, with the exception, perhaps, of Ratcliff-highway [in the East End]

William Frederick Windham: A carte de visite from around 1861, when the young heir was attracting attention in the notorious Haymarket of London.
(NRO ref: MC580/1, 780x1)

on certain occasions' - but the Norfolk squire's screeches made even him stand out. His physical appearance was hardly that of a dashing young beau: a later description has him as 'a young man with round face, bullet head, and short black moustache'. Windham was better behaved in the cafes, and Insp Holden recalled later that he had never seen him in the company of street prostitutes.

But that did not mean the young Norfolk squire was not falling prey to the many sharks who swam about the district. Indeed, Windham's behaviour made him an irresistible target. Bystanders would laugh at the strange-headed man with the rough country accent, but they would be delighted when they discovered it was accompanied by a desire to buy 'sham' (champagne) for everyone.

Another London policeman, Sergeant Edward Oliver, recalled how 'the women all used to get round him, and he would treat them, and they would ridicule him. He always created a great deal of excitement in every house he went into.' His colleague Sergeant Kay met Windham in one of the 'flash houses' in Panton Street in the summer of 1861, where he saw him deep in conversation with a barmaid. On seeing the sergeant, Windham shouted out: 'Here come the bobbies!' and struck Kay on the back with his cane. Normally, of course, this kind of behaviour would have had a sequel involving a police cell, but Kay - like the other policemen - let Windham be. 'I did not think he was right in the head,' he explained. 'None of the police ever took any notice of him.'

All this implies that Windham had been cut adrift and left to wallow in the fleshpots of the Haymarket. But the truth was that his companion Horrocks, the Court of Chancery and his mother and guardians were still trying (admittedly some parties rather harder than others) to make something of the troublesome young squire. In the National Archives at Kew there is a court document from January 1860 which shows exactly how much of a headache Windham was proving to be. His uncle Lord Alfred asked for permission to stand down as a guardian - which was granted - as he could no longer cope with his wayward charge. The main reason for the behind-closed-doors hearing, though, was for Lady Sophia to persuade the Court of Chancery to give her permission to take her son back under her control. The previous two years, her attorney insisted, had been 'spent in a manner worse than useless, and the minor [ie Windham] has lost considerably in moral feeling and his conduct has become more self-willed and uncontrollable'. Horrocks had told Lady Sophia that her son 'never studies and rarely (if ever) opens a book' and was under 'no proper control'.

And so an order was made that Windham should accompany his mother and 'travel abroad for one year certain and should visit the different Capitals of Europe and, introduced at the Courts there with a view to his learning the languages and preparing himself by frequenting Society of the First Class, especially that of Ladies of high rank, for his future position'. As an optimistic statement of personal improvement it was admirable, but as a reflection of reality it was ridiculous. Windham the attentive, polite, gentle courtier, some some of latter-day parfait gentil knight? It just could not be; and so it proved.

Windham's relationship with Horrocks had already descended into mutual hatred. Despite this, Horrocks continued to be his companion until June 1860, and the policy (such as it was) of moving Windham from resort to resort continued. His reputation in the Haymarket proves there were still plenty of opportunities for him to slip away to London to get into mischief. And he later mentioned that he had been to Paris six times, but only once with his mother. It is hard to believe he spent these visits in cultural excursions. While on his coastal meanderings in England, though, he could still behave with propriety. A 'clean and tidy' Windham stayed at a house next to the Esplanade Baths at Ryde in April 1860 for three weeks, and again in May 1861 for nearly a fortnight.

It was a similar story at the Royal Kent Hotel in Sandgate (in Folkestone) in 1859, and again in March 1860 when Windham stayed there for a fortnight with Horrocks. Windham was there to associate with the officers at the Shorncliffe barracks, as he still had thoughts of a military career. To this end he wrote to Sir Edmund Lacon, Colonel of the East Norfolk Militia and Great Yarmouth MP to ask for a commission, which was granted by the Lord Lieutenant.

Windham - without telling the hated Horrocks - joined the militia's headquarters in Yarmouth in 20 April 1860 as a lieutenant, and enjoyed the training, especially the drill, at which he practised up to five hours a day. Dedication, clearly, and yet the other side of Windham was to break out while he was in the Norfolk town. Solicitor W C Reynolds remembered later how Windham had called in to his offices about the long-running Chancery case involving his mother. It was the first of several encounters with the young squire over the next few days, which included seeing him 'blubbering like a great child' at a local hotel late one night; hardly the stuff of martial legend.

In spring 1860 Horrocks at last parted company with Windham, the Court of Chancery appointing Joseph Peatfield in his stead. He was instructed to take Windham on yet another meandering series of travels from June around England, Scotland and Ireland. Their week-long stay in Edinburgh was not a happy one, Windham scandalising two landladies and their servants by making loud cat and cockerel noises and by shouting and jumping around his room. Within days he was so notorious that people would follow him in the streets.

Peatfield and Windham eventually returned to Felbrigg in early September, where they stayed until 4 February 1861. Windham soon disgraced himself again, offending the great and the good at the Norfolk and Norwich Festival Ball the same month by drunkenly making a 'great noise' and even trying to borrow a policeman's whistle so he could blow it and cause panic in the crowded hall. Their stay back in Norfolk came to an abrupt end after reports reached Peatfield of Windham getting involved in a fight with a showman in Aylsham (in which he received a black eye). Peatfield immediately ordered Windham to pack his bags and they travelled down to London. Windham was furious, accusing Peatfield of being 'a sneak and a spy'.

Lady Sophia, who regularly wrote to the General about his nephew's actions, was sufficiently alarmed by now to plead with her brother-in-law to return home from India. While in London Peatfield went to see the banker Robert Hook, a relative by marriage and who had been appointed another of Windham's guardians, and was promptly ordered to take him to the Channel Islands. There is a snapshot of their stay in the Channel Islands, thanks to the 1861 Census. Peatfield and Windham were staying at 5 College Terrace in St Peter Port, Guernsey, the only guests of Mary and Maria Owen. When it came to giving details of his profession, Windham clearly already had his mind on what would happen only three months later. He told the census clerk: 'landed proprietor'.

In March the General responded to his sister-in-law's plea and left India, where he had been in command at Lahore. He arrived back in England in May and tried to get Windham to travel abroad once again with a companion, but by now Windham was beginning to fall out with the man he had once admired, and came to believe that the General was secretly working against his interests. In the spring there was a widespread rumour in Norfolk society that Windham had high hopes of marrying a lady (unnamed) of good family. There was certainly no direct evidence for this rumour, and what family letters exist in the Norfolk Record Office make no mention of this.

There are, however, two possible references to it. One of Peatfield's friends, the Rev T J Baty, later told how he had met Windham in late May, with Windham spinning an extraordinary tale of how he had employed a policeman to check on the chasteness of a lady he was engaged to - a 'lady of position' (whom he did not name) who had since married an army officer. The clergyman did not seem to think there was any truth in Windham's claims, putting it down to another of his 'useless, causeless, objectiveless' lies. But another local cleric, the Rev Dolphin on Antingham, later told he had heard how Windham had confided in him that he was to be married to a 'lady of good family'.

The Reverend Baty had encountered Windham in lodgings at Duke Street in London. And it was here that some of the most bizarre episodes in the Windham saga were to be played out, ones which would be of crucial importance in subsequent events. The lodgings were run by a Mr and Mrs Llewellyn, with Peatfield and Windham arriving on 27 May, having spent a couple of weeks at the Bedford Hotel.

According to Peatfield's later account, he had been asked by the General and his fellow guardian Hook to 'let him [ie Windham] be his own master'. It was to be a disastrous decision. Peatfield was to stay on at the Llewellyns' until 12 or 13 August - in other words, just after Windham's 21st birthday - but effectively he had lost the remainder of what little control he had over the squire-to-be the moment the General's request had been made. The General told Windham he was trusting him to be on his best behaviour 'as a gentleman'. It was to be a forlorn hope.

AND NOW the destinies of Windham and Agnes finally began to converge. Windham, like most people, was fascinated by the talk sweeping society about the 'pretty horsebreakers'. While at Duke Street he invited his Felbrigg estate bailiff, Martin, to stay for a few days. There were frequent lunches, often champagne-filled - for which a glass or two would no doubt have been raised to Gladstone who had cut the duty on bubbly that year - during which Windham spoke of his fascination with the ladies who lived in the 'shady groves of the Evangelist', ie St John's Wood. Windham told Martin: 'I would rather marry a "pretty horsebreaker" than a lady.' It was an idle statement, but was to turn out to have an ominous resonance.

It is possible that Agnes, despite moving in higher social circles, might have heard something of the stories beginning to circulate widely of the strange young country squire in the Haymarket. But her first encounter with Windham took place not in the drunken debauchery of the Haymarket - Agnes would hardly have allowed herself to be seen there - but in the genteel environs of Ascot.

Founded in 1711 by Queen Anne, racing had gradually evolved at the heath near Bracknell over the decades until the four-day Royal Ascot became the annual - and indeed until 1939 the only - fixture at the racecourse. We do not know which day they first met, but it seems most likely that it was 'Ladies' Day', when the Gold Cup is staged, then, as now, the busiest day of the meeting. Thursday 13 June 1861 saw what was claimed to be the biggest crowd ever seen at the course. For three hours the railway platforms of the nearest stations disgorged their cargo of race-goers - Windham probably being one of them - with roads through Windsor Park choked with carriages including, it must be assumed, Agnes'. There were so many people, The Times' correspondent reported, that the Grand Stand was 'uncomfortably full, and hundreds of the fairest of creation were unable to obtain even the slightest view of the racing'. The sunshine blessed all the day's racing, as indeed it did for the whole of the festival.

Agnes' carriage might not have been in the enclosure opposite the Stand - that was reserved for 'the privileged' - but the rest of the running ground was 'alive with vehicles of every description'. At 1pm the first of the day's eight races set off,

Agnes Willoughby (Rogers): Pictured on 21 March 1861, a few weeks before her fateful meeting with Windham. *(NRO ref: MC580/1, 780x1)*

but the first three races were merely the appetisers for the Gold Cup. At 2.30pm the seven runners were saddled up, including the favourite, 1860 Derby winner Thormanby, with a strong field including St Leger victor St Albans, French hope Royalieu, and Dulcibella, winner of the Cesarewitch. The 'vast host of spectators' saw second-favourite St Albans and stablemate Plumper make the running, only for Thormanby to ease into the lead at two miles and win at a canter.

Agnes, an excellent judge of horseflesh, would have enjoyed the fine display by the thoroughbred. Perhaps, in her carriage with her latest gentleman-protector Garton and his friends, her thoughts had strayed back to two nights earlier when her lover Giuglini had made yet another triumphant appearance on the London stage. Whatever thoughts were in fact going through her mind, they must have been abruptly interrupted by the sight of the unprepossessing young man before her. In the later words of Windham's counsel, Sir Hugh Cairns: 'Mr Windham was very much struck with her, and, to use an intelligible expression, fell "over head and ears *(sic)* in love with her".

'The lady at first was not at all anxious, or desirous, to leave the position she was in and to enter into marriage. The gentleman had no objection that she do so. The matter was a matter of negotiation for some time, the gentleman saying that he was willing, if the parties themselves arranged it, to resign any claim he had on the lady and after her marriage to discontinue any acquaintance with her.'

The Times' report concluded: 'Soon after five o'clock the curtain fell on as glorious and Ascot Cup day as ever was remembered.' The fate of the Gold Cup had been decided for 1861. And so, it was to turn out, had the destinies of a Norfolk estate, a society courtesan, and a very strange young squire.

5

July-August 1861: 'A Gentleman of Position and Fortune'

'A FAST GIRL fails to catch a lord and master
Because some other girls are rather faster...'
Punch, 6 July 1861

'An annuity is a very serious business; it comes over and over every year, and
there is no getting rid of it.'
Mrs Dashwood, in Sense and Sensibility (1811) by Jane Austen

FROM THE FIRST, it was down to money.

Windham's legal team was later careful to try to paint the Ascot meeting and subsequent wooing of Agnes as a love match, but if love was indeed there, then it was one-sided. Within a few days, Agnes had visited her solicitor, James Bowen May, and told him she was to be married. Bowen May advised her she would be better off to stay as she was, under the protection of her gentleman and with her current handsome income.

His advice was not heeded by Agnes, who returned a few days later to say that she had had an offer of marriage from a 'gentleman of position and fortune' whom she named as Windham. She told her solicitor she had not made up her mind whether to accept. The sticking point was that 'she did not care for him' and would only give up her allowance if some 'very advantageous arrangement' were made for her present and future needs, and for those of her two younger sisters. The solicitor was to claim later that he had advised her to ignore Windham's offer, 'which was not likely to turn out happily'.

On 29 June, while she was still 'making up her mind', Agnes took Windham along to her favourite jeweller, Emmanuel of Brook Street. She was no stranger to its wares, one of its salesmen, Henry Dore, later testifying that Agnes had been there at least once before in the company of another man. It was to be the first of a series of visits, during which Windham almost invariably ended up buying Agnes some new and expensive

Emma Rogers: Agnes frequently cited her welfare and that of her sister Thirza as prime motivations for pressing for a generous settlement from Windham.
(Helen Denney)

gift. At first the presents were relatively small - from 29 June to 8 August they amounted to £211. But as soon as Windham came of age, and could pledge the full weight of his estate in collateral, the value of the gifts grew rapidly.

These jewellery purchases provoked much comment later, being cited as clear evidence of Agnes' avariciousness. That Agnes had a taste for jewellery is indisputable. But the reasons for this extended beyond mere greed: Agnes was thinking ahead, as usual. It was by no means certain for most of that summer whether the marriage settlement would be secured. Agnes was ensuring that, if the courtship did collapse, then at least she would walk away from it with some material compensation.

Part of the reason for her love of jewellery was, of course, to do with fashion.

As someone who caught many an eye on Rotten Row, it would have been strange indeed if she did not set the fashion in the salons and opera boxes too. Agnes' liking for drop pearl earrings echoed the tastes of one of the great fashion icons of the age, Empress Eugenie of France, wife of Napoleon III. While the emperor's territorial ambitions and meddling in the wars of Italian unification were beginning to cause disquiet in the corridors of Whitehall, Eugenie's influence on international matters was altogether more benign. Her striking blonde hair became so fashionable that gold-coloured hair powder became a popular beauty product in the 1860s. Agnes, of course, was lucky enough to have no need for such artificial aids.

There was also an element of self-advertisement. Agnes shared a characteristic shown by her predecessor of two generations earlier, the society courtesan Harriet Walters, who had also flaunted her status in her opera box. Jewellery provided a way of advertising her wealth, thus demonstrating to potential suitors the level at which they would be expected to equal - or better. And there was one final reason: jewellery provided portable and easily redeemable wealth in an emergency. It was to become clear in late 1864 just how much Agnes relied on her personal 'Bank of Diamond'.

WINDHAM, meanwhile, was still at the Llewellyns', where a pattern of long and drink-filled lunches - and worse - had begun. It was suggested later that the General deliberately let Windham stay at the Llewellyns' lodging house (which was close to the Haymarket flesh-pots) as part of a carefully-worked-out plan to spark proceedings, as soon it was obvious that the callow William was incapable of managing his own affairs. Such an analysis, although possible, does not take into account the General's well-established character. He was, after all, a headstrong man of action, likely to act on the spur of the moment, however inadvisable. In June he was appointed colonel of the 46th Regiment, but his planned return to India was now delayed as the family crisis surrounding his nephew deepened.

What exactly went on while Windham was at Duke Street - where he stayed, with some gaps, until 29 August - was to be the subject of much later debate. It is not clear when his landlords became aware of Windham's infatuation with Agnes, but the fact that Windham was now (July) to be seen in the very public confines of her opera box several times a week meant that there were plenty of opportunities for tongues to wag. David Llewellyn said he had heard of Windham's plans by the end of July, a fact which would have been promptly reported back to his paymaster (the General) and which must have filled Windham's uncle with alarm.

Both David and Augusta Llewellyn asked Windham about the rumours, only for the young squire to at first flatly deny any such liaison, and then to insist that Agnes was a clergyman's daughter who had been left money in her father's will. He even claimed it was a case of mistaken identity, with 'his' Agnes not the same as the notorious St John's Wood version. Even when her identity was established, Windham continued to deny he wanted to marry her, saying he merely wanted to use her as a whore. Windham told the Llewellyns that he frequently visited Agnes for the purpose of sleeping with her, but had sometimes had to come back to Duke Street because he had found another man there already.

ON 1 AUGUST, Agnes returned to see Bowen May again, but this time with Windham. The solicitor later claimed that he had no inkling that the prospective bridegroom was under age. He was lying. He knew perfectly well that he was, as Windham told him at this meeting that he was not due to come of age until a week later. Bowen May thought that Windham was not talking 'in any very serious way'. The solicitor met with Windham alone on 4 August and asked him: 'Are you really in earnest about being married? Because I think it right to tell you that the lady is a kept mistress and is very extravagant. She keeps two or three horses and is used to hunting.' Windham replied: 'I know all that and am much obliged to you.'

On 8 August Windham and Peter Hansell, now the receiver of the Felbrigg rents, went to the estate where they met with a London solicitor called

Agnes Willoughby (Rogers): Pictured in mid-1861. Her marriage settlement was a matter of hard bargaining with the heir-to-be of Felbrigg.
(NRO ref: MC580/1, 780x1)

67

Jackson, who had been appointed by the Court of Chancery, and the General. The following day - the day the new squire came of age - as the group sat in the library at Felbrigg, Mr Jackson made his proposal: that the whole estate should be put into trust until 11 October 1869, when Hanworth's mortgage would be paid off, with Windham living at Felbrigg for a purely nominal rent until then or on an outlying farm. Windham seemed utterly baffled by the suggestion.

According to Hansell, he gave no sign that he understood it at all. Jackson then spent the rest of the day trying to persuade the new squire, backed up by Hansell, who explained patiently to Windham how the suggestion would focus his financial resources and increase his income. They were wasting their breath. The only answer Windham gave was: 'Then I cannot cut down my trees!'. From the family's point of view it looked a reasonable agreement to ensure the continuity of the estate, but for Windham it appeared very different, appearing to be more of an arrangement intended to guarantee the General's welfare and not his. It did not help that there was no-one at the meeting who might have been considered an independent advocate for young Windham.

And so Windham came of age. In normal circumstances, the accession of an heir to such a fine and important landed estate would have been accompanied by a banquet, music and general jollity. But these were not ordinary circumstances. In the event, the new master of Felbrigg spent the day at someone else's celebration, a regatta at Cromer.

There was no fête at Felbrigg.

ONCE MORE, on 13 August, Bowen May warned Windham about Agnes. But Windham replied brightly that Agnes' protector had been quite easy-going about the possible marriage and had promised to break off any relationship and not speak to her. Later that same day Agnes ushered Windham back to Emmanuel's. Now that Windham had come into his inheritance, there was little to hold her back. Between August 13 and 25 the besotted young squire spent £4,163 18s 6d on jewellery for his lady love, the equivalent of perhaps £180,000 in today's money.

On 20 August the pair returned to Bowen May's office to say they were definitely intending to be married in September or October. Bowen May's account of the meeting shows Agnes' clear-headed - or hard-headed - assessment of her situation. Windham said his income was £3,000 a year but would be £14,000 to £15,000 one day. Agnes said: 'If I marry him I must have £1,000 a year settled.' Her intended replied: 'At present I can't give that, for my income is so little to what it will be.' At this point Bowen May intervened and told Agnes she ought to be content with £500 - which she 'ridiculed'. His suggestion of £600 met a similar response, with Agnes saying 'Do you think it likely I will give up £2,000 a year for such a settlement?'.

After more negotiation Windham eventually proposed £800 a year immediately, with £1,500 once he came fully into his property. Agnes was minded to reject this too, but was eventually persuaded by her solicitor. 'Mind,' she added, 'I am to have the allowance so I can will it away.' Bowen May responded that it was usual for marriage settlements to be a life interest in favour of the wife; in other words, when she died, the allowance died with her. But Agnes was adamant. 'I am going to marry for the benefit of my sisters, and I must have it so that I can will it to them, or do as I like with it.' Windham, in contrast, said he had no-one to concern himself about, as his mother already had an allowance from the estate. Agnes insisted the draft agreement be written out at once. 'Oh yes,' replied Windham, 'better put it in black and white, and then she will be satisfied'.

Although there was nothing unusual in a marriage settlement - historian F M L Thompson observing that they 'accompanied all marriages in the landed classes as a matter of course' - the negotiations were usually a matter of discussion between solicitors and parents. The object of a settlement, under the protection of trustees, was to secure some measure of financial independence for the bride-to-be, whose possessions would otherwise fall under her husband's power according to the long-standing principles of common law.

But Agnes' settlement had two unusual characteristics: its generosity - not just in its size but in its lasting in perpetuity, and the fact that Bowen May had not followed the standard procedure. The Windham case gives us a rare insight into the actual negotiation of a mid-Victorian marriage settlement, but it would be difficult indeed to claim it as anything like the norm. Towards the end of the 20 August interview, Bowen May eventually persuaded Agnes to accept £800 a year 'without any reference to the future', and Windham - naive as ever - asked him to act as his solicitor too ('all the lawyers are out of town'), paying him £200.

WINDHAM'S appearances at the Llewellyn household began to be more and more sporadic. Around the time of this meeting with Bowen May, Windham disappeared from Duke Street. On 26 August, Windham and Agnes returned yet again to the solicitor's office. Agnes was determined to have the last word. Bowen May expected the pair were there to call off the engagement, and said as much. But Windham said instead that he had made up his mind to give Agnes the original, generous, settlement. The question of trustees was then raised. Bowen May suggested an old school friend - irony of ironies - Windham's uncle, the General. Windham, naturally, rejected him out of hand, saying, 'He wants to get hold of my property; we are not friendly.' It was Agnes' idea for James Roberts to be one of the trustees. At this stage Windham had not met him, but offered no objections as he was a 'wealthy man'. By any criteria, Roberts was a colourful character. He had been declared bankrupt a few years earlier, but had since grown wealthy on the combination of the proceeds of his several brothels (hence his nickname, 'Bawdyhouse Bob'), a timber merchant (hence his other nickname, 'Mahogany' Roberts) and government contractor. He made a reputed £5,000 a year and lived in style, with a Piccadilly address. Agnes' doctor Dr Whidbourne was then suggested as the second trustee. On the same day - 26 August - the Great Yarmouth solicitor Reynolds saw Windham dressed as a railway guard on Cambridge station. He asked him: 'Windham, how can you make such a fool of yourself?', and received the reply 'I must see these fellows do their job properly. I am going to be married next week.'

Windham turned up for the final time at Duke Street the following day, returning - extremely dishevelled - in Agnes' carriage. It was now impossible to keep news of the impending marriage secret. The Windham family solicitor Chappell had called round to Duke Street saying that Vice-Chancellor Wood wanted to see the young heir urgently about the marriage settlement he was proposing. Llewellyn at once telegraphed Felbrigg.

Later that evening the General, then staying at nearby Hanworth Hall, called in Mrs Martin and her husband, and asked them to go to London immediately to try to reason with his nephew. As long-term family confidantes, he felt they were in the best position to make him see sense. They arrived at Duke Street about 5am on 28 August and immediately talked with Windham. One of their gambits - and one clearly drilled into them at Hanworth - was to threaten that the General would get up a commission of lunacy against him. Windham replied: 'He is up to that, is he? On what grounds?'. At first, they thought they had succeeded, Windham promising them he would go back with them to Felbrigg.

Another of Windham's uncles, Captain John Henry Windham, was not so easily fooled. He wrote from Cromer to Hansell saying how his brother (the General) had been telegraphed, 'requesting him to come to town to prevent Mr Windham's marriage with Miss Agnes Willoughby's sister (sic). The General and Mr and Mrs Martin have prevented it - for the present.' He continued: 'Gla thinks this very fine woman to be modest, but he is such a fool & it is only putting off the evil day.' Windham was still denying on 28 August that he had any intention of marrying Agnes. He told Mrs Llewellyn that she could stay on with Jack [Garton, her protector] for all he cared.

On 29 August the marriage settlement was finally signed. Agnes was careful to have a clause which stipulated that the jewels 'should remain to her separate use.' Not for the first time - or the last - Agnes had got her way. That night - on the eve of the marriage - Agnes' lover slept with her at her house, although Windham was later to

The fateful marriage: A copy of the marriage certificate of William Frederick and Agnes, obtained by Felbrigg solicitor Peter Hansell for his extensive scrapbook on the young heir. *(NRO ref: MC580/1, 780x1)*

claim, pathetically, that her soon-to-be-ex paramour had slept in the same house but not the same bed. The fact that the gentleman in question had his boots outside Agnes' door did not seem to register.

On the very same day that Capt Windham had sent his letter - 30 August - came the news that the family had dreaded: William Frederick Windham, Squire of Felbrigg, had married Agnes Rogers.

6

31 August-October 1861: 'Our Infatuated Nephew'

'MARRIAGES.
On the 30th ult., at St Anne's Church, St John's Wood, by the Rev. Henry
Wm Maddock, WM. FREDERICK WINDHAM, Esq., of Felbrigg Hall,
Norfolk, to ANN AGNES, eldest daughter of the late Wm. ROGERS, Esq.,
of Basingstoke, Hants.'
Norwich Mercury, Wednesday 4 September

IN FACT the marriage announcement in the Norwich Mercury was incorrect. As the marriage certificate makes clear, the ceremony actually took place at All Saints' Church, with both participants described as being 'of full age' with William's rank given as 'Esquire' and Agnes' - whose address was given as 10 Blenheim Place - left blank.

Witnesses to the marriage were G F Whidbourne, and J Bowen May. Bowen May's part in the contracting of the marriage was already clear, but Whidbourne's involvement was apparently more innocent. He was painted in the reporting of subsequent events as a co-conspirator but the reality - at least from the tenor of his later evidence and behaviour - seems more that of an innocent man sweet-talked into an embarrassing situation. Dr Whidbourne, a London GP, had accepted Agnes as a patient in 1860, and then a week before her wedding she had asked him to be a trustee for her marriage settlement. He had eventually agreed to do so, after Bowen May had promised him it would be 'little trouble'. It turned out to be anything but.

Whidbourne was further persuaded to give Agnes away - filling the role which would have been taken by her late father - but turned up to the wedding with reluctance, as he was suffering from painfully dislocated ribs. When he arrived at Agnes' house in St John's Wood on the morning of 30 August he was surprised to be asked by her to examine her husband-to-be. It later transpired that Agnes had heard from Windham's surgeon Johnson that he had been ill and wanted confirmation. Windham, whom Whidbourne had never met, claimed that he had 'chafed himself' and asked for the doctor's advice. Whidbourne, by now no doubt thoroughly bemused at being asked for a medical opinion on what had been a purely social call, examined him briefly. Windham asked him if there was any objection to being married, seeing as he had not suffered from venereal disease for six months. Whidbourne said there was none. It was not exactly the most romantic of pre-nuptial preparations. It also, incidentally, suggests that - contrary to Windham's boastful claims to the Llewellyns - Agnes was not yet sleeping with him.

But why, then, did Agnes even consider going through with the marriage if she at least suspected Windham might have such a condition? The answer, surely, is in the urgency of the situation. She must have very real fears that Windham was about to be removed by his family and sent back to the confines of Felbrigg. Put simply, Agnes was prepared to take the gamble.

The pair then returned to the rest of the party, which consisted of Agnes' mother Ann, her sisters Thirza and Emma, who acted as bridesmaids, and her older brother George, later described by the doctor as 'dressed respectably, though rather common in his manners'. There were a few other men in the house ('between 30 and 40 years of age... and not gentlemen') but Roberts was not one of them. Bowen May, as Agnes' solicitor and the fellow wedding witness, was also present. Whidbourne accompanied Agnes and her sisters in a brougham carriage to the church. All the wedding party gathered round the altar for the vows. Windham was described as 'lively, not melancholy' during the ceremony and 'quiet and tranquil' afterwards. The doctor stayed long enough to toast the newly-weds, then left, no doubt with a mixture of relief and bemusement.

The Windham family, unsurprisingly, took an utterly jaundiced view of the nuptials. Captain Windham, writing to Hansell a day after his previous letter, fumed: 'The Bride is the celebrated Horse breaker Mrs Willoughby. Her name in the

Newspaper is only a Sham, one for the occasion. The Martins did all they could and got Gla away once but he was afterwards kidnapped & the poor fool is married.'

'POOR FOOL' or no, William set off with his new wife Agnes for a honeymoon in Paris, arriving there at midnight on Saturday 31 August, and staying at the Hotel de Menrice in the Rue de Rivoli for ten days. The party consisted of the newly-weds, one of Agnes' sisters (almost certainly Thirza), plus Windham's valet William Badcock, and Agnes' maidservant. They had a suite of apartments on the first floor and dined at the table d'hote, a waiter later reporting that there was 'nothing unusual' in the conduct of any of them. 'They rode about during the day and went to the theatre in the evening, just the same as other people,' he said. But the waiter, Jean Souney, made one telling observation: 'Mr Windham seemed to be very fond of his wife but she did not appear to care so much for him.'

Windham was painted in print and gossip as a besotted fool, as indeed he was. But there is also evidence that he had taken a more thoughtful approach to Agnes' status. He may have been in denial, or acted like he was, about Agnes' colourful past as a society courtesan, but he also tried to make sure the slate was wiped clean by their marriage. 'I told her whatever she had done before marriage did not signify,' he said later, 'but she was now my wife' and should therefore behave respectably. Unfortunately, Windham had miscalculated again. While they were on their honeymoon Agnes was desperate to go to the celebrated open-air dance hall Le Jardin Mabille. It was everything that Agnes loved: showy, risqué - it was famous for its can-can dancers - and frequented by the famous (Harriet Beecher Stowe and Mark Twain were just two of its many curious visitors). Windham told her she could not. Agnes obeyed him - this time. Windham might have fooled himself he had the upper hand but, as his counsel Karslake was to state baldly the following year: 'From the moment he married her he had no control over her of any sort or kind. She did what she liked, went where she liked and would listen to no remonstrance on his part'.

ON 4 SEPTEMBER, Windham wrote to Martin from Paris: 'We shall be down with you on Tuesday next. Yates will be down on Monday, and will bring further orders. I want two rooms - one for my wife and self, one for her maid, and one for her sister. Get the piano tuned; get a man from Norwich. Good bye... Have the east bedroom and dressing room for my wife, and the thoroughfare room for her maid.'

The newly-weds and their party returned to London from Paris and stayed for a night at Morley's Hotel before heading to Felbrigg. While they were in London, Windham took the opportunity to have Bowen May carry out the second part of his legal task - a document to 'bar the entail', that is to say, overturning the provisions of

Felbrigg: Pictured around 1861. Agnes' arrival as Windham's wife marked an example of social mobility on a grand scale - but her new position immediately sparked opposition from all classes of local society. *(NRO ref: MC580/1, 780x1)*

William Howe Windham's will which allowed the property to pass to a nominated relative, a common practice designed to secure the integrity of the estate for another generation. During the evening of the same day (Tuesday 10 September) the new lady of Felbrigg finally headed off on the long train and carriage journey to North Norfolk. The rail journey from London with her husband turned out to be hardly routine. In fact, when it became public knowledge a few months later, it was to provide one of the juiciest morsels of scandal of the whole affair.

Railway guard Joseph Ford had become familiar with Windham because of his habit of travelling back to Norfolk on the night mail train and sometimes working as a guard. So there was no chance of Ford mistaking his man, or missing what happened, on the night journey to Norwich on 10 September. Mr and Mrs Windham and another man - it turned out to be Roberts - travelled in the same first-class carriage as far as Broxbourne. When they pulled into the station, Windham asked Ford to lock his wife and Roberts in the carriage so they would not be disturbed. The guard peered into the carriage - and saw a makeshift bed. Agnes drew down the carriage's blinds to hide them from prying eyes, and the discreet arrangement lasted all the way to Norwich. As for Windham, he was with the driver at the front of the train, enjoying himself immensely and blithely ignoring the infidelity happening further along the train. He acted as if he were the friend and Agnes and Roberts the newly-weds instead. The rest of the party - Agnes' sisters and the servants - travelled in another carriage, but they could scarcely have been unaware of the strange goings-on.

ARRIVING at her new domain in the early hours was hardly what the new Lady of Felbrigg would have wished. At the end of the tiring carriage drive from Norwich, Agnes would have swept through the entrance gates built by her new husband's father, probably sensing rather than seeing the dark bulk of the Great Wood on her right as the carriage travelled onwards in the gloom. As she approached the house there would have been the glimmer of oil lamps as the household servants came to the end of their long vigil waiting for the squire and his lady. At last the carriages would have drawn up at the front of the house. And then a parade of bowing and curtseying servants, and a bustle of crinolines up the stairs, and so to bed.

But next morning, surely, the squire's lady would have wasted no time in sweeping down the dark staircase, stepping through the modest entrance hall and moving outside to, at last, look back to the house for the first time and savour her triumph. And triumph it was - the village sawyer's daughter had leapfrogged the barriers of class, privilege and social approbation to complete an astonishing transformation. But it was not to be the end of her journey.

Agnes' arrival at Felbrigg immediately caused division and desertions within the household. Windham's old confidante and whist partner Mrs Martin moved out at once with her husband to Home Farm. At least she remained on speaking terms with the young squire. Other servants, however, soon left for good. Even though she was now the wife of the squire of one of the most stalwart of Norfolk country families, Agnes was, naturally, far from being accepted in the county's politer circles. The reaction of Sir William Foster was typical. He 'absolutely declined' to be introduced to Agnes, because she was a person of 'not very good character'. Windham had told him in reply, 'I assure you she is a lady', prompting Sir William's response, 'I must have something more than your *ipse dixit* [say-so] on that subject'. The marriage, he said, had 'caused a strong feeling against him in the county'.

THE NEWLY-WEDS' first official house guests (apart from the now ever-present Roberts) were Whidbourne and Bowen May. They arrived on Saturday 14 September and stayed until the following Wednesday. Neither had been invited entirely for their personal pleasure. Whidbourne had already attended Agnes three times since her arrival back from Paris for what was described as 'derangement of the stomach'.

Bowen May, meanwhile, had been given one more legal task from Windham: that of preparing his will. Although later torn up by Windham, its contents were startling:

Windham's property was to pass to Agnes for life, with the remainder to any children. Should there be no children, Lady Sophia would inherit. If Lady Sophia were dead, then Thirza and Emma Rogers would inherit, with the first to marry taking the name of 'Windham' and the coat of arms. And so, as the Lukins had become Windhams in 1824, so would the Rogers. It was a remarkable indication of Windham's utter rejection of almost all his many relatives.

On Tuesday 17 September the General made the short journey from Hanworth to visit his nephew. Whidbourne was introduced to him and heard Windham and his uncle discuss an exchange of land for about an hour. Later that day the General met Agnes for the first time, although their conversation is not recorded. Whatever was said, and it is hard to imagine it was anything more than the iciest of formalities, it did not alter his growing determination on a fateful course of action.

A physician from nearby Cromer, Mr Buck, was sent for by Windham on 21 September after he complained of feeling sick. Buck gave him some medicine, and when he came back the next morning to see his patient he found him at breakfast with Roberts and Agnes' two sisters. Windham started to tell him about how he felt, but when Buck asked to see him alone, Agnes stepped in to stop him. She asked Buck: 'Don't you think his relatives are poisoning him?', to which Buck replied: 'No, by no means.'

The next day, 23 September, Buck called again to see his patient. Agnes took him to the billiard room and told him he could not see her husband, as he was asleep. Undaunted, Buck tried again at 4pm. This time, however, he did not even get past the door. The servant merely handed him a letter which read: 'Dear Sir - My wife prefers me having her medical man to attend me, and he is now here. I am sorry for this, but she will have it. Yours truly, W F WINDHAM'.

Six days later Agnes abruptly left Felbrigg. Windham later explained her disappearance: 'She went away without me and went to Dublin. She said her doctor recommended her to go there'. She had already tired of being lady of the manor - and of her boor of a husband - and so headed off to Ireland with her lover Giuglini and his opera company.

THERE ARE two photographs of Agnes, both taken a few months before her marriage, and which form part of the Hansell archive, now in the Norfolk Record Office. One of the pictures has her in a side-on pose in one of her famous riding habits, showing off her trim figure. In the other, Agnes is facing the camera and stares back frankly; nothing of the 'proper' demureness of the mid-Victorian genteel young lady here. In both of the pictures her blonde hair - darkened by the photographic process - is concealed inside a hairnet. Only the wearing of the fashionable crinoline

- still very much *à la mode* despite its impracticality and increasingly-reported intrinsic fire risk - and drop pearl earrings give a hint of the much-touted lady-about-town. This photograph was probably one of several which were exhibited by some of the more enterprising London shopkeepers later that year. The Belfast News Letter recalled in December 1862 how 'crowds were assembled all day long round the shop of a well known alderman in Regent Street' and in the elegant Burlington Arcade where, the paper pointed out, many in the curious crowd would be 'dreadfully shocked if an introduction to the original were suggested, but who elbow and push each other to gain a glimpse at [her photographs].'

We have a vivid account of Agnes in her showy prime in a pen-portrait by the Dublin correspondent of that same paper, made in October but not widely reprinted until early February the following year. The correspondent writes: '[She] was a constant attendant at the Theatre Royal, Dublin, during the series of operatic performances... in which Signor Giuglini and Madame Titiens *(sic)* were the "particular stars", [but] I have read no description of the syren who bewitched the owner of Felbrigg Hall...

" 'Twas Saturday night; the house was crowded from the pit to the galley to hear the latest creation of Verdi's genius, Un Ballo in Maschera. In the second act the attention of the fashionables in the boxes was attracted by the entrance of a party into the right-hand stage box on the first tier. A young lady, a decided blonde, with deep blue eyes, and a profusion of bright, fair, wavy hair, simply but elegantly arranged, advanced to the front of the box with a rather bold air.

'She was of middle height, and her features were intelligent - piquante and pretty rather than handsome. She stood for a moment at the box front, and as her eyes... glanced confidently round the house, an attendant removed from her shoulders a black velvet mantle trimmed with magnificent sables which even a Prussian millionaire might have envied.

'Her fan and bouquet - of choicest flowers - being duly deposited on the cushion, she turned round ere she took her seat, and displayed to the best advantage certainly one of the most exquisite-fitting dresses I have ever seen. Her figure is remarkably good, and shown by her dress of rich white silk - made *a la* Raffaella - and cut square, rather low, and but half concealing a very fair, well-shaped bust, and revealing a beautifully-rounded arm. Confining her hair, which she wore in a plain, full broad braid or band, was a coronet of sky-blue velvet, ornamented with diamond stars. Her necklace, earrings, brooch, and bracelets were of diamonds, with a radiance so brilliant as almost to light up her graceful figure.

'Many were the inquiries, "Who is the lady in the stage-box?". By and by it was whispered around the house: "Her name is Windham, she is very wealthy, is a frequent denizen of the stage-box during the present engagement and cherishes a *penchant* for a celebrated Italian tenor."'

There can be few better examples of the maxim 'to see and be seen', and is by far the most vivid account of Agnes in her pomp. The contrast with her demure appearances in her opera box at the Lyceum only a few months earlier are startling too. While Agnes was staying at the elegant Monk's House in the Irish city, Windham was haunting his old dens of vice in the Haymarket. A policeman, Inspector Holden, met Windham on the streets at 2am a day or two later. It was not an edifying sight. The young Squire of Felbrigg was talking about his mother having married a young man and how they were conspiring with the old General to rob him of his property. 'The tears ran down his cheeks, and he was frothing and foaming at the mouth,' Holden later recalled.

ON HER RETURN from Dublin, Agnes had been 'suffering severely' for several days, and consulted with Dr Gwyn on 8 October. It was later on that same evening that the doctor witnessed an incident which spoke little of any remaining tenderness between the newly-weds. Windham was driving Dr Gwyn back to Felbrigg from Norwich in his brougham when there was a violent thunderstorm. Windham stopped the coach about 10pm to attend to one of the carriage's two horses. By now Agnes was becoming alarmed by the storm and when there was a crack of thunder, she jumped out of the coach and started to run.

Windham, who had the advantage of a muscular build despite his incipient stoutness, chased and caught up with her after only a few yards. Agnes protested she wanted to travel in the 'safer' luggage van travelling behind. Windham would have none of it, saying such a vehicle was not a fit one for the 'lady of Felbrigg Hall to ride in', took her by the waist and put his petite and struggling wife into the brougham despite her cries. Gwyn got back into the carriage and tried to calm the still-frightened Agnes for the remaining hour or so of the journey.

Windham, by now, had bought her another huge tranche of jewellery for Agnes. In October he spent £5,419 16s 1d, bringing his total spending on jewellery for her to £13,785 - equivalent to around £600,000 in today's money. The reason for his generosity would emerge a few months later. But it was all to no avail. Agnes stayed at Felbrigg only four more days, then vanished again.

IT IS DIFFICULT to be exact about the moment when the General first conceived the idea of trying to obtain a Commission of Lunacy against his wayward nephew. It may have been in his thoughts from at least 1860 while he was still serving in India. It was certainly so by late August 1861, as is clear by his instructions to the Martins.

The principle that the Crown should look after the affairs of lunatics had been established as far back as the reign of Edward II. But attempts to legislate to deal with the situation had been piecemeal at best. Two classic cases - which were both to be invoked in the Windham hearing - showed the powers of the law at work. The first involved Lord Portsmouth in the early years of the nineteenth century. Easily-led and generally weak, the young heir was cuckolded by his wife's doctor, who fathered a child by her. Lord Portsmouth's relatives took action when they saw the helplessness of the young peer and the growing influence of the doctor over the estate. Lord Portsmouth was found incapable by the jury.

The second took place after 1828 regulations extended the principle of regular independent inspection of the system, establishing the officers known as Commissioners in Lunacy. Drawn from the ranks of doctors and lawyers, they were to check, reduce and eliminate abuses, and to improve treatments for patients. It also allowed, crucially, for the setting up of hearings which could hear controversial or contested cases before a jury of experts. The subsequent quoted case took place in the early 1830s and concerned a Miss Bagster, a 'young lady of fortune', who had eloped with an unsuitable lover. Her family tried to annul the marriage on the grounds that she was of unsound mind. They won, backed by the opinion of a Dr Sutherland, whose son, also a doctor, was to figure in the subsequent Windham inquiry. The jury agreed that Bagster's passionate, sometimes 'indelicate' actions, and wilful actions - and an intellect at the level of a seven-year-old's - made her incapable of looking after herself. And, far more to the point, her money.

The law was amended in 1853 to iron out perceived anomalies. One extensively-reported case from 1858 involved a Mrs Mary Ann Ruck, who was attempting to have her husband Lawrence committed to an asylum. Ruck had accused her of being a prostitute and having had two children fathered by another man who had then been murdered. In a foretaste of what was to become a feature of the Windham case, proceedings were frequently punctuated with laughter, as the public gallery lapped up the bizarre details of Ruck's behaviour. But the order was made, with the successful lawyer being a flamboyant QC, Montague Chambers, whose success was not forgotten when the General eventually sought an advocate to lead his case.

ARMED WITH legal opinion on these and similar cases, the General then began the process of sounding out the views of both the close and extended members of the Windham and Hervey families, to encourage them to join in a petition to secure the hearing. The Hansell archive contains a series of replies to the General's no-doubt persuasive letters, beginning from around 16 September - in other words before he had even met Agnes. One of the first replies, on 9 October, was from his fellow guardian

Okehampton
Oct 18. 1861

My dear Charles.

For many years I have been of opinion that our Nephew was a youth of unsound mind. I have always given to my friends this reason, as an excuse for his mad behaviour. His conduct at school, at his father's funeral & at your

Gathering support: In the autumn of 1861 the General carried out an urgent and extensive letter-writing campaign to garner support from the wider Windham and Hervey families for his intended actions. This letter from James Hunt Holby is typical of the reaction he received. (*NRO ref: MC580/1, 780x1*)

Hook, with the support of his wife Kitty (Catherine), who wrote from Arlington Street in London: 'I think the course you propose taking is the only one that can save our unfortunate nephew W F Windham from absolute ruin, and is as humane as it is wise.'

A sister of the General, Cecilia Baring, wrote in similar, although more extensive vein, from Gunton Park in Norfolk on 17 October. 'It is,' she wrote, 'a most painful admission to make, but, I think you fully justified in taking the steps you are about to do. From his very early youth Gla was singularly strange and excitable... increasing as he grew older - I have long thought him incapable of self-government, and, I do now feel persuaded that the best act, which the most affectionate friend or tender parent could perform towards him, would be to place him under restraint, and to deliver him, by such measures, from the dishonest and disreputable hands into which he has now fallen. I see no other course left in such extremity.'

James Hunt Holby wrote from Okehampton on 18 October: 'For many years I have been of opinions *(sic)* that our nephew was a youth of unsound mind. I have always given my friends this reason, as an excuse of his mad behaviour - His conduct at school, at his father's funeral & at your reception in Norwich ought to satisfy any unprejudiced mind as to his unfitness to go alone - his late proceedings quite justify your taking any steps to place him under such restraint as the Law will admit of.' His views were support by his wife Horatia, who wrote with similar sentiments on 29 October.

The Marquis of Bristol took five weeks to reply, and when he did on 27 October he was supportive although cautiously pragmatic. 'To annull *(sic)* the marriage, to save the estate from ruin, & to rescue our infatuated nephew from the fangs of disreputable & dishonest associates are, of course, objects of immense importance.' But, the marquis went on to say, there were 'several matters' on which explanation might be required and that he had briefed his solicitors to raise them.

The petitioners' list was formidable indeed: led by the General, it included his brother Captain John Henry, sisters Cecilia Ann Baring and Maria, Dowager Countess of Listowel and her son the Hon Richard Hare and his wife Mary. On the Hervey side of the family, the petitioners included the Marquis and his brothers Lord Alfred Hervey and the Rev Lord Arthur Hervey. The list was joined by more members of the extended family: Robert and Kitty Hook, the Hunt Holbys, and finally John and Caroline Foley. A long list, then - but it was that very strength in numbers which was to, paradoxically, prove an Achilles' heel of the petitioners' case.

Conspicuous by her absence was William's mother. Not that the General had not tried - and tried, indeed, with all the persuasive powers at his disposal.

On 15 October he wrote to his sister-in-law:

My dear Sophia,

You are, perhaps, aware that your son William is now in great difficulties as to money, and that he will in all human probability be absolutely ruined before many months are passed. His approaching ruin has been brought about by himself, in spite of the best advice the Vice-Chancellor or his family could give him, and I see no way of saving him, to say nothing of his property, but by getting him declared incapable of managing his affairs. I have for long had my doubts upon this question of his mind, but, as I am not his nearest relation, I have refrained hitherto from taking any steps in the matter. As I am about to proceed to India I must now do so, or he and everything he has will be lost ere my return. The first person I consult is you, and to you I must declare that, should he be proved lunatic, I will have nothing to do with either the person or the property of my nephew. Indeed, in India I could not; therefore the family in England, particularly yourself, must arrange it; at any rate it must be clearly understood that I will have nothing to do with him. The steps I may be compelled to take arise solely from a desire to save him from his associates, who, in the short period of two months, have nearly brought him to ruin. From what I learn from all those who are best acquainted with him, his mental capacity is beyond a doubt.'

The General was, of course, being a little disingenuous when he told Lady Sophia he had consulted her first, having already sent - and received - letters about the matter from other family members. It was clearly an attempt to put emotional pressure on his fey and indecisive sister-in-law. It was plain, too, that he was already fully aware of how his actions might be misconstrued, so made the (honourable) insistence that he did not want to benefit financially from any lunacy decision. Lady Sophia's solicitor then met with the General's, and indicated she would be communicating 'her determination' to join in with the petition. All seemed well - until her solicitor, Chappell, asked to speak alone to the General on the matter a few days later.

When they met - on 20 October - the General was handed a long legal document, listing seven pre-conditions about which Lady Sophia was adamant, the most startling of which were insistences she and her husband should have full control of the estate and that Lady Sophia be guaranteed £10,000, with interest, if a lunatic Windham should die without children, or if the General came into possession of the lands. There was nothing here of a mother's tender concern for her only child. Nothing, either, of the emotional hand-wringing she had performed at the Court of Chancery to gain the sympathy of Sir William Page Wood. What mattered - all that mattered - was the money.

The document made chilling reading, and the General was duly chilled, expressing his 'disapprobation' of it. But he agreed to take it away for his solicitor Field to look at. The next day, the General wrote back to Chappell. His letter was to the point: 'The question is simply this. Am I acting rightly as an uncle and a testamentary guardian, and a well-wisher to the young man's future interest, or am I not? If I am, then she [Lady Sophia] ought to concur at once, particularly as her family wish her to do so. If I am not, it is her duty to fight against me to the last. With these feelings I must decline discussing the paper you gave me. You must remember that I have always solemnly declared myself most willing and desirous to secure the comfort, honour and well-being of my nephew.'

The General continued that he would 'never oppose' any just claim on the estate - provided the courts saw fit to do so. And always, he stressed, 'remembering that not one shilling directly or indirectly comes to me'. If it came to a question of who should run the estate, then it was 'proper and honourable' for Vice Chancellor Wood to do so, bearing in mind his 'intimate knowledge of my nephew's affairs'. Chappell tried, unsuccessfully, to persuade the General on 23 October and 12 November. He then told him Lady Sophia had decided to remain neutral during the ensuing proceedings, and also asked the General to return the 20 October document. But the General, knowing full well its significance, refused. He told the solicitor: 'I am very sorry, Mr Chappell, that Lady Sophia should have directed you to give me such a paper.' He replied: 'Well, sir, you know how she is very poor and distressed...'

Lady Sophia's hesitation was not shared by Mary Hare, who wrote from Stoke two days later on 29 October. Her reply to the General was to the point: 'I lose not a moment in answering yr letter. Most heartily do we join in the prayer of the petition... I hope that you will succeed & wish that Felbrigg were yours. It makes me quite sick to think of all the fine old trees being cut down.' The reference was not lost on the General. For here, should an unsuitable marriage, shady associates and reckless spending not be enough to persuade the petitioners to support his action, was the first direct evidence that the physical integrity of the Felbrigg estate itself was under immediate attack.

7

October-December 14 1861:
'A Capital Bargain'

'Undoubtedly Mr Windham has been most grossly deceived.'
Mr Cole, Windham's solicitor, 23 November 1861

THE FULL story would only emerge in detail later, but for William's relatives it was enough to know the woods of Felbrigg were under threat, and that on 25 October an agreement had been signed by the young heir which seemed to seal their fate. For the woods were truly one of the glories of Felbrigg. William Windham I had begun the process in earnest in the late seventeenth century, planting more than five thousand oak, birch, ash and sweet chestnut trees. By the 1760s William Windham III was to emulate him, with his agent the visionary Nathaniel Kent masterminding the famous Great Wood, separating the north side of the Felbrigg estate from the growing settlement of Cromer.

It was now barely two months into Windham's tenure of Felbrigg and already the carefully-nurtured estate enlarged by his father was beginning to crumble. In late October Norwich land agent and valuer William Butcher was called in by the solicitor Chappell - at this time acting for both Windham and Lady Sophia - to value the farms on the Felbrigg estate, as a 'large sum of money' was required to pay the young squire's debts. In the end the trustees of the estate were forced to sell around £65,000 of settled estates to pay the immediate debts. As part of the drive to raise cash, Butcher travelled round the estate from 25-28 October, marking more than 530 oak trees which he thought could be felled without damaging the estate too much. He did not meet Windham until the afternoon of the final day. When he did talk to him, he was astonished to be told: 'You have been too slow; I have sold all the trees; I have sold £5,000 worth to a Government contractor'. Windham told him he had signed the contract the day before, and would receive £500 a month.

It was the ever-influential Roberts who had persuaded Windham to sell the trees. As the Windham affair became the stuff of anecdote in later years there were claims that Roberts had 'sold' Agnes to Windham in exchange for the timber. The truth, as we have seen, was more convoluted than that, although it was certainly the case that the young heir needed little persuasion to part with his trees. Selling off standing timber was a long-established practice by impecunious young landowners to raise ready cash when they came into their inheritances.

Windham had been contemplating doing this for months, as is shown by his outburst during the 9 August meeting; Roberts merely provided the impetus to make the idea a reality. Windham later explained: 'My father had always cautioned me against getting into the hands of the Jews [ie moneylenders] and I was determined not to do so and Mr Roberts was with me at my estate in the country when one day out riding he said: "Why should you borrow money paying interest upon interest when you have the money here upon your estate? You've so many trees there being spoilt and I can introduce you to a timber merchant who would not attempt to cheat you in taking the timber in a lump, but would pay you so much a foot for it."

'Of course I consented and he accordingly introduced me to Messrs Lawrence and Fry, who are very respectable timber merchants and who paid me £1,000 down, agreeing to give me some £350 a month, up to £3,000 a year for four years, or £20,000 in all. He said: "The trees have not been cut for so many years that, far from the estate being injured it would be much benefited by having the timber cut down." 'And Windham added: "You may depend upon it I shall take care they do not cut down anything that would injure the estate."'

IT WAS SOON claimed that the real buyer of the timber was Roberts himself, but the nominal purchaser at least was Robinson and Co, a timber business at Mark Lane in London. Roberts' only direct interest was a one per cent commission for introducing Windham to the brokers - a maximum of £200 over four years and probably much less - although his real interest, of course, would have been in then

Felbrigg trees: It was the fear that one of the chief glories - and valuable assets - of the estate was to be removed that explained the urgency of the General's legal efforts.

parting the young squire from his share of the sale. The 25 October contract, signed at Felbrigg by Windham, and witnessed by Agnes, assigned to William Lawrence and Walter Fry the 'whole of the timber which may be cut on his Norfolk estates' over the next four years at the rate of at least £5,000 per year.

But only a day after signing it, Windham was already muddled about the details. Rather than the £500 per month which he had told Butcher about, he had actually agreed to being paid only £350. Without the benefit of legal advice Windham then fell even deeper into the trap. The final clause of the contract said that the contract 'does not contemplate any trees being cut down of small size *unless absolutely necessary*' [my italics]. And who would decide this necessity? An umpire appointed by both parties, again without any likelihood of legal advice and therefore likely to be a puppet for the contractors. There was, too, one name conspicuous by its absence from the contract:

that of Roberts. By December Windham had even forgotten whether the down payment to him had been £500 or double that.

Butcher - who would only find out about the detail of the contract months later - told Windham: 'I hope you have done no such thing, because if you have it will ruin the estate.' Windham simply shrugged and replied: 'I have made a very good job; don't you think I have made a capital bargain?' Windham's legal team later tried - not very convincingly - to portray the contract as perfectly reasonable and the price offered as fair, and therefore the actions of a rational man. But Butcher was unconvinced, and even more so when he discovered later how the trees had been measured, two-thirds up from their bases. The trees here were narrower than at ground level, so Windham was being under-valued on every single tree by a factor of 25 per cent - and that was on top of the below-market value price he had agreed to accept for the timber. In short, he was being fleeced, and the estate was poised to lose one of its chief glories to pay for his fecklessness. It was one of the gravest crises in the history of Felbrigg.

IN FACT, ornamental value aside, much of the timber on the estate turned out to be poor quality - to use the assessors' slang, 'shaky'. A timber valuer went to look at the estate on 17 November for Lawrence and Fry. He did not like what he saw. Much was poor quality, and the cost of transporting it to the London markets prohibitive. In fact, he believed the brokers would have to spend the enormous sum of £4,000 before they made any profit. Although the contract claimed up to £20,000 of timber could be felled, the true figure was more like £7,000.

What was a bad deal for Windham was also now looking a poor one for the brokers too. And by now both the brokers and the buyers had got wind of exactly how controversial the sale was likely to be. In the end, the bad publicity led both of them to walk away from the affair - but not soon enough to avoid being dragged into the subsequent lunacy proceedings as witnesses. The General offered to pay back the £1,000 they had advanced to Windham, but even though they were not out of pocket, both firms must have rued the day Roberts had contacted them. As for Windham, he was adamant that he had done the right thing. 'I did not make a bad contract about the timber at Felbrigg,' he insisted in December. 'I left it to Messrs Lawrence and Fry. They are very respectable men, and they treated me honourably.'

BY NOW, Windham had other matters on his mind. When Agnes had left Felbrigg before to pursue Giuglini she had at least returned a few days later. But by the end of October she had been gone off a second time, this time for three weeks already, with no word from her about when - or if - she would return. Windham finally found out about Agnes' infidelity when the Dead Letter Office sent back two letters she had sent to Giuglini at the wrong address, while Agnes was away hunting. Windham was furious when he discovered the passionate letters were addressed to her 'dear darling Antonio'. Agnes followed her 'dear darling' to Dublin, Glasgow and the north of England. As Windham's counsel was to later put it: 'She was acquainted with a person of whom she was much fonder than Mr Windham and went with him to Dublin and elsewhere, and lived with him in open and barefaced adultery.' Even Windham could bear the humiliation no longer. He angrily destroyed the will which Bowen May had drawn up, and set off in pursuit.

On 1 November there was a brief distraction for Windham from his marital troubles. He was in London, being interviewed by Mr Hancock, Chief Surgeon of the Charing Cross Hospital as part of the build-up to the threatened court case. During their interview the surgeon expressed his sorrow that Windham's wife had left him. He replied, very calmly: 'Yes, she has. But I know where she is and I have employed a detective to trace her and I going to Scotland this evening to bring her back.' Hancock warned Windham against using any violence, in case it was used in evidence against him.

The Norfolkman answered: 'You need not be afraid. I can be firm without being violent. She knows that I have right on my side. I shall tell her that I am acting under my lawyer's advice and that law gives me great power as a husband and I shall therefore tell her to come home without making any piece of work.'

It was actually two days later - 3 November - that Windham went with Dr Gwyn on the night train to Glasgow in pursuit of the errant Agnes, who was with Giuglini and the opera company. It was to be a fruitless quest, bordering on farce. When they finally reached her hotel Windham was told she had just set off back to London - from which city Windham had just made a long and tiring journey. The landlord told him she had behaved 'with propriety' during her stay, but Windham was in no mood to be satisfied with that. He stormed back to the station with an exhausted Dr Gwyn in his wake. They had been precisely 40 minutes on Scottish soil. Back in London they found Agnes at the Euston Hotel, where she had arrived with her French maid early on 4 November.

That evening Windham and Dr Gwyn went round and insisted on seeing Agnes. She was dining with a man who was later revealed as her solicitor. The hotel's manager, Robert Wheeler, heard a 'noisy altercation' take place until 2am, when all three men left together. Agnes stayed in the hotel until 6 November, with Windham dining with her two or three times. Once Windham tried to get into her bedroom, but Agnes refused. Windham made so much noise that the manager gave Agnes notice to leave.

Things took an even more bizarre turn on a later evening. The Windhams, Gwyn,

Windham's current solicitor Berry Hutchinson and a Dr Neil were dining together when Windham came rushing down the stairs, screaming at Wheeler: 'They are killing a man in the room; they have knocked out his eyes, which are hanging down his cheeks, and the blood is flowing from him like rain.' Wheeler - who already knew something of Windham's tendency to lie - told him he should have stayed upstairs and stop the 'murder' taking place. When Wheeler went upstairs he found Hutchinson rolling on the floor complaining of Gwyn damaging his eyes by throwing a bottle at him. But when Wheeler looked he found Hutchinson was completely uninjured. Windham had by now fetched the police, but the case never went to court.

What had caused the row was Windham discovering that Dr Neil was actually in the General's pay. The General, Wheeler later claimed, had been to the hotel 'once or twice to see either his nephew or Mrs Windham'. Significantly, Wheeler also said later that the General had made an 'offer to save his nephew'. So did the General offer to buy off Agnes? It seems eminently possible, and one certainly in keeping with his impulsive character. But if an offer was made, nothing became of it; Agnes was far too shrewd for that. She knew she was in a strong bargaining position. The General certainly did have to spend some money on his visit to the hotel, however, smoothing over the 'flowing blood' incident by paying Dr Neil's bail - and some 'hush money' to Hutchinson.

Windham was staying at the Piccadilly house of his friend Roberts. Sometime after 5 November Augusta Llewellyn said she had tried to see him at the house, but Roberts acted 'like a keeper over him'. Roberts had at first refused her permission to see Windham, telling her with considerable chutzpah, that she should not come 'dunning [cheating] Windham'. Eventually he had allowed Windham to see her, but only after taking the precaution of locking the outside door so she did not try to take him away from the house.

While in London, Windham continued his series of interviews with medical men. During these sometimes long and tiring sessions, the young squire let slip much about his state of mind. Dr Harrington Tuke talked to Windham several times in November, the interviews totalling 14 hours. On 12 November Windham seemed confident and sure of his case. The principal mover, he told Dr Tuke, was the General, but he did not think he would dare to pursue the matter. 'The old general,' he insisted, 'knows I am quite well.' Dr Tuke was impressed by the young squire's knowledge of proceedings and his estate. Windham had many comments to make on the various affidavits being made against him, dismissing Mrs Llewellyn's claims as 'a pack of lies'.

Windham claimed to Dr Tuke two days later that he had not knowingly passed his 'certain disorder' to Agnes, and added: 'I loved her too much for that. It has made a dreadful quarrel between us; she is so dreadfully angry about that.' His extravagant October purchase of jewellery was thus explained - he had been trying to say sorry.

Windham's embroidered version of his wedding day medical examination was that Whidbourne had shaken him by the hand and added - 'almost with tears in his eyes' - 'My dear boy, you are all right, you need not be under any alarm.'

BUT TOWARDS the end of November and the beginning of December, Windham's confident exterior was beginning to crumble. One bizarre rumour doing the rounds by now was that Agnes had run off with a railway guard. The reality was that she was now living openly with Giuglini. She had left the Euston Hotel and by December moved in with the singer at Bilborough House, St John's Wood. Her servant Mary Ann Decker later recalled: 'I was sent for to light the fire in the bedroom. She and Giuglini were in bed together at the time. He lived in the house for a fortnight or three weeks.' When asked how often she had seen them in bed together, Decker replied simply: 'Every night'.

Agnes and Giuglini then moved on to Liverpool, Manchester and other cities. When they returned to London, where they lived for several weeks at 34 Clarendon Gardens, Paddington, Giuglini would come at night and go in the morning. 'They lived there as man and wife,' Decker said. It was hardly discreet. But then again, most of London society seemed to know about the relationship already.

It was all too much for Windham. Inspector Holden, who had come across the blubbering Windham in the Haymarket in late September, found himself with a repeat performance, with the Norfolkman this time crying about how Agnes had run away and 'robbed him of £13,000 of diamonds'. Windham was forced to advertise to repudiate his estranged wife's debts. Agnes blithely ignored him, continuing to spend - and having the bills sent to Windham. On 13 December alone Windham received a bill of more than £300 for silks, with more accounts arriving all the time.

In late November or early December Windham paid one last visit to the Llewellyns for supper. He acted like a beaten man, subdued and contrite. He told the couple he now regretted his marriage, but apart from saying 'I was drawn into it' he refused to say any more. By now affidavit was relentlessly being piled upon affidavit. The wheels of justice were beginning to turn ever quicker.

IT FELL TO the Lords Justices' Court, in a hearing behind closed doors at Lincoln's Inn on 23 November, to make the final decision whether to hold a Commission. The Lords Justices had to decide whether there was, prima facie, a case. They were as keen as everyone else to know Lady Sophia's view of the matter. Lord Justice Knight Bruce asked her solicitor Mr Jessell directly:

'Does the Lady support the [aims] of the Commission, or does she oppose it?' Jessell's reply, alas, did not match his Lordship's for either brevity or unambiguity. 'I can best give your Lordship an answer to your question by saying that the instructions I have received are - that, having regard to her position as respects her son, she does not wish any opinion as to the state of his mind; but she desires most earnestly that protection may be thrown around his property and person, in order to prevent the course of extravagances which he has just entered upon; I think these instructions will answer your Lordship's question as satisfactorily as I am able.'

On the same day, Windham's solicitor Mr Cole fought a rearguard action by trying to prove that the timber affair had not been de facto evidence of insanity or incapability. 'A gross fraud was practised upon him,' he explained. 'Undoubtedly Mr Windham has been most grossly deceived; and he is able and intends to take proceedings for the purpose of obtaining relief against the deception.' And no doubt in a rehearsal for a line of defence to be taken at any commission, Cole tried to show that the move to sell off the timber had been an example of financial prudence, not recklessness.

Felbrigg, he explained, took £16,000 per annum to 'keep up' - but Windham had only £3,000 income per year until 1869, 'less £1,500,' he added simply. He carefully avoided explaining that it was precisely because of Windham agreeing to hand over half his yearly income to his new wife that he was now in such desperate need of ready cash to service his debts. Their lordships were unconvinced, and made their decision: the commission would go ahead. They formally directed 'an inquiry before a jury as to the state of mind of Mr Windham'.

IN THE first week of December two events happened which guaranteed that the glowing embers of public curiosity were to be fanned into a roaring flame. The first involved a bizarre public appeal, ostensibly from Windham himself. Someone had been pasting the following handbills around the streets:

'TO THE PEOPLE OF GREAT BRITAIN'
'I call upon you as an Englishman, and I appeal to both sexes and all conditions
of life, to aid and assist me by your voice and influence to protect me from a
conspiracy to defraud me out of my property, rights, and privileges, by those
who ought to shelter and protect me. You, I hope, have all read the startling
disclosures only partially made in "The Daily Telegraph", more will come, at all
events, by affidavits obtained by extraordinary means. My immense property
has been *pro. tem.* confiscated, and upon the grounds that I am a lunatic,
although the eminent Drs Tuke, Sutherland, Hancock, Seymour, Babbington,
Stevens, Gwynn *(sic)*, and others, have sworn affidavits that I am perfectly sane.

The motives for this conduct and false accusation are very transparent, as, by my death or lunacy, my property will pass into the hands of my uncle, Major-General Charles Ashe Windham, who has been the great mover, with others, in this false accusation, which, were they to succeed, would be to me far worse than death.

'The greatest murderer is to be tried with open doors, and his property is not confiscated until he is proved guilty. Mine is now confiscated, and the preliminaries of my trial were, contrary to my wishes, held with closed doors. It came upon me so suddenly, that I am startled that any body of men and women could club themselves together to perpetrate such a great iniquity, that I appeal to you all to rally around me. Let your cry be "Justice!". I ask no more. You, or your flesh and blood, may one day be similarly circumstanced. That no doctors' certificates can doom a man to everlasting imprisonment as a lunatic, for it takes a very short period for a perfectly sane man to become insane with the appliances that can be brought to bear by well-paid officials of asylums.

'Numerous friends have proposed that a public meeting shall be held at the Freemasons' Tavern, in the first instance, where resolutions will be proposed and seconded. After that a monster meeting will be held in Hyde Park, in order to satisfy the wishes of thousands who have already expressed their determination to stand by me in this hour of peril. I now give you the names of those who have signed the petition, which is causing me this injury [the placard listed the petitioners and their addresses]. The preliminary meeting will be immediately held at the Freemasons' Tavern, which will be announced by advertisement in "The Daily Telegraph" and other papers. In the mean while I shall thank you to send me your signature (by letter), so that your names may be placed on a memorial [a written statement of facts with a petition], which will also be produced at the meeting for signature, and afterwards presented to the Queen, praying her gracious Majesty to use her royal prerogative to protect a sane subject of her realm from such diabolical interference.'

WILLIAM FREDERICK WINDHAM.

Felbrigg Hall, Norfolk.'

The handbill had been concocted by Roberts, and if it were aimed at building up public interest in the case, then it could hardly have failed to succeed. One of the placards went up in the Anglesey pub in the Haymarket and attracted such a crowd that a policeman had to order it to be removed. In all, 5,000 copies were made by a printer in Paddington, who was - almost inevitably - never paid for his trouble. Even though there is no evidence that the public meeting at the Freemasons' Tavern ever, in fact, took place, let alone the 'monster meeting' at Hyde Park, Roberts had managed to skilfully blend a patriotic appeal for fair play, hints at vast wealth, medical torture, self-interest and even a suggestion of royal approval for the campaign. The call for mass meetings, and the careful printing of addresses of all the petitioners, added a further element, that of the veiled threat of mob rule. But the real undercurrent was of family betrayal - and family villainy.

And there was a particular reason why this aspect would have resonated with the public. Only the year before, the nation had been gripped by the serial publication of perhaps the greatest sensation novel of the Victorian era, Wilkie Collins' The Woman in White. Even prime minister Gladstone had found himself bewitched by the tale of false imprisonment, alleged lunacy, coercion and fortune-hunting. Surely, the book's Sir Percival Glyde, the acme of dissolute moustache-twirling fictional devilry, now had a real-life parallel in the form of the General?

Claims that the petitioners were conspiring to have Windham locked up so they could then fall upon his estate were to bedevil their case throughout. The actual evidence, as seen in the October correspondence, shows that, at least for some petitioners, there was a genuine concern for Windham's well-being. Unfortunately, those letters have remained unpublished until now and, as the academic Robert Claiborne once observed, what actually happens often matters less, in the long run, than what people think happens. Windham discussed the Roberts placard with Dr Harrington Tuke on 5 December, saying his solicitor was angry with him over it. Dr Tuke told Windham the placard was 'calculated to do great mischief', to which Windham replied: 'Oh, as long as it was not libellous, I said to Roberts he might print it'. Dr Tuke said he was wrong to have brought the names of the ladies into it, and Windham said he would try to do something about it. The next day he returned: Roberts had outwitted him, and distributed the placards all over London.

THE SECOND fillip to public interest happened in the Vice-Chancellor's Court. As befitting a decisive military man of action, the General had opened another front in his campaign. He now tried to have Agnes and her solicitor Bowen May brought before the court for contempt for 'procuring the marriage of a ward of Court immediately upon his attaining twenty-one, with a woman of bad character, and inducing him to execute settlements for her benefit of a considerable portion of his property'.

The General had launched the case because the Lords Justices' Court hearing had revealed the events leading up to the wedding. The General clearly hoped that a successful order for contempt - with its unambiguous implication of legally-proven skulduggery - could only aid the petitioners' case in the fast-approaching commission.

But only one of his targets had stayed long enough to remain in his sights. Agnes'

94

second departure from Windham and Felbrigg at the end of October had meant the General's agents had not been able to serve the order. Ironically, the General would have been able to serve the order on Agnes in person at the Euston Hotel in early November. So, on Wednesday 4 December it was Bowen May alone in court. But more to the point, as far as the general public were concerned at least, the contempt order was to be heard in open session - and thus, at last, supply the first, definitive (and reportable) juicy morsels of scandal to back up and reinforce what had been whispered round dining room and bar, in corridor and clubroom, across the nation for weeks.

The hearing heard how Windham, described as 'a young gentleman of large fortune', had married 'a kept woman' ('Agnes Ann Rogers, otherwise Willoughby', Agnes having by now changed the order of her first names). The solicitor first met her in 1859, and according to his affidavit, she was 'at that time living with a man who allowed her £2,000 a year'. Bowen May then went on to tell the court about her visit in June 1861 and the various meetings in August, being careful to explain how - naturally - he had tried to talk the couple out of marriage. When Agnes had mentioned Windham, he claimed it was the first time he had ever heard of him and he had been 'quite ignorant of his being under 21, or a ward of court'. He had, he conceded, heard 'something' about a hearing in August about a suit in Chancery, but claimed that, being extremely busy with his practice and not being an expert on Chancery matters, 'it had never occurred to him' about Windham's legal status.

This was too much for the General's men. Surely, they argued, May had now condemned himself out of his own mouth. For, despite knowing the character of 'the woman', Windham's immaturity, the financial implications of the settlement and the sheer unsuitability of marriage, May had not contacted Windham's family or the family's legal advisers. It was no good claiming, they said, that the wedding had taken place after Windham reached 21; his conduct over the 'infatuated young man' amounted to clear contempt for the legal process.

Defending Bowen was a man who would come to dominate the legal duelling over the coming weeks and months: Sir Hugh Cairns, QC. Frankly, he claimed, 'there was not a syllable of evidence' to prove contempt, conspiracy, or anything else. It was a typically robust defence from an advocate who would demonstrate a terrier-like ability to snap at - and on - the heels of any weakness in the opposition's case.

WHO, THEN, was this pillar of Windham's defence? There are a number of evocative carte-de-visite photographs of Sir Hugh taken shortly before the Windham case. They show him with a striking look of incipient disgust in the lines trailing from his high-bridged nose to his downturned mouth; a mouth meant for censure and the reluctant uttering of distasteful evidence. An obituary of Sir Hugh in 1885 was to comment on his coldness, pointing out his 'lack of geniality' and 'limited sympathy' with the feelings of the ordinary Englishman. His puritanical Christian beliefs, honed through his patrician Ulster background, also did not brook any deviation from the norms of moral behaviour.

But coldness was one aspect Sir Hugh McCalmont Cairns, QC, was not to bring to his appearances in the Windham case. Far from it - his life as a leading Tory politician (he was solicitor-general in the 1858-59 government, a post achieved aged just 38) meant that some commentators were to claim a political dimension to the Windham case, strengthened by the fact that the General was a successful Liberal candidate for East Norfolk.

There was no doubt that by recruiting Sir Hugh to their cause, the Windham camp had secured an immense legal and political heavyweight. Born of solid land-owning Ulster stock in 1819, Cairns was twenty years younger than his flamboyant rival QC, Montague Chambers. Called to the Bar in 1844, Sir Hugh was elected as Belfast MP in 1852 and rose quickly up the ranks, his legal career flourishing alongside his political one. He became a QC in 1856, and his later Cabinet post only served to boost still further his legal practice.

Sir Hugh's advocacy on behalf of Bowen May was only partially successful, however. In that 4 December hearing, Vice-Chancellor Wood admitted that, yes, Bowen May had not committed contempt, as everything significant connected with 'this unhappy marriage' had taken place after Windham's 21st birthday. But if Bowen May had secured the promise of marriage before 9 August, well, that was quite a different tale. The vice-chancellor said it was Bowen May's 'plain duty' to have let the Windham family solicitor know. But alas, he sighed, 'the mischief was done, the marriage had taken place, and nothing could be gained by further inquiry'. The vice-chancellor concluded: 'Mr May knew all throughout that Mrs Windham never displayed the slightest affection for her intended husband, yet he is content to see this infatuated young man about to marry a woman of worthless character, who feels an absolute repugnancy for him, without taking any step to protect him.' In a stinging rebuke, he concluded that Bowen May was 'content upon this flimsy statement of an intention to change his solicitor to act for this young man without the slightest communication to the guardian or solicitor. It was deeply to be regretted that a solicitor of this Court should have acted in such a way.'

WINDHAM was to be examined by two more medical men, Dr Mayo, President of the College of Physicians, and Dr Forbes Winslow, who eventually tracked him down to Roberts' house in Piccadilly. Windham was an emotional wreck by the time the doctors examined him on 11 and 14 December. The first interview lasted more than two hours, the second nearly an hour. They were not happy occasions. Windham went through the whole sorry tale of his marriage, the venereal disease he had given Agnes, her lovers (pre- and post-marriage) and the amount of his debts - at least £20,000 and rising daily, as his estranged wife's bills came in. But he refused to disown Roberts, even when the affair of the timber was raised, or the spurious placard, or even the matter of being cuckolded by his 'friend'.

There was one final legal preparation to make. On 11 December Sir Hugh, appearing before the Lords Justices, asked that £2,000 be freed from Windham's estate to pay off his former solicitors (the shedding of legal advisers would become a recurring theme for the rest of his life) and to help him 'properly defend' himself before the commission. And so now the stage was - at last - finally set.

Sir Hugh Cairns QC: Taken in May 1861, a few months before the Windham hearing. A fast-rising member of the Tory political establishment, his role in Windham's defence was to spark accusations of political influence. *(NRO ref: MC580/1, 780x1)*

8

16-19 December 1861:
The Commission

'CHARGE OF LUNACY IN HIGH LIFE'
Headline in the Penny Illustrated Paper, 30 November 1861

FATE, however, had one more trick in store to force the Windham case, temporarily at least, from the public's mind. There were many other stories competing for their attention, the work on the pioneering 'Metropolitan Subterranean Railway' and the latest eruption of Vesuvius being two of them. But these stories were dwarfed by the diplomatic crisis which threatened to drag Britain into the American Civil War. US President Lincoln's navy had stopped a British steamer and removed two Confederate agents. The action had prompted troop manoeuvres in Canada and a flood of jingoistic telegrams from naval reserves around the country offering to take up arms.

But in turn even that, though, was thrust from the news columns by what one paper described as 'The National Calamity'. Queen Victoria's husband Prince Albert had fallen ill with a fever, but a 11 December bulletin said he was 'unattended by unfavourable symptoms'. In reality the prince was declining rapidly, and late on 14 December, he died. The news stunned the country, promoting outbreaks of grief not seen since the death of the grand old Duke of Wellington in 1851. At least on that occasion, the commentators noted, the Duke had been increasingly aged and the nation prepared for his demise. Albert, however, had been in the prime of life.

But the British legal system, in particular, waited for no-one and nothing - not even the death of a prince - and so the Commission began its deliberations as planned on Monday 16 December, with the early newspaper reports of the Windham case encased in a thick border of mourning black. The great and historic setting of the Court of Exchequer near the medieval Westminster Hall in the Houses of Parliament was crowded, and it (and the Westminster sessions house, where the inquiry later moved) was to remain so for the whole inquiry.

The petition was read out. It sought to prove that William Frederick Windham was a lunatic on 1 August 1861, or 'at any other or what subsequent time thence down to the present'. If the public gallery was crowded, then so was the space set aside for the advocates. For the petitioners, there was Chambers, supported by Hume Williams and Edwin Field, with Peter Hansell of the Norwich solicitors. On Windham's side, there was Sir Hugh and Karslake, plus Mr Milward, with London firm Gregory and Co as his solicitors. In addition, Mr Coleridge QC was watching the proceedings on behalf of Agnes, while Charles Russell was doing the same for Lady Sophia, too ill to attend. The General was there from the start, and indeed for the whole of the case until Sir Hugh's opening speech for Windham.

What, then, of the team for the petitioners? Leading their case was the larger than life Montague Chambers, QC, a person well versed in dealing with high-profile cases, and also to controversy, both within the courtroom and outside it. Born in 1799, he was called to the Bar in 1828. By 1845 Chambers was a QC and appearing in a series of major cases. During that year, for example, he represented one John Taswell at a Slough inquest into the death of Sarah Hart, of Salt Hill. Public feeling ran so strongly that a human barrier of policemen was needed to try and protect the defendant from a baying mob.

Chambers' appearances were nothing if not varied. In the same year he acted for an earl trying to halt the route of a railway line; in a case for slander; and for a railway company against the Duke of Palmella who claimed it had lost a valuable box of plate. By 1847 racier fare was the order of the day, Chambers being involved in a number of cases which were to anticipate in lesser or greater degree the 1861 Commission. At the summer assizes in Croydon, Miss Sarah Mary Hoare had brought a suit against Captain Dickson for slander. Chambers, appearing for Hoare, found himself in full retreat after counter-claims that she was 'an adventurer and a female Jeremy Diddler [trickster]'. Hoare was 'nonsuited' - that is, had her claim struck out by the judge for lack of evidence. But Chambers finished on the winning side in 1850 when representing a Fleet Street bookbinder, accused by Eliza Cuffley - a girl of 'considerable personal attractions' - of making her pregnant. Chambers produced evidence that, despite her claims to be a pauper, she was dressed expensively and was a known frequenter of public houses, the clear inference, of course, being that she was a prostitute.

By 1852 Chambers was moving in political circles as well as legal ones. In February of that year he put himself forward as a Liberal candidate for the seat of Greenwich. But despite the inevitable and considerable outlay involved in a nineteenth-century husting - Chambers even having hired his own brass band - the electors were unimpressed, despite the candidate having made a rousing speech to the crowd in which he said that he had 'been tainted with being a lawyer but was not ashamed of his profession'. A second attempt, in 1853, however, did prove successful.

Perhaps Chambers' most high-profile (and successful) case of 1852 was appearing for Robert Frederick Brownlow Rushbrooke, of Rushbrooke Hall in Suffolk, in a suit against Capt George Nathaniel Broke, accused of seducing Mrs Rushbrooke. The jury agreed with Chambers and awarded the wronged husband the considerable sum of £3,000 in damages. In 1859 Chambers' political career received a setback when he was again rejected by the voters of Greenwich. By the time the Windham hearing was beginning, he was into his sixties and - as a contemporary photograph shows - the acme of mid-Victorian respectability, with white and occasionally wayward hair and the jowls of a prosperous late middle-age.

In contrast with Chamber's general air of benignity, accentuated by the pince-nez which he wore in court, his chief opponent in the case, Sir Hugh, was to cut an altogether more forbidding appearance. Sir Hugh was aided in his case by John Burgess Karslake, who had only become a QC a few months earlier. Aged forty, he was born into a legal family. An 1873 watercolour by W Vine, one of the famous Vanity Fair series, and now in the National Portrait Gallery, portrays him as a rather sharp-faced, though dapper man. He was to prove an incisive questioner in the weeks to come.

In charge of the hearing was Sam Warren, whose round spectacles gave him an owlish though diffident air, reflected in the studious though often ineffectual way he was to handle proceedings. He had an unusual background, being a former MP and author as well as a lawyer. His most popular work was 1842's Ten Thousand A Year, but he also wrote 'Passages From A Diary of a Late Physician' in Blackwood's Magazine. He had resigned as Midhurst MP in 1859 to take up the appointment as a Master in Lunacy.

MASTER WARREN began by addressing the jury - 23 lawyers and medical men - about the issues they would have to consider. The assembled reporters had to strain hard to hear his voice, which barely rose above a mumble. There were, he said, essentially, just two issues to consider: whether Windham was 'at the present time of unsound mind', and if so, whether he had been of unsound mind on 1 August or any subsequent occasion.

Chambers began the petitioners' case with a dramatic flourish. He sought, and won, a ruling from Warren that 'ladies should not be present, as it would be his painful duty to lay before the jury details that would be unfit for females to hear' (at which point the assembled newspaper shorthand writers must have discreetly but urgently double-checked that they had a plentiful supply of pencils). He then began to summarise what he described as Windham's 'very melancholy' early history. Chambers said that from the outset Windham was unlike other children.

He had not the same intellectual powers... a deficiency of intellect, not amounting to anything like raving mania, but rather to imbecility,' he said. The issue was not a clear-cut one of people such as Windham being 'absolute idiots'.

Montague Chambers QC: A flamboyant character, whose successes in a series of varied and high-profile cases was carefully noted by the General. *(NRO ref: MC580/1, 780x1)*

Indeed, they might have 'exhibitions of talent' in some areas such as memory. But, he stressed, the overall effect might still be for the individual concerned to be 'incompetent to take care of themselves, or to manage their affairs'.

It was a fine distinction, and one which the general public, and much of the press, struggled to grasp over the coming months. For them the issue was clear: either Windham was a lunatic (as the petition and the name of the commission stated) or he was sane. Chambers mentioned that one aspect of young Windham's 'deficiency of mental power' was his fondness for 'very low company and low pursuits'. 'He was quite fond of going among the servants and did acts quite inconsistent with the position of a young gentleman,' he said.

At his first school, aged nine, he had shown himself prey to 'dirty and nasty habits with regard to his person [and] expressed himself in filthy language'. His behaviour had not improved by the time he was sent to Eton in 1854, and so the Rev Henry Cheales was brought in to help him at school and accompany him on his holidays. He was a difficult pupil, Chambers continued, resorting to telling the 'most transparent untruths' and gorging himself at meals to the point of vomiting, behaviour which earned him the nickname of 'Mad' Windham.

There was worse: 'He had a great fondness for screeching, shouting and hooting in a way likely to alarm people both in and out of doors. He had sudden and extraordinary fits of passion without any adequate cause. Upon a sudden, when he had been previously tranquil, he would break into a violent passion with persons with whom he had no quarrel and he still continued his dirty habits,' he said. At Eton he exhibited 'strong animal instincts or passions'. While back at Felbrigg he showed 'a cruel and barbarous disposition' in his dealings with animals, and on a stay in Torquay his manners provoked complaints by the ladies there. He would 'burst into fits of blubbering', even when aged 17.

Chambers told how Colonel Bathurst was then appointed as Windham's next companion, but had only lasted a few months. While visiting Spa, it was noticed that Windham's clothes were 'frequently so disordered that he appeared to be unconscious of the ordinary decencies and proprieties of life,' Chambers added. Windham had since continued to tell ridiculous lies, and had behaved in a dangerous way in a dog-cart, crashing into a Norfolk inn. Now Windham had decided he wanted to be in the army, and took to calling himself 'Captain' Windham, 'and seemed to imagine that he was the greatest man in England in regard to military affairs'.

The counsel now produced another coup-de-théâtre, coming to an incident, 'which, if unchecked, was likely to endanger the lives of other people'. Chambers explained that Windham was very fond of trains, 'and desired to work the brake and act as a guard. Sometimes he actually got upon the engine without the permission of the driver, and started the train. 'Once, at the Cambridge Station, he took off the guard's belt, blew the whistle for the train to start, and the engineer, thinking it the proper signal, set the train in motion; and had it not been stopped, in all probability it would have run into another train,' he added.

OF ALL THE things which Montague Chambers mentioned in his opening remarks - and later on the same day there were to be more salacious titbits - this was the one which was calculated to cause the greatest public concern. It was not a point of quaint eccentricity; it was far more serious than that. The Victorian age was a time of enormous technological change and a huge increase in industrialisation. But the steam-driven surge towards new markets and a burgeoning economy rarely went hand-in-hand with modern safety concerns.

Open almost any Victorian newspaper at random and it is likely it will contain a lurid account of an industrial or mining disaster or its aftermath, or the report of the 'melancholy death' of some worker dragged into machinery.

The greatest manifestation of this rush for progress was the railways. They changed the nineteenth-century world as utterly as computers have changed ours. Listen to The Economist from January 1851: 'It is here that our progress has been most stupendous - surpassing all previous steps since the creation of the human race....we have reached in a single bound from the speed of a horse's canter, to the utmost speed comparable with the known strength and coherence of brass and iron. The railroad is the Magna Carta of the [poor's] motive freedom.' The success of the Manchester-Liverpool rail link had pointed the way to the enormous financial benefits of linking centres of population with a cheap, efficient and reliable transport network.

Master in Lunacy, Mr Commissioner Warren: Sam Warren, lawyer, best-selling writer and former MP, rapidly found himself hopelessly out of his depth as the Windham case began. *(NRO ref: MC580/1, 780x1)*

But the task of reaching that acme of cheapness, efficiency and reliability was sometimes not so easily detectable when there was profit to be made. The 1840s and 50s were full of stories of boom, corruption, commercial skulduggery, and - rather as in the 'internet bubble' of the late 1990s - fortunes made and lost in spectacular style. At a time of relatively lax safety legislation, it was a cause of alarm to commentators that railways, although undoubtedly one of the wonders of the modern age, had also hugely increased the potential for large-scale loss of life and injury. In September 1861 there had been yet another two crashes on the railway network only a few days apart, at Kentish Town and at Brighton, the latter claiming a shocking 23 lives. The Brighton crash had prompted one newspaper to write a stinging editorial, headlined unequivocally 'SLAUGHTER ON RAILWAYS'.

Earlier in the year Punch had commented pointedly: 'As ninety-nine percent of the accidents that happen might be prevented were more labour and more vigilance employed, and were not too often a cheese-paring of expense, it clearly is high time to call a spade a spade, and speak of RAILWAY MANSLAUGHTER by its only proper name'.

The Eastern Counties Railway, on which Windham did most of his travelling, already had a poor reputation for safety and efficiency. After an 1854 crash which killed two people near Thetford, the paper demanded to know why travel on the line was so 'dreadfully hazardous' and attacked the 'utter incompetency' of the company's management, branding them 'monopolists, [presenting] dangers to the safety of the public either from sheer incompetent management or incomplete means'. Strong words; little wonder, then, about the alarm which Chamber's revelations about Windham would have on the general public.

MONTAGUE CHAMBERS now moved to the last year or so before Windham came of age. He told how two more companions - Messrs Horrocks and Peatfield - had tried to rein in his behaviour by taking him travelling. To no avail: 'He seemed insensible to shame, and unconscious of the improprieties he was guilty of,' he added.

In May 1861, he said, the General returned to England, prompted by the urgent concerns of his sister-in-law. General Windham urged his nephew to travel abroad to gain maturity and prepare himself for coming into his inheritance but, claimed Chambers, other influences on Windham were now at work, trying to persuade him that the General was secretly plotting to prevent him marrying and having children so that the estate would fall into his hands. Peatfield had lodged Windham with the Llewellyns of Duke Street, St James', with the instruction that he should be 'relieved from restraint as much as possible, that he might try how to manage his own affairs'. But, said Chambers, he continued to scream and shout in the street, eat like a pig (and, indeed, make noises like one), vomit, and carry on his other dirty habits.

The newspaper reports at this point drew a veil over the next part of the speech, merely saying that 'the learned gentlemen described other instances of want of cleanliness which are not fit for publication'. The court transcript is not so coy: Chambers actually continued: 'At other times he would go into a bath when he had been driving an engine, or anything of that sort; but besides that it will be lamentable to record, as the servants will tell you, that despite a water closet close to his bedroom, to which he could, with the greatest of ease, have used, his bed was found saturated. Sometimes... the calls of nature have been answered in the bed and upon the sheets'. The QC then mentioned Windham's habit of pretending to be a policeman in London and Norwich, to the extent of making 'arrests' in the street. And now, he said, he would show that Windham was 'utterly senseless of decency and honour' and it was with these details in mind that he had asked for the ladies removed from the court. Chambers then continued: 'In July, 1861 [a mistake, it was, of course, June] he met with a lady, calling herself Agnes Willoughby, but whose real name was said to be Rogers. He met her in the Ascot week, with a person named Roberts, who appeared... on terms of improper intimacy with Miss Willoughby.'

'[She] was not the chastest of the chaste; her favours in love affairs were not few; she was known to the police; she was known to gallants. On the 30th of August... Mr Windham was married to Miss Willoughby, alias Rogers, although both he and the lady knew at the time that he was suffering from a foul and infectious disease.' Chambers went on to mention the 'very hasty' and 'curious' marriage settlement and the '£12,000 or £14,000' in jewellery which Windham, or 'the victim' as he called him, was persuaded to buy.

Turning to the affair of the timber, he said Windham had been led to part with it to Roberts for a third of its real worth. 'Mr Windham knew no more of its value than he did of the gold mines of Australia,' he said. 'In actual fact he seemed utterly incompetent to what he had been doing.' And when the two distinguished doctors, Dr Mayo and Dr Forbes Winslow, had interviewed him in early December, they were struck by Windham's 'utter deadness to anything like a notion of decent propriety or sense of honour'.

The QC outlined some more of the links between Windham and Roberts, reading out the notorious placard. Chambers concluded by reminding the jury that when Windham came to be examined before them he might be able to impress some that he was 'sufficiently reasonable to continue to control his own actions', but warned them that this would not be the case. In short, this was an inquiry demanding 'the most careful investigation on the part of the jury'. Not all the jury would make it through to the final test.

THE FIRST witness was Dr William Nicholls, the Norwich doctor to whom William Howe Windham had turned for advice. Dr Nicholls told the jury how he had been quickly convinced that the young boy was weak in intellect. 'He was always slavering at the mouth and had all the accompaniments of that condition of mind indicating idiocy, and I should have thought would ripen into idiocy in after age,' he said. In cross-examination he said the boy was unable to speak or articulate properly. He told of his next encounter with Windham in 1858, when the teenager was introduced to him at a public ball in Norwich. 'He shook hands with me and immediately burst into an idiotic laugh,' he said. Sir Hugh pressed him on exactly what he meant by 'idiotic'. Very loud,' he replied, 'and in a manner unlike the laugh of any person of sound mind. It was such a laugh as would attract the attention of the bystanders... I came to the conclusion, from what took place that evening, that he was unable to take care of his person or to manage his affairs.'

Quizzed by the master, he went on: 'The laugh of an imbecile is louder, more shrieking, and unmeaning, that that of a person of sound mind.' Windham's laugh was to become a recurrent theme in the weeks ahead, frequently quoted in evidence. But as the case wore on, it became less of a serious point than one of those which itself sparked laughter from the public gallery. The matter of the laugh, in short, itself soon became laughable.

The second, and final, witness in what had been an eventful first day was Windham's former private tutor at Eton, the Rev Cheales. He told how he had been appointed in August 1854, the month young Windham turned 14, and stayed with him almost until Easter 1857. 'His powers of attention and learning were very small,' he said, but of similar concern was his personal behaviour. 'His habits were not cleanly. I frequently called that to his attention. His hands and face were very constantly dirty. He showed great gluttony at his meals, and would sit with the saliva running from his mouth at such times.' Young Windham frequently cried at the least opportunity, exhibit 'violent fits of passion' and frequently used 'violent abuse, couched in the worst possible language - profane and filthy'.

'I have also seen him dance about the room, moving his head about and screaming,' he added. 'When he went into society he was rude and noisy. He was rude in his manner to ladies'. Once, said Cheales, they were at a party at Torquay and Windham had 'seized a gentleman by the whiskers and held his head against the wall, laughing and screaming. I was obliged to release the gentleman then.' The clergyman talked too, about his habit of frequenting Eton railway station. 'I used my best efforts to instruct him, and to improve his manners, but without success,' he admitted.

The court adjourned at 4.30pm. There was plenty for the jury and the gallery to talk about: loathsome diseases, railway misbehaviour, scarlet women, manic laughter, gluttony, impersonation of police offices, cruelty to animals, and more. And it was only Day One. The Windham case promised to be just as sensational as everyone had hoped.

CHEALES' EVIDENCE continued the next day, going into more detail about Windham's lessons at Eton, and his slavering. 'I complained to his mother at Felbrigg of his dirty habits, and she said I must try and cure him,' he said. He talked about the abortive efforts to introduce Windham to polite society by getting him used to the company of ladies on trips to Torquay on three visits between 1855 and 1856. They were a failure and there was also the unfortunate incident of Windham seizing a gentleman by his whiskers.

'Mr Windham was about sixteen when ladies complained to me of his rudeness,' he said. 'I have seen him follow ladies about the room, shouting and endeavouring to lay hold of them - I suppose in sport.' The clergyman then told the jury about Windham's accident to his hand at Eton station. Cheales' evidence concluded in slightly surreal fashion as he denied that Windham's imitation of a steam whistle had anything to do with a song by the Ethiopian Serenaders, a group of 'negro minstrels'. That comment provoked laughter in the public gallery. There was to be plenty more.

The next witness was another clergyman, the Rev Edward Hale, a mathematics teacher at Eton since 1850, and a private tutor to Windham from Easter to Christmas 1856. 'He was the "densest" pupil I have ever had,' he said simply, 'and while under my care he never made any visible advance.' Hale added, using the Eton slang, 'he rather funked me'. Up in the gallery, inevitably, there was another laugh. Hale concurred with Cheales' observations about young Windham's slobbering, but also referred to what the some accounts coyly glossed over as 'a very indelicate habit'. The Times was a little more direct: 'He used his hands in a disgusting manner'. They were talking, of course, about masturbation, which for Victorian audiences was seen as clear evidence of moral turpitude, allegedly leading to weak muscles, damp hands, even consumption - and, yes, madness. W Acton, in his influential 1857 work The Functions and Disorders of the Reproductive Organs, even concluded: 'Self-indulgence, long pursued, leads ultimately to... early death, or self-destruction.'

Hale, for one, was in no doubt of Windham's abilities, or rather the lack of them. 'I considered him incapable of managing himself, or his work,' he said, adding that he had been the worst pupil in his eleven years at Eton. The other boys, he added, encouraged him to be disruptive in class, and it was through this behaviour that he gained the 'Mad Windham' nickname.

Another Norwich physician, Dr Donald Dalrymple, then went into the witness box. A Fellow of the Royal College of Surgeons, he told the court that he had known the Windham family since William's childhood. His conclusion, he added, was that 'I do not think him fit to go into the world to manage himself for his own safety, and the safety of others. He is certainly not fit to manage his money.' He mentioned Windham's lies, his 'outbursts of passion' and his association with the servants.

Dr Dalrymple also told the jury what had happened on the day of the General's ovation in August 1856, with the youngster's continual 'shrieking and halloaing'. Worse, when he went into his bedroom later than evening to check on him, he found him 'in a state of nudity'. The papers spared their readers the subsequent details. Dr Dalrymple covered him up with his bedclothes and put out the light.

Windham was, he added, also badly behaved at the Volunteer Militia review in 1861 and at a party in Brundall, near Norwich, in July of that year.

Dr Dalrymple was frank about Gla's father and his 'hot-tempered' nature, and also about Lady Sophia's 'excitable' personality. William Howe Windham, he said, had allowed his child 'to amuse himself pretty much as he liked... the parents continued to spoil the child and allow him to have the run of the house.' And now the child had grown up, and Dr Dalrymple was concerned for his future. He told Chambers: 'I don't think he has the capacity to protect himself from the traps and lures that might be laid for him in society. He has an impulsive nature, that in my opinion would lead him to do wrong or mad acts.'

He was followed by another Norwich medical man, and one who also specialised in mental conditions. Dr James Johnson told the hearing about another civic occasion at which Windham had created a disturbance, the Norwich Sessions Ball in 1859. The next witness was the Rev Thomas Goodwin, who explained how, while visiting Torquay in 1857, he was asked to look after young Windham for two or three weeks. It was a brief, but memorable experience, and not for the right reasons. The clergyman found the 16-year-old rude, uncouth, dirty and thoroughly strange. 'He was very excitable in demeanour,' he said. 'I have seen him jump over chairs, jump on his mother's shoulders and try to ride her like a horse, I have seen him suddenly leave off reading and run round the garden screaming.' Sharing a table with him was even worse, with Windham picking the food straight out of the serving bowl with dirty hands and pushing large pieces into his mouth.

The final witness of the day was yet another of Windham's former paid companions, Col James Bathurst, formerly of the Coldstream Guards and now in charge of the 19th Middlesex Volunteers. He told how he had been engaged by the family in 1859, taking Windham down to Plymouth for three months, and then chosen by Vice-Chancellor Wood to accompany the young heir for another six months over the summer in a Continental tour. But he was forced to admit: 'I cannot say that I got him to behave as I wished him to do'. The only literature which made any impression on his young charge was one of the Ingoldsby Legends, that once hugely-popular 1847 collection of tall tales and ballads from the Rev Richard Harris Barham, of which the best-known is The Jackdaw of Rheims.

And the only thing which Windham could remember about that was the couplet - which drew the biggest laugh of the day from the public gallery - 'The Rotherham monk/ Got jolly well drunk'. In fact the colonel's memory was playing him tricks (as was The Times' reporter, who had 'The modern monk/ got jollily drunk'). The actual quotation was from A Lay of St Nicholas ('But Roger the Monk got excessively drunk'). Ironically, one of the other tales in the book, The Witches'

Frolic, was about the 'wild and roving' Rob Gilpin, 'forever in the alehouse boozing/ Or romping - which is quite as bad/With female friends of his own choosing.' The moral of that particular tale was also lost on the young Windham.

There were more unseemly associations with the servants, more casual cruelty towards horses, more 'foul and disgusting language' - which the colonel repeated in court - and more handing over of douceurs to railway guards so Windham could ride in the vans and even operate the train's brakes. But the Colonel's evidence showed that Windham's amorous side was now being stirred too. 'He was always,' he said, 'as far as I could judge, falling in love. At a dinner in Plymouth he got excited and made himself very conspicuous. He had had some little joke with a lady, and he continued to call out the name of the lady and to repeat the joke.' The lady in question soon wanted nothing to do with the peculiar young heir. The colonel concluded, in the last comment of the day, 'he is certainly unfit to manage his private affairs'.

The evidence so far may have shocked (and titillated) newspaper readers across the land, but Windham was apparently unconcerned. On 18 December he bumped into a Mr Connor, yet another former tutor, in Palace Yard. He told Windham he thought it must be an anxious time for him. Windham replied that he was not making himself very miserable and he had no doubt about the result. 'He seemed to be in good spirits,' Connor concluded.

BEFORE THE colonel resumed his evidence on the third day, Master Warren told Sir Hugh that he was 'seriously distressed' at the likely length of the inquiry. He had, he told him, already signed and sealed more than 200 summonses to witnesses, including one to Russia. 'The expense of such inquiry is necessarily frightful,' he added, saying that everyone in the court had an interest in completing it as soon as possible. The court would, of course, be closed the following Monday because of the funeral of the Prince Consort, and General Windham was under pressure from the Horse Guards to go to his command in India. Commissioner Warren then dropped strong hints that he, too, had other business to attend to after 1 January. The implication was obvious.

But Sir Hugh was too wily a campaigner to respond to the commissioner's hint for brevity. All he could say, he explained, was that he had no idea of the likely length of the petitioners' case. His own course would be 'guided in a great measure' by the other side. Colonel Bathurst was then cross-examined by Sir Hugh. He had spent, he said, upwards of £200 per year on Windham's clothes and pocket money, but his young charge was always short of cash.

George Farrow, a registrar at the Court of Chancery, told how he had met Windham at the gaming table in Spa in 1859. The youth was 'throwing his money around'. 'His conduct was the talk of Spa', he added. Sir Hugh said, to laughter: There is not much in that. I dare say Spa is sometimes sadly in want of something to talk about.' To which Chambers muttered, to more laughter, '...And Mr Windham was the very man to give it something to talk about.' All this amusement was too much for the Master, who interjected: 'The newspapers of this morning report with great accuracy certain bursts of laughter which took place yesterday. I hope nothing of the kind will take place again. The inquiry is a very painful one, and I trust that out of respect for public decency, if for no other reason, we shall in future have no such unseemly ebullitions of feeling.' His comments had absolutely no effect. Within seconds, there was more laughter.

Mary Wilkinson, another visitor to Spa, then told the court that she had stayed in the same hotel as Windham. He had 'conducted himself like a child', bursting into tears for the slightest cause. His relationships with the other women staying at the hotel had caused concern, she added. The widow said Windham had told ridiculous lies, including a claim that he was armed with a pair of pistols. 'I considered him a vain, silly child,' she added.

The court then resumed its examination of Windham's paid companions with the evidence of Edgeworth Horrocks - coincidentally the brother of Mary Wilkinson - who was appointed to succeed Colonel Bathurst in October or November 1859. He met Windham at London, and then returned to Felbrigg where he stayed until June 1860, a few weeks before Windham's 20th birthday. In between they made another trip to the South Coast, this time to St Leonard's. By now, Horrocks said, 'his great subject was ladies' and he had told an elaborate (and false) story, about how he was going to convert to Roman Catholicism so he could marry a young woman of that faith in the resort. And here, too, was an indication of Windham's liking for the lowest - as well as the highest-born - women: 'Wherever I took him,' he added, 'Regardless of a lady's position or rank, or whatever her character, good or bad, he would after a few weeks, and sometimes after a few days, make her an offer of marriage.'

He added that his stay with Windham almost had disastrous consequences. On a visit to Aylsham in his dog-cart he was thrown out when Windham drove it furiously into a yard. 'He used to beat the horses very cruelly. Sometimes he would cuddle them as if they were his children, and even kiss them, but afterwards would ill-treat them again.' 'He ate like a brute,' he continued, pointing out Windham's liking - to more laughter - for dumplings. 'The genuine Norfolk dumpling is very large and he would eat a whole one,' Horrocks added, in all seriousness. He had carried on his association with 'the very lowest persons', boasting to them that he was the 'great Mr Windham of Felbrigg'. On one bizarre occasion he had gone into a pub in St Leonard's wearing a military greatcoat and telling the barmaid that he had been ill-treated but that he was going to kill his tormentors with something he had hidden under his coat.

Horrocks had a three-stage method of trying to deal with his difficult charge: firstly, by saying he would write to the Vice-Chancellor, then by preparing to leave Felbrigg, and finally 'threatening to thrash him'. On at least one occasion, he admitted, he had done exactly that. 'He would not come to lunch once,' Horrocks explained. 'He was in the housekeeper's room and I went for him. He refused to come. Lady Sophia told me to go and bring him. He said "I shan't come unless I am made." I boxed his ears well and he threw himself down, and, putting his head on the doormat, yelled and screamed as if I was killing him.

'Mrs Martin came out and said "What are you doing with my dear boy?"... He then looked up and said, "I'll shoot you, you ------!" I said, "You had better try it." When he got up his face was covered in blood.' Horrocks was more than ten years older than Windham, who also had the advantage of being stouter, but he had not tried to defend himself. But Windham had tried to take his revenge by complaining unsuccessfully to the Vice-Chancellor about Horrocks' behaviour. He admitted, when pressed by Karslake, that he had once told Windham that his uncle the General would come back to put him in a lunatic asylum.

WINDHAM arrived in court for the evidence of two of his uncles at the start of the fourth day of the hearing - which also happened to be Agnes' 21st birthday. It was the first time most people in the public gallery had seen the now-famous Norfolk squire. According to one report, Windham conducted himself with 'the utmost propriety and decorum. At some passages of the evidence a faint smile passed over his features, and he occasionally communicated with Mr Karslake while that gentleman was cross-examining the witness.'

The papers reported on Windham's appearance: 'He appears to be a young man of considerable physical strength, about the middle height, of a full habit of body, with inclination to corpulency. He has a dark complexion, and wears his hair parted down the middle. The defect in his upper lip, to which so many allusions have been made, is partially concealed by a moustache, but is still plainly visible, exposing some of his teeth.'

The drama of the first day of the hearing had been steadily dissipated by the succession of clergymen and ex-military men relating their largely similar experiences during their period in charge of the troublesome Gla. But the drama returned on the fourth day with the appearance in the witness box of some of the leading members of the Hervey clan, both signatories to the petition which had sparked the inquiry. Windham's uncle, the Marquis of Bristol, began his evidence by talking about young Gla's visit to his father's house in Brighton around 1847 or 1848 with Lady Sophia.

During his stay, which lasted around a fortnight, young Windham's mother seemed, he said 'very anxious to keep him in order', even carrying a 'little whip' in her hand when they came down for meals.

Windham had called on the Marquis at his London house twice since Easter 1861 and had stayed for dinner, behaving himself 'remarkably well' apart from his foolish way of laughing. Their next encounter had been when he saw him riding on his own in Rotten Row in August, when the Marquis noticed he had a 'very remarkable appearance'. 'His face wore an expression of mingled fun and folly,' he said. 'He seemed to have a childish pleasure in being on horseback in the Park, where there were so many people about, but I also detected an expression bordering on idiocy.'

His brother Lord Alfred Hervey gave an account of a family meal which the 13-year-old Windham had attended. Lord Alfred's wife had rebuked Gla for reaching into a pie dish and pulling out a portion instead of using a knife and spoon. She refused to let him have any of the pie, at which he 'seized a large carving knife, and rushed at her with it'. Luckily, Lord Alfred had stepped into the room at that moment, grabbed a hearth broom, and then hit Windham on the legs to make him drop the knife. Gla had then rushed out of the room, yelling. The next time Lord Alfred had seen him had been at William Howe Windham's funeral, when he found young Windham's conduct 'very peculiar'. Lord Alfred said Windham's behaviour appeared to have improved when he attended two family dinner parties in May 1858 without incident. But Windham had mysteriously disappeared at the end of each meal. The second time, his uncle had returned to the dining room and found Windham in his shirt-sleeves helping to clear the table.

I immediately called him out of the room and was very angry with him,' he added. 'He would go to my brother's house and behave something like a gentleman, but immediately after dinner he would go away somewhere else and conduct himself in the most outrageous manner,' he added. Lord Alfred added that Windham's lies were persistent and 'objectless' - lying for lying's sake. 'I do not think he was amenable to any influence by fear,' he said. 'I am of the opinion that he is totally incapable of taking care of his property, and his general habits are that, if not placed under proper control, his life will probably be shortened.'

Now it was Karslake's turn to cross-examine, and point by point he forced Lord Alfred on the defensive. No, he admitted, he had no personal knowledge about the likely outcome of Windham's life - he had formed his opinion after reading the various affidavits. And, no, he had not directly seen him in 'low haunts of vice'. But he was adamant his nephew was a liar, spoilt, and feckless.

One comment from Lord Alfred would have far-reaching repercussions. 'As a matter of fact,' he admitted, 'General Windham would get the estates supposing my nephew had no children'. Those members of the public who remembered the infamous placard would recall its claim, amid all the hyperbole, that Windham's family was plotting to take his property.

Joseph Peatfield, the final companion for Windham appointed by the Court of Chancery, was next to give his evidence, having travelled all the way from St Petersburg where he was now a private tutor. He had taken on the job of looking after Windham in spring 1860 and he had been told to travel with him through England and Scotland. After returning to Felbrigg in early September and spending the winter there, they were off on their travels again then back to London in May 1861, to the Bedford Hotel, and then to lodge at the soon-to-be-infamous Llewellyns'.

The 2nd Marquis of Bristol: Windham's uncle told how Lady Sophia resorted to carrying round a 'little whip' to keep her errant son in check. *(NRO ref: MC580/1, 780x1)*

It had, as usual, been a tale of bad behaviour and rowdiness. His charge was frequently drunk - sometimes 'foaming at the mouth' - violent, and abusive, Peatfield claimed. Things came to a head on 4 February 1861 at Felbrigg, when reports of Windham being involved in a fight at Aylsham came back to the hall. Peatfield ordered him to get ready to go to London; Windham told him to 'go to hell' and that he was 'a sneak and a spy'. Peatfield told Windham he would be in contempt of court if he did not obey instructions, and called in the housekeeper Mrs Martin to witness his disobedience. The housekeeper's husband eventually persuaded Windham to go. Peatfield went on to tell the court how the General and Mr Hook had asked him to let Windham be his own master from the middle of May onwards, as there were only 12 weeks to go until his long-anticipated 21st birthday. His nephew had then behaved, said Peatfield, 'in a terrible manner on many occasions'. Soon the court was to hear detailed claims of exactly how bad the 'terrible manner' was.

Under cross-examination from Karslake, he admitted that he had once said that 'Windham had plenty of brains if chose to apply himself' but said he could reconcile those comments with his assessment of Windham as being incompetent because of his constant 'peril' in money affairs. Oh, and the several occasions he had danced on billiard tables. The fourth day ended with Peatfield unequivocal about the effect of Windham's stay in London. 'From the time he went to the Llewellyns he cast off his allegiance to me,' he said. But what was the Llewellyns' view of what had happened? That, and much else besides, would be revealed the next day.

The proceedings were crowded every day, even - as the Daily News reported - including 'several members of the aristocracy'. And no wonder, for with the exception of Prince Albert's funeral (which took place on Monday 23 December), this was the greatest free show in town.

9

20-26 December 1861:
The Llewellyns

'I have given it to him pretty strong, and his lady love too'.
Quote attributed to Augusta Llewellyn, 20 December

WITH THE benefit of hindsight, if there was a day on which the commission's verdict was decided then it was Friday 20 December, Day Five of the inquiry. Much had been made of Windham's unsatisfactory childhood in the previous days, but the critical period was after 27 May 1861 when he lodged with the Llewellyns. This was the time when he had fully succumbed to the debaucheries of the Haymarket, fallen for Agnes, and become entangled in the manipulative world of 'Bawdyhouse' Roberts. Over the span of 14 weeks the future of the centuries-old Windham tenure of Felbrigg changed from merely uncertain to that of being in critical danger.

In the morning the jury heard from Thomas Partridge, a friend of Peatfield, and from one of Windham's Edinburgh landladies, Mrs Jesse England. Both confirmed the essential details of Peatfield's evidence, with stories of shrieking, strange laughter and furious carriage-driving. When Augusta Llewellyn came to give evidence,

Windham made his second appearance in two days, once again paying close attention to the proceedings. And her evidence was soon worthy of study. She told how she and her husband David, a wine importer, lived at 35 Duke Street and had been asked by a neighbour to take in Windham during Epsom Derby week. With the exception of certain intervals, Windham remained with her until 29 August. 'I had, therefore,' she said, 'full opportunities of noticing his conduct, habit, and manners.' Her verdict on Windham was plain: 'I formed the opinion that he was not in his right mind.'

Windham, she said, was not just dirty in his habits but so filthy that her husband had to force him to take a bath. Not that he stayed in the bath very long; on at least three occasions, she claimed, he had 'jumped out... and ran as far as the dining room with no clothes on.' Fortunately the three female servants in the house were upstairs and did not witness his nakedness. When Mrs Llewellyn threatened to tell the General of his behaviour, she said he had sworn at her and threatened to 'rip up her bloody guts' with a carving knife. 'I left the dining room as soon as I could,' she added, unnecessarily. Windham was careless with his money, constantly asking her husband - or 'Old Bob Ridley' as he called both the Llewellyns after the title of a song he was then obsessed with - for a loan.

His table manners were as shocking as his want of cleanliness. Frequently not getting up until 10am, his breakfast could last more than two hours. There now followed one of the most famous and quoted claims about Windham's behaviour: 'His favourite dish was poached eggs, of which he consumed a large number. I never knew him take less than eight. The largest number I ever saw him eat was 12.' On one occasion, she claimed, he even vomited in her lap, a statement greeted with laughter from the public gallery.

He often ordered dinner but stayed out late, sometimes not coming back at all. 'I do not believe he told me the truth during the whole time he was in the house - not even on the most trivial occasion. I feel confident he did not know the difference between truth and falsehood.' Once when he was at the dining table he moved about on the edge of the table as if he were riding like a woman on horseback. 'He called out, "My dearly beloved Agnes - Agnes" and pretended to be riding in the Park,' she added, inevitably to more laughter.

She said he had disappeared from the house around 20 or 22 August, not returning until 27 August. 'I remember him coming home with only one sock on. He was very black. He said he had been driving the engine. His foot that had the sock off it was cut,' she said. 'He was very ill, and I went to the doctor's for him... I have never seen him in such a state before.' He had come back in Agnes' carriage, she added. Mrs Llewellyn said Windham had talked to her about Agnes on several occasions, the last time being 28 August, the day before he left Duke Street. She had told him it would be a shocking thing to marry a person like Agnes, to which he replied: 'I never intend to marry her or any such whore. I have had all I want with her, and she may stay on with Jack [Garton]'. And yet he had told Mr Llewellyn previously that Agnes was a respectable clergyman's daughter. Mrs Llewellyn further claimed Windham had told her Agnes had been seduced by Lord Willoughby, and that was why she styled herself 'Miss Agnes Willoughby'.

This was too much for the Master, who interjected: 'It is only due to Lord Willoughby to state that there is not the slightest foundation for Mr Windham's statement'. Mrs Llewellyn went on to say that Windham had come back to Duke Street for supper about five to six weeks before the commission, the first time since leaving on 29 August. 'He was then worse than ever,' she said. 'He cried quietly. He seemed more silly and more stupefied than before, and mentioned his marriage, expressing regret at what he had done.'

Augusta Llewellyn's account had been startling stuff. And yet the more perceptive members of the jury could be forgiven for starting to detect that, rather as she claimed Windham's breakfast habits had been, Mrs Llewellyn was guilty of over-egging her evidence. It now fell to Karslake to try to expose this, and with expert and forensic questioning, Sir Hugh's junior attempted to do exactly that. After running through some of the facts of the house at Duke Street and Windham's arrival, he moved to his real subject: the question of who had made, or not made, affidavits, and what was their motivation behind doing so.

Mrs Llewellyn said she had not met the General until the middle or the end of June, although she admitted that her husband had known William Howe Windham. She had seen the General three more times before agreeing to make an affidavit to his solicitor, Mr Field. She said her younger sister, Eliza Dignam, had also gone with her and had offered to give evidence but, Mrs Llewellyn said, it was so similar to her own that Mr Field told her it would not be necessary.

The General, too, was there in Field's office. Augusta Llewellyn denied Karslake's suggestion that he had said: 'That's right; I am glad to hear you put it in that way.' And, on leaving the solicitor's office, her sister had not said: 'How came you to make such false statements as those?' or that she had replied: 'I have given it to him pretty strong, and his lady love too'. Karslake then handed up two letters to Mrs Llewellyn, asking her to read them carefully.

Yes, she admitted, those were letters that she had sent - one on 30 October, the other on 20 November - and both to her sister Eliza who had been 'the entire destroyer of my happiness'. Mrs Llewellyn said the letters concerned a 'very painful and distressing' family matter and begged the court that she would not be asked about them. But Karslake pressed the matter, eventually forcing her to read out the November letter in open court.

In it Augusta Llewellyn had referred to suffering 'continued bullying and want of money', and asked Eliza to pray for her 'joyful widowhood' as a man named only as 'Edward' would then want to marry her. She added: 'I see the General very often and he would like to see you... the poor General looks very ill...'. Mrs Llewellyn refused to read out the earlier letter, but admitted that the words 'heartless, wretched coward', which Karslake quoted at her, referred to her husband. At this point the jury intervened, asking that Karslake stop this 'irrelevant' line of questioning. Karslake agreed to do so, but said the questioning had every relevance, as the jury would eventually discover.

With this teasing comment, he turned back to probing Mrs Llewellyn on the detail of her evidence and her affidavit. On the matter of Windham being forced to have a bath, for example, she conceded that she had never actually witnessed her husband doing so. But she - and two of her two servants - had seen the young squire run naked out the bathroom. She insisted he used to tear his nightshirts to expose himself - 'all the housemaids knew it, and used to laugh at it'. Windham was careless with his money and his possessions, but she said her husband kept scrupulous accounts of how much Windham owed them. Mrs Llewellyn denied that Windham had ever said to her husband: 'I say, Bob, this is sticking it on rather strong.' She added: 'He was a man of very exuberant spirits. I could term him nothing but a mad man.'

DAY SIX, Saturday 21 December, began with the Master ordering the several women present in the court to withdraw; a sign that more distasteful evidence was on its way. Once again, Windham was in court to hear the proceedings, this time staying almost the whole day. The Times noted: 'He joined in the laugh which occasionally arose in court, but at certain parts of the evidence, to which it is unnecessary to make any more particular allusion, his face slightly flushed and he dropped his eyes to the ground.... Once or twice he scribbled a note - writing very fast - and handed it to his solicitor, who was sitting below him. Perhaps it would not be incorrect to state that more than one question was put to the witness in cross-examination at his suggestion.'

Agnes' solicitor Coleridge then stood up to cross-examine Mrs Llewellyn. Like Karslake, he was keen to leave the jury with the impression that the Llewellyns had been involved in a deliberate plan to make Windham's behaviour look as bad as possible. Agnes was convinced that the family were conspiring against Windham. Yes, Mrs Llewellyn agreed, there was champagne drunk at lunch, but she never saw her husband drunk. 'He is a most sober man... he is a most passionate man, he is a Welshman,' she added, to laughter. And, yes, she and her husband did argue frequently, mostly about Windham.

But she never said to him 'You are sucking the poor boy dry, and while he has any money left you'll stick close to him.' She had travelled with Mr Wood - clerk to the solicitor Field - to see the Llewellyns' charwoman, Pritchard. Their purpose was to gather support for her claims of Windham's habit of dirtying the bed. She had said to Mrs Llewellyn that he had not seen any evidence of it, but Mrs Llewellyn had explained that away by claiming she herself had set things straight by changing the sheets.

But Pritchard's view of their meeting was very different. She claimed she had told Mrs Llewellyn that it was impossible she had done any such thing, and that Mrs Llewellyn had replied: 'That blackguard Windham has been and married a worthless woman, and she is going to bring him a child, and we want to do what we can for the General. If you come and speak against Windham, and say he is a gorger, the General will put you and your husband into a good position; but you must keep it quite quiet.'

Mrs Llewellyn also denied that when she was making the later affidavit in Field's office the General had ever turned to her and said 'I am very much obliged to you for the capital evidence you have given, and I have never heard half of it before', or that her sister Eliza had immediately told her she had never heard this 'evidence' either. Mrs Llewellyn denied the General had then gone on to say 'This little woman [ie Eliza] might break down on cross-examination.'

Coleridge then turned to the matter of the wine Windham had been sold by David Llewellyn. Mrs Llewellyn denied all knowledge of her husband selling £34 worth of wine to Windham in August, or of him sending another £260 of wine to Felbrigg on September 16. But she did admit that her husband was currently suing Windham for unpaid bills. After the implications of exaggerating and distorting the facts, fleecing the hapless Windham of his cash and cheating him over wine - not to mention the unsympathetic portrait the evidence had painted of the General - Coleridge's cross-examination now ended on an even more sensational twist. Augusta Llewellyn had painted a picture of herself as the altruistic moral adviser to Windham, cautioning him against marrying the unsuitable Agnes. But now she said, yes, she had known Agnes' close associate Roberts. Curiouser and curiouser; it was all fast becoming a closely-knit web of connections and intrigue.

Her ordeal in the witness box was still not over. Montague Chambers rose again to re-examine on behalf of the petitioners. His first question, although intended to be friendly, actually weakened Augusta Llewellyn's picture of the Duke Street establishment as being an oasis of moral rectitude. Yes, she conceded, she had had to dismiss one of her servants, Kate Babbage, for going to bed with Windham. And how, continued Chambers, had the defence managed to obtain her private family letters to her sister? This gave Mrs Llewellyn the chance to try to explain how she knew Roberts, and also give the facts behind the cryptic references to Karslake about Eliza being the 'destroyer of her happiness'. Her sister had first met Roberts on a visit to Cremorne Gardens - a well-known pleasure garden - and... but here the questioning was stopped as 'not being evidence'. She tried a different tack: Roberts had got hold of her sister for 'a bad purpose' - not spelled out in court but clearly to procure her for one of his brothels - and Mr Llewellyn had sent her away, but she was still trying to protect her younger sister.

She had been to Roberts' Piccadilly house three times and had seen Windham each time. The first two times Windham had told her that her husband's account was with his solicitor, but on the third occasion Roberts had tried to stop her seeing Windham, agreeing eventually but insisting on locking the street door. When she was finally alone with Windham, he told her that his wife had run away, casually adding that the moneylenders had closed in and that Agnes was now locked up in Glasgow Gaol - all nonsense. Windham agreed to go over to Duke Street to talk to Mr Llewellyn, but he never did.

Chambers then tried to play down Karslake's implications of a conspiracy. Had General Windham said he would provide for her and her husband? 'Major-General Windham has never offered me a sixpence,' she said. 'He has charged me to be most particular in stating the truth and never made any such offer. It is a foul accusation.' She repeated her claim that she and her husband had not cheated Windham. 'His weekly book was presented to him. He never added it up or made any objections to the items.' Windham, however, was reckless with his money - 'he considered himself almost the richest man that ever lived'.

Now, at last, she was allowed to stand down. It had been a gruelling cross-examination, forcing her to try to justify every statement she had made, point by point, while trying to defend herself against implications of perjury and conspiracy. Mrs Llewellyn was also forced to deny that the couple had milked Windham of his money. The cross-examining counsel, especially Agnes', had also planted a certain image of the General in the jury's minds. A conspiring, blustering General - yes, a Sir Percival - prepared to stop at no lie in order to discredit his nephew. And far from being the complete strangers to the Windham family it had first appeared there were now strong links: The unhappily-married Augusta was on intimate terms with the General (how intimate was left up to the imagination) while her husband had known both the General and Windham's father. Now it was time for Augusta's husband David - this Welshman full of passion - to give his evidence. What would he let slip?

LLEWELLYN BEGAN by telling Field that he had not heard any of his wife's statement to the court. He said he had been a wine merchant's agent since 1846 and had known William Howe Windham and his son around 1850, but not the General, whom he said he never seen until he came round to Duke Street at the end of June or beginning of July. His tales about Windham's behaviour were similar to his wife's, and he claimed he had even used a whip on his lodger on one occasion to try to get him to cover himself up. Windham's lies had included telling how he had arrested a man who blocked the Norwich-Cromer road, and how - this once again to laughter - the court which heard the case had jailed the miscreant for four years after Windham had addressed them.

Llewellyn said the first time he had heard Windham talk about Agnes Willoughby was when he claimed to have been riding with her in Rotten Row, where they had a 'jolly row' with 'Skittles'. Windham, he said, had been quite unashamed about his 'improper intimacy' with Agnes, and how he had arranged to stay at her house to sleep with her, only to be forced to come back to Duke Street because another man was already there. Whenever he stayed out all night he had told Llewellyn he had 'been with the girls' - ie the Haymarket whores - or he had been with the police. Windham had at first claimed that his Agnes was respectable, later changing his story, but still laughing off claims he wanted to marry her, saying he only intended to 'use her for a time'.

Sir Hugh then cross-examined Llewellyn, who told of the financial arrangements for Windham's stay at Duke Street. 'He was quite satisfied with what he had,' Llewellyn added. He had not, he insisted, supplied Windham with large quantities of wine until he came of age. Some - 'upwards of £200' - was sent to Felbrigg on 20 August, including his 'very good and very cheap' champagne at £3 a case. The cellars at Felbrigg had been empty when Windham came of age, he added. Windham had been on 'very good terms' with him, Llewellyn claimed. He told the hearing that Windham had a fiery nature.

'When he was in a passion he would do almost anything, so that it would be dangerous to go near him,' he said. 'He would swear and threaten to kill anyone. I have seen him bite his lips [and nails] till the blood came... he would halloa, hoot, and scream till he was black in the face, and was almost fit to drop.' Llewellyn told Sir Hugh that he did not know his affidavit about Windham's behaviour would end being used against his former lodger.

'I did not know the affidavit was made for purpose of getting proceedings in lunacy against Mr Windham,' he insisted. 'I thought it was made to protect him and his property from the vile hands he had got into.

'I thought it was for the purpose of having his person and property taken care of, but not for the purpose of taking his property from him.

'I am well aware,' he added, 'that Mr Windham was suffering from a loathsome disorder while in my house. He has talked obscenely in my presence; he has also spoken very indelicately before Mrs Llewellyn.' The final part of his evidence before the court adjournment for its Christmas break was to explain why he had thrown Eliza out of the house. 'It was when I found her sitting on the bed with Mr Windham that I turned her to the door.' The Llewellyns' evidence so far had answered many questions about Windham's behaviour in those last, crucial 14 weeks. But it also raised many more, including one the jury might well have considered as they enjoyed the festivities: why, if Windham had been such an appalling and troublesome guest, had the couple not simply ordered him to leave?

THERE WAS little Christmas respite for those involved in the inquiry. Windham went back home to Norfolk where he gave a dinner for his tenantry on Christmas Day, and ended up the worse for drink. But even here, in the heart of his estate, there was to be no peace from the prying attentions of those who wanted to bring him down, as revelations in a future week of the inquiry would make clear. The case resumed in the Court of Exchequer on Boxing Day, with Master Warren again beginning proceedings by warning of his increasing anxiety over their likely length. The inquiry was now in its seventh day, and yet had only been dealing with witnesses at the rate of three per day. 'I, for one, hope we will get on quicker in future,' he sighed.

David Llewellyn was back in the witness box, with Agnes' solicitor Coleridge - who had proved so effective in his interrogation of Mrs Llewellyn - posing the questions. From the start he put Llewellyn under pressure and made him angry by insisting on asking about his sister-in-law Eliza's activities. Coleridge then tried another tactic to goad the witness: his previous appearances in court. The Welshman admitted he had been a defendant in a court action Smart v Llewellyn, but claimed it was a conspiracy involving a 'set of swindlers' who had 'concocted' the claim. Yes, there was an award of £150 damages made against him, but that was down to the poor-quality jury and his counsel 'selling' the case. He had gone into the witness box at his own insistence and had ended up not paying 'a single farthing'.

Llewellyn admitted he had been involved in another case, Dignam v Llewellyn, when his estranged sister-in-law had successfully sued him for £30. But, he told the jury, Eliza had been 'put up to it' by her brother, and 'did it out of spite because I turned her out of my house'. Llewellyn insisted once again that Windham had never complained about his bills. 'I have no doubt I could have overcharged him with impunity if I had been inclined to do so,' he concluded. Llewellyn then stepped down. Like his wife, his experience at the inquiry had been a bruising one.

Hume Williams, for the petitioners, made his first appearance by examining the

Rev T J Baty, another friend of Peatfield's. He had visited his friend in Duke Street, where he had also met Windham. The latter had told him the wild tale of having 'Sergeant Joy, of the detective force' following his fiancée (not Agnes) to discover if she were chaste. The clergyman backed up the Llewellyns' claims of Windham's lies, swearing, odd table manners and howls 'like a madman'.

Next to give evidence was the Llewellyns' former cook and kitchen maid Ellen Moore. She told Chambers she had seen Windham running around naked one day. She used to poach from four to eight eggs for his breakfast. 'He ate more like a pig than anything else,' she said. One of Windham's fellow-lodgers at Duke Street, War Office clerk Mr Corbellis, said he had never met the young man but heard his strange laugh frequently and he had no doubt that 'there was something wrong in his head'.

The inquiry was finished with the affairs at the Llewellyns - for the moment. The final witness of Day Seven was the Aylsham solicitor Scott, who repeated the claims of Windham's behaviour at his father's funeral and the General's 1856 ovation. Scott had 'no doubt' Windham was a person of deficient intellect and 'was not to be trusted'.

10

27 December 1861-1 January 1862: The Trees and the Trains

'Mr Windham did not appear to understand the value of his trees in the least.'
Norwich land agent William Butcher, 27 December 1861

'To marry under such circumstances is an act which no man would do unless he were drunk, drugged, or insane.'
Dr Forbes Winslow, New Year's Eve 1861

THE EIGHTH day of the inquiry began in bizarre style with a story from bootmaker Thomas Atkin, who spoke of an incident when Windham pointed a pistol at his chest and said he would fire... unless Atkins stood him a bottle of champagne. 'But it was merely a frolic,' he said. 'I know he meant me no harm.'

Mr Breeze, landlord of the Black Boys hotel in Aylsham market place, confirmed Horrocks' account of the accident when Windham crashed into the building, and also of Windham's fight with a showman after another collision. Windham had ended up in yet more trouble during a ball in the Norfolk town when he got into a squabble with police and told Breeze 'the ------ peelers wanted to prevent me getting the inn yard but I would have driven over them if they had not got out of the way.' Windham still owed him for horse hire going back to 1859, he added.

Metropolitan police inspector William Holden, next in the witness box, told how he had known Windham since late 1859 or early 1860 because of his late-night shouting and screaming in the Haymarket area, and his pretence of being a policeman. Insp Holden then recounted of his two late-night encounters with the tearful young heir that autumn, when Windham had sobbed how his family were conspiring against him, and how Agnes had robbed him. 'He was always in a crying mood and frothing at the mouth,' he said. Windham would try to catch him by the arm and tell him 'Now, then, Holden come along and have some champagne - you are a jolly old cock'. Holden's statement inevitably garnered more chortles from the gallery.

Windham's other obsession - the railways - was the theme of the next witness, Henry Wigley from Norwich. He was now a detective with the Norfolk city's police force, but before then had been an inspector on the Eastern Counties Railways. He had become familiar with Windham in both his roles. Windham was 'constantly' on the platform at Norwich Thorpe Station, running up and down and shutting and closing the carriages. In reply to a question by the Master he said the railway authorities had 'never' remonstrated with Windham for his actions.

'Was not such conduct calculated to interfere with public safety?,' the Master asked.

'It ought to have been,' was the reply. 'It was improper for him to act as a railway servant, but I did not interfere because I was not then in the company's employ.'

As a policeman, Wigley frequently saw Windham swearing at people and claiming to be a London detective. He told the court about Windham's bad behaviour at the Festival Ball in the city the previous September. He added - to yet more laughter - 'I have travelled with the lunatics from the county asylum at Thorpe. They were always very quiet, but Mr Windham is always in a wild sort of state.'

NEXT CAME the first details for the jurors about one of the key incidents of the previous autumn, the affair of the Felbrigg timber. Norwich-based land agent William Butcher told the court of his involvement in measuring up the timber on the estate back in late October, and his shock at discovering Windham's intentions. Butcher had measured up 536 carefully-selected oaks which had a value of £2,586; many of the rest would only be fellable after 40-50 more years. And there were large quantities of sweet chestnut, beech, fir, plus some sycamores, ash and elm trees to take into account. 'Mr Windham,' he concluded, 'did not appear to understand the value of his trees in the least.'

Butcher's assessment was underlined when Chambers produced a paper with a flourish and read some of the details of the notorious October contract. The price Windham would receive was 12d per cubic foot for the larger trees, and 8d for the smaller ones. 'Was that,' Chambers asked, 'a reasonable bargain?' Of course, as all good advocates should, he already knew the answer.

'Certainly not... the first price is fully one and sixpence below the market price, and the second fully ten pence below,' said Butcher. In other words, Windham was selling his larger oaks for only 40 per cent of their true value and his smaller trees for 44 per cent of their worth. And the hapless squire of Felbrigg was already being cheated of a quarter of the price of his trees because of the unfair way they were measured. If the trees were cut down 'the place would be left exposed to the sea, and would become quite a bleak and barren spot'.

The evidence of the final witness of the day - Sergeant Edward Oliver, of the Metropolitan police, was lighter in tone, at least at first. He told how Windham used to treat the girls of the Haymarket to champagne. 'That is what Mr Windham did, and I suppose such ladies like to get hold of a young gentleman like Mr Windham,' he added, to laughter. But then added: 'If I had heard of Mr Windham committing murder or any other crime, I should not have been surprised, for I never considered him accountable for his actions.' Now there was no laughter at all.

DAY NINE - Saturday 28 December - began with the Master making a cryptic reference to private letters being written to him about the case, which was 'most improper, almost amounting to a misdemeanour'.

The hearing proper heard more evidence about the notorious timber sale. The contract was produced in court and, after some hesitation, was agreed to have Windham's signature. After it was read out in full to the court by the Clerk, Henry Sandford, a land agent at Cromer, was called. He said the contract was even more unfair than the jury had heard the day previously, as the large oak was actually worth three times the price being offered. If the contract were carried out there would not even be enough timber left to carry out maintenance work on the hall.

If Butcher's evidence had been the dramatic highlight of Day Eight, then Day Nine's most striking feature was the story of Joseph Ford, a former guard on the Eastern Counties Railways. On 24 August 1861 Windham had stopped Ford on the platform at Shoreditch and given him a carpet bag, saying there was champagne inside. When the train reach Broxbourne, Windham went into the guard's van with Ford, put on his great-coat and belt, and then worked as a guard all the way back to Norwich.

Windham, Ford, and a friend of Ford's, who was also in the van, got through three bottles of champagne and a bottle of sherry on the journey back. 'Mr Windham showed me two rings, asking me whether I thought they were good ones,' Ford said. 'He said his missus as was to be had given them to him; and he had been with her all afternoon. He did not mention her name.'

He then told of the incident in September when Agnes and Roberts had spent the journey on a makeshift bed in a closed carriage while Windham had blithely rode with the engine. When the train came into Norwich, Roberts gave Ford a tip of half a sovereign for keeping the carriage-door locked. 'I spoke to Mr Windham about Roberts and his wife being locked in the same carriage together,' added Ford. 'He only laughed.' And so to all the other defects of Windham's character could be added one more: a willing cuckold. Agnes' relationship with Roberts was also brought into focus. Tellingly, Agnes' counsel Coleridge did not dispute any of this. He merely asked Ford about the habit of people travelling the mail train using first-class carriages.

What really concerned the jury was not any outrage to morals, but the evidence of malpractice on the railways. As already outlined, there was already widespread public concern at their safety record, and the efficiency of the Eastern Counties Railway was a perennial issue. Ford had talked about guards being bribed, of passengers riding on the engine or the guard's van - all banned practices. He had even spoken of Windham actually working the engine levers and starting the trains.

This was too much for the jury. One of their number stood up and said, to applause from the gallery, 'I trust that after what we have heard today, railway companies will in future be more careful of the lives entrusted to their charge. They ought to see that their rules for the working and management of trains are strictly observed by their officers.' Chambers said the railway company had been told about the incidents and had promised it would not happen in the future.

The Master had had enough. 'I hope this discussion will not be carried further,' he spluttered. 'We are here to inquire into the state of mind of Mr Windham, and not to investigate the conduct of a railway company.' It was yet another sign - not that Warren would ever admit it - that the efficient handling of the commission was starting to slip away from him. The next two witnesses were both railway employees. Both spoke of other incidents - at least a dozen in the past year - where Windham had been seen acting improperly on the railway. On 3 December he had nearly caused a crash at Haughley station in Suffolk by trying to blow his whistle to start the train. Railway inspector Joseph Goody had had to knock it out of his hand to stop him.

Robert Wheeler, manager of the Euston Hotel, told the court about Agnes Windham's eventful stay in his hotel in early November - the 'blood flowing like rain' incident and all the various rows. Wheeler said he had spoken 'in very strong language' about Agnes and her conduct to Windham, telling him that it was obvious that she loathed him and why did he not have the sense to see it. 'Mr Windham made some idiotic remark, laughed in an idiotic manner, and did not seem to understand the meaning of what was said to him,' Wheeler added. 'From what I have seen of him, I believe him to be a mere child - an imbecile'.

There was a brief coda to the day's proceedings when Norfolk policeman James Hudson took the stand. He said that Windham had claimed to be a detective, and he had also heard Windham saying that to some 'rough characters'. And that was all he had to say.

An incredulous Sir Hugh rose and said: 'Surely you have not come all the way from Norfolk to tell us so little?'

'I don't know anything about that, sir.'

Coleridge then could not resist rising too, and adding: 'Mr Hudson, having cost £100, you may now go.'

THE TENTH DAY of the commission heard from the Great Yarmouth solicitor Reynolds, who told the court about his various encounters with Windham on East Anglian railways, and how his firm had helped the young heir draft an affidavit for his Chancery case in 1860. Mr Reynolds was left deeply unimpressed by the 'blubbering' 20-year-old. He had also seen him at a private musical party making 'absurd noises' on the staircase, and again at a ball in Yarmouth when he attracted the attention of everyone in the room with his uncontrollable laughter.

PC Charles Brown then told the court of more Haymarket antics from Windham, including wanting the policeman to lock up some of the street-walkers. 'There are too many women about here,' he told the bemused PC. 'I won't have so many'. When the laughter had died down, PC Brown explained how the women tried to shrug off Windham's hand pushing on their backs, telling him: 'Go away you fool, you are not right in the head.'

Before the next witness was called Chambers accused his rivals of 'doing everything they could to prolong the inquiry'. Sir Hugh, 'with some warmth', denied the claim. Their grew ever more heated until Master Warren stepped in to remind them both that they were 'gentlemen of great eminence' engaged in a 'delicate and painful inquiry'. Chambers withdrew his claim, and Sir Hugh expressed himself 'perfectly satisfied'. It was a reminder that the atmosphere in the hall was becoming decidedly chilly between the legal teams.

The next witness, the Norfolk solicitor Hansell, brought the necessary gravitas back to proceedings with his sober account of the financial situation of the Felbrigg estate. As the receiver of the estate's rents since January 1859 he knew better than anyone exactly how much the young squire was worth. After expenses had been taken into account, he said, Felbrigg would yield about £1,200 a year, to which could be added the shooting rights and the lease of the house. From 1869 - when the mortgage on Hanworth would be largely paid off - it would rise to about £4,000 a year.

He then talked about the meeting in Felbrigg Hall's library on the morning of 9 August, the day Windham came of age, and the suggestion that the estate should be put into trust until the young squire was 29. The General, Hansell said, had declared his support for any idea of the Chancery court-appointed Jackson's 'if it was the benefit of the estate and his nephew'. The Jackson proposal would indeed have hurt the General in the pocket to the tune of around £600 a year, he claimed.

Under detailed cross-examination from Karslake, Hansell admitted that if Windham should die without heirs then the General would inherit. This was a key admission. Hansell said the whole of the Felbrigg Hall property - house, park, and ornamental timber - was worth about £80,000 or £90,000.

That was the income side of Windham's accounts; now for the debit. The court now heard from Henry Dore, a salesman at Agnes' jeweller, Emmanuel of Brook Street. He told of the frequent visits of Windham and Agnes to the shop, beginning on 29 June and ending on 18 October, and the total bill (which had not yet been paid) running to £13,785. 'Mr Windham always looked carefully at the items before he bought them, and frequently cavilled at the price,' he said. But such, of course, were Agnes' charms that she usually got what she wanted. Once, he said, Windham had summoned him to Felbrigg to attend to a musical box and a 'self-acting organ' which needed repair - oh, and to bring some jewels with him. Dore took £12,000-worth, from which Windham bought diamond and emerald ornaments to the tune of £5,000, including a £2,800 diamond bracelet. Dore said Windham then turned to his wife and said: 'Here, Agnes, I give you these to make up for what I have done to you.' The next witness, Dr Illingworth of Arlington Street, told the commission that at the time of his marriage Windham was indeed suffering from a 'loathsome disease' and knew - or had at least been told - that 'he was in no fit state to marry'. But, of course, Windham had ignored him.

DAY 11 of the inquiry - held on New Year's Eve - drew together some of the threads of the previous day. It was not a pleasant story. The Cromer physician Buck told of his rebuff in late September when Agnes had pressured Windham into stopping him visiting. Not surprisingly, perhaps, Buck was in full support of the petitioners, branding his former patient an 'imbecile'. He revealed he had seen Windham on 19 August 'with a touch of a bad disease'. Buck had warned him he would probably be ill 'for a very long time' and warned him not to communicate it.

But the evidence of another medical man, and an acknowledged expert in mental health, would be of far greater import to the hearing. Dr Forbes Winslow told how he and Dr Mayo - with Dr Bright as witness - had had the long interviews with Windham on 11 and 14 December. It was a sorry tale, with any attempt at note-taking rendered useless by Windham's erratic streams of consciousness. Dr Winslow told the court how he had talked to Windham about the state of his marriage, and questioned him about the 'misconduct of his wife before their marriage, and referred to her alleged impurity'. 'He said he was fully aware she had been kept by several men, but he did not see why that should be an objection to his marrying her, as other persons - men of rank and distinction - 'had done the same thing with impunity.'

And now the evidence of the previous day was at last brought together. 'I referred to the state of his bodily health previously to his marriage, and I said that I was informed that he was suffering at that time from an aggravated form of a particular disease. [Windham] said the character of the disease had been mistaken.' It was yet another of Windham's casual lies. He contradicted himself immediately.

'A remark was then made to the effect that he had communicated the disease to his wife,' Dr Winslow continued. Windham said he had given her some jewellery - 'between £13,000 and £14,000' - as compensation 'for the injury he had given her'. The doctor then continued - in a comment which says much about mid-Victorian view of such matters - that he had remarked to Windham that 'it was an unusual thing for a husband to compensate a wife for ill-treatment of such nature, and I also observed the amount was a very large one.'

He had then turned to the question of two of Agnes' lovers, the man with whom she had been living [Garton], whose boots were outside her door on the morning of her marriage, and her adultery with the man described clumsily as 'Mr -----, No 2' - Giuglini, of course - to which Windham replied that it was because of this adultery that he was now determined to begin divorce proceedings.

Windham told Dr Winslow about his debts. It was sorrow heaped on sorrow. He had no idea how much he owed, 'certainly £20,000 and it might be much more'. Agnes had continued to spend wildly, knowing, of course, that legally her debts were still her husband's concern. 'Fresh bills were coming in every day, and he was in such a state of alarm that he was actually afraid to open his own letters.'

Dr Winslow had then tried to get Windham to accept he had been swindled over the timber and that the real buyer was not Messrs Lawrence and Fry but his friend Roberts. Not even the fact that Roberts had told Windham during a row that he had slept with Agnes before her marriage seemed to make any difference to Windham's opinion of 'Bawdyhouse Bob'. 'When he told me Roberts was a good fellow he giggled and laughed, and when he referred to the sobriquet under which Roberts was generally known, he laughed loudly, as if he thought it was a good joke,' he continued.

THIS WAS good stuff, of course, for the readers snapping open their copies of their newspapers over the breakfast tables of Britain. But what did it really say about Windham's state of mind and fitness to run the estate? That was a difficult question, which Dr Winslow now attempted to clarify. He was unequivocal. Windham was 'in [such] a degree of mental imbecility, that he is a person of unsound mind, incapable of managing himself or his affairs'. That verdict, he said, was not inconsistent with Windham being able to write letters or settle small accounts.

Now it was Sir Hugh's turn to put the questions. Dr Winslow admitted that he based his questioning on affidavits gathered by the petitioners, and not those collected on behalf of Windham. But he insisted: 'I do not believe that Mr Windham is capable of managing himself. I say so because I do not think a man is capable who could contract marriage while suffering from a foul disease, and

Dr Forbes Winslow: During two long interviews with Windham in December the doctor heard a long and rambling account of infidelity, debts, and worse. *(NRO ref: MC580/1, 780x1)*

when he knew that the paramour with whom his wife had been living slept in the same house with her the night before the marriage [and] who could act... as an engine driver and a railway guard.'

Warming to his subject, he rounded once again on 'a woman of such a character' - he could not bear to use her name - with the comment that it made a 'material difference' that her lover should sleep with her on the eve of her marriage to Windham. 'To marry under such circumstances is an act which no man would do unless he were drunk, drugged, or insane,' he added.

Dr Winslow's barely-concealed (if concealed at all) hatred of Agnes was clear. Windham had scandalised society by his actions, but was scandal the same as madness? Dr Winslow was already back-tracking by the time the day's proceedings drew to a close. He admitted he could not tell 'where sanity ends and insanity begins' and, in response to a question from the Master, said he would have been reluctant to say Windham was of unsound mind if he met him without any knowledge of his previous actions.

NEW YEAR celebrations for those taking part in the inquiry were necessarily muted, as the first day of 1862 saw them all back in Westminster Hall for Day 12. Dr Winslow was asked exactly how he would define Windham's alleged imbecility. The doctor replied that he believed he had amentia - 'not downright idiocy, but something intermediate between idiocy and lunacy'.

He was careful to distinguish it from dementia, which in this era was simply a synonym for madness. Windham would not, he said, need to be put in an asylum but instead put under the firm control of someone who could effectively supervise his behaviour. In reply to a question from the Master, he again said that it was difficult to define lunacy. But, in a way, that was not important; what mattered were the actions and conduct of the person concerned.

Dr Mayo supported his colleague's assessment of Windham. Not only did the young squire have a 'very weak' intellect but also had a 'very impure' mind. Dr Mayo said Windham's 'utter and entire shamelessness' when questioned about his wife was remarkable. Like Dr Winslow, he said the best way of dealing with Windham was not to lock him up but to 'put him in the hands of a person who would prevent him meddling with affairs'. He cautioned against the jury being deceived by examples of Windham behaving normally. They were, he said, more likely to be the product of 'cunning, rather than to a sense of self-respect or the decencies of society'.

At this point the succession of medical men was halted by a surprise witness: Augusta Llewellyn. Sir Hugh Cairns insisted she was recalled to the witness box, and he went straight to the point. Yes, she had a brother, Conway Dignam, but she had not seen him since May or June the previous year. After their mother died, he ended up begging. 'He is a dissolute, worthless, lazy fellow, and never earned a shilling in his life,' she said.

No, she said, she had not seen him in September, October, November or December.

No, she had not said to him 'I know of a capital thing you can do nicely. Did you ever hear of young Windham? His uncle, the General, has begun to try to bring him in insane, and if you swear for the General, it would be the making of you, and you would not require a situation [job].'

No, she had not said to him either: 'The General will have his money, and not his nephew. What you will have to swear is this - that you lived with Llewellyn, as clerk, and had ample chances of hearing young Windham's hideous noises, and seeing his mad ways.'

She denied, too, that he had replied 'Oh, Augusta, how can you try to bring a younger brother into such a mess? You are aware that I know neither the General nor young Windham, and I would not try to get myself into trouble by false swearing for you or twenty generals.' Or that she had then said: 'You are very foolish; you know as much as other people that you are on the General's side'. She denied that she had invited him to commit perjury like this or had any such conversation.

Chambers then rose to try to come to the rescue of Windham's former landlady. Her brother, he said, was a 'ragged beggarman' who had lived off their mother until her death in June 1860 and had never worked before or since.

'Before I came here today I had the most remote idea of the kind of questions which were to be put to me,' she said. 'I solemnly swear that the conversation which has been detailed is totally false.' The landlady added with a flourish: 'May I die in your presence if I do not speak the truth.' At this point the witness 'who said she was suffering from ill-health and who had given her evidence with considerable warmth, immediately left the court.'

After the drama, it was back to the medical men, with the court now hearing from Dr Southey, who admitted he found Windham a hard case to classify. He refused to say conclusively that Windham was not fit to run his estate. 'He is a person of weak intellect, thought I should hesitate to express the opinion that he is not capable of managing himself or his affairs,' he concluded. It was hardly the rousing end to their twelve days of evidence which the petitioners would have hoped for. The final act of the day was the reading of the famous - or, more accurately, notorious - marriage settlement.

Now it was time for Sir Hugh to have his say.

11

1-3 January 1862:
'A Charge Most Cruel'

'The thing is grossly incredible.'
Sir Hugh Cairns on the Llewellyns' evidence

SIR HUGH began by summing up the twelve days of the evidence so far. 'The petitioners have raked up and paraded before the world the events of a life of 21 years,' he said. 'They have exposed to the public gaze, and that in no dim or hazy light - they have pictured to the public view - and that in no delicate touches - the youthful vices and follies and frailties of their relative, the subject of this inquiry.' While this had been going on for days, he explained, Windham's counsel had been forced to sit in 'constrained acquiescence', with the exception of the cross-examination they had made to 'correct the errors into which the witnesses had fallen, and to elicit the facts which they had withheld, and to explore the inconsistencies with which they were chargeable.'

Now, at last, he was free to address the jury on behalf of Mr Windham. He wanted them to consider two requests: to bring their 'calm, dispassionate, unbiased and judicial' verdict on his remarks. 'Short of the issues of life and death, there is hardly any issue more momentous than that involved in the present inquiry,' he continued portentously. 'No more important issue, with one exception, could be submitted to a jury, or fall to be decided upon the fate of any fellow-creature.'

The second issue, he said, was that the jury would 'extend to him their indulgence' while he tried to defend Mr Windham from a charge most cruel, most unjust and most unjustifiable.' With these rousing words, as Sir Hugh must have hoped, the public gallery erupted in loud cheers. And as the cheers rang round the courtroom, the petitioners' hearts must have collectively sank. Here, surely, was evidence that the tide of public opinion was ebbing from them and flowing instead to Windham.

Sir Hugh resumed by saying the jury was not here to decide if Windham were of unsound mind, but 'whether he is incapable of managing his affairs by reason of unsoundness of mind'. The difference was important, he added: a man might be incapable of looking after his property because he had a preference for 'literary or other pursuits' rather than the management of his estate. 'But in England a man cannot be deprived of his personal liberty or his property on the grounds of incapacity until a jury of his countrymen are satisfied, first, that he is incapable of managing his affairs, and secondly, that his incapacity arises from unsoundness of mind,' he added. He reminded the jury, too, that the presumption must always be in favour of sanity.

Windham's case, he continued, was not an ordinary one. This was not insanity accompanied by delusions, but a case of imbecility. 'If the mind is not there, or only there in a certain small and limited quantity, no desire on the part of the individual to show a greater amount of mind... can supply him with what Nature has denied him.' Much had been made, he said, about the size of the property at issue - but, frankly, whether it was £100 or £20,000 did not matter in the slightest. It was also important, he added, in his final comment of the day, that the jury should ignore any remarks on Windham's sanity made by witnesses who had spoken already in the inquiry.

The crowded public galleries, and acres of newsprint given daily to the proceedings, are eloquent testimony to the public fascination. But another reaction, from the upper echelons of polite society at least, can be seen in a letter to a newspaper from Old Etonian Morton Price, complaining about the school being mentioned in the 'disgusting Windham case'. He may have found the case repellent, but for everyone else, it seemed, it was a source of almost-hypnotic fascination.

IF THE end of the day's proceedings had interrupted the flow of Sir Hugh's speech there was no sign of it when he resumed the next morning, Thursday 2 January - Day Thirteen of the Commission. He began in persuasive style. The petitioners, he said, had enjoyed a 'very great advantage' in gathering their evidence. The petition 'garnished with an array of names... of very considerable position and distinction in society' who could wield considerable influence in finding 'every jot and title of evidence which could be obtained in their favour'. Windham, on the other hand, 'stood alone against the family, with the exception of his mother' [although he could have added, of course, that she was not exactly fully supportive of her son either]. The situation seemed to Sir Hugh to be the introduction to this country of 'the terror of domestic life aboard', the family council. So here we have appeals to British fair play, but also the corruption of traditional family values of mutual support, and even - Heaven forfend - importing foreign ways of behaviour.

It was a good start, calculated to appeal to the John Bulls among the jury. Sir Hugh continued by saying how the 'decrees' of the family council had been made to 'command' every scrap of evidence they could find. But if the family had really been interested in 'sincerely and fairly' taking the opinion of an English jury [John Bull again] they could have simply consulted independent medical advisers and left the court to make up its own mind.

Instead, he said, they had gone about 'overlaying the case with the flimsy and ridiculous evidence of railway guards, policemen, lodging-house keepers and other persons, deposing to acts, some the most trivial and some the most disagreeable'. Sir Hugh had thus taken the bold - but risky - step of simply ignoring the vast bulk of the petitioners' evidence, strengthening his stance by carefully choosing those witnesses which might be said to be of the lower orders or associates with criminals - or both. The claims which had been made by these witnesses, he continued, were 'most disagreeable, not to say disgusting, description [of] all the boyish acts, follies, and vices of their youthful relative'.

This evidence, he said, it had put off friends and supporters of Windham from coming forward because they would have feared being 'mixed up' in some of the revelations. Time, too, had been on the petitioners' side; the General had a consultation as far back as September about the commission, and the petitioners had had more than three months to gather their evidence, even from as far afield as Russia. Windham, in contrast, had had just three weeks to prepare his case. And the law of lunacy as it stood had barred the one person from appearing in the witness box who could have denied or explained away many of the claims made so far. And that person was William Frederick Windham himself.

IT WAS now time, said Sir Hugh, to look at the different periods in Windham's life. His childhood, he said, had featured 'the misfortune' of his being an only child. A spoilt one too, in the fullest meaning of the word - 'at once indulged and irregularly and capriciously restrained' by his parents. He loved the world of outdoor pursuits but not of learning. 'After he left Eton he had nothing which could properly be called education,' he said.

With no siblings or companions, it was natural he should turn to the servants' quarters for fellowship. He was 'passionate' and 'excitable' and had 'rustic manners' about which he was given no kind of training. There was no mixing with young ladies; there was his 'fairly and frankly' admitted slovenliness in clothes; there was his laugh and voice - much of which could be explained by the formation of his mouth, as the jury would hear; there was his great power of imitation.

'It was also a fact,

Powerful: Part of the transcript of Sir Hugh Cairns' speeches in the Norfolk Records Office. His skilful appeals to the British sense of 'fair play' impressed the jury.
(NRO ref: MC580/1, 780x1)

which could not be disputed, [that] his was a boy's boisterous animal spirits,' Sir Hugh conceded. As for his mind, well, it was 'not a powerful one, but little more could be said on the subject'. He said it was 'ridiculous' to say Windham was incapable of managing his own affairs even if his mind was shown to be below the average mental standard.

Sir Hugh then tackled another prop of the petitioners' case, his client's 'eccentricities'. The first, 'a taste for the management of railways and the society of railway guards', far from being uncommon, was in fact shared by many of his contemporaries at Eton. The claims that Windham had acted as a railway porter had not been proved. 'It was impossible to account for such tastes; they were eccentric, but not proofs of unsoundness of mind,' Sir Hugh insisted. Windham did, in fact, perform the railway work 'extremely well', which was in itself 'no small proof of competency and of the power of acquiring knowledge'. With one exception - which would be explained -

there was never any suggestion that the 'slightest appearance of an accident [was] likely to occur in consequence of any incompetency on his part'.

Windham's other eccentricity, 'a fondness for walking about with the police and imitating their actions', was evidently meant as a joke ('though, perhaps, a bad one'). Sir Hugh said that, 'owing to circumstances which were greatly to be regretted' and - he added pointedly - 'for which his guardians were in no small degree responsible', Windham had gone through a 'season of London dissipation'. During this period he was frequently in the Haymarket, 'the noisiest part of town', where he took a fancy to making an acquaintance with the local police. Was it really a proof of insanity, he asked, that a young man should want to imitate them to show he 'appreciated them to a high degree'?

Now Sir Hugh played another brilliant trump card. He was, he confessed, much surprised to hear Mr Chambers say on Wednesday that the petitioners' case was now closed, as there was one kind of evidence that was 'conspicuous by its absence'. He had assumed (or so he claimed) that the case would not be closed until every one of the petitioners who were physically able would go into the witness box to give support to their case.

But, he pointed out, in fact only two - the Marquis and his brother Lord Alfred Hervey - had done so, and what they had had to say was not of 'the least consequence'.

'It was,' he insisted, 'the positive obligation and duty of every member of the family... to some forward and tell in open court all that he knew - to state whether he knew anything or merely acted on hearsay.' Surely it was right, he added, to draw conclusions from the fact that they had not done so. Sir Hugh said, and almost certainly with considerable accuracy, the petitioners had in fact really stayed away because 'they were afraid of telling that they never saw their relative, never associated with him, never informed themselves about him until a time came when they thought the property was in question'.

Mr Chambers had claimed in his opening remarks that the General could not gain from the property, he added. But, Sir Hugh insisted, the facts said otherwise: if his nephew was declared an imbecile - 'and his marriage null and void' - then the General would benefit from the Felbrigg estate income. And what if Windham were declared insane and given, say, £3,000-£4,000 a year for his 'comfortable maintenance'? That would leave [after 1869] £8,000 a year surplus income. If Windham lived for, say, another 40 years that would mean an accumulation of between £300,000 and £400,000 (worth around £13-£17 million at today's values) - 'a very pleasant thing for the next of kin'.

'And who were the next of kin?,' he asked. 'The other petitioners.'

He was not going to impute motives, Sir Hugh continued (having just done exactly that), but those who carried on an inquiry of this kind ought to be above not merely blame, but suspicion, 'and they were not above suspicion if they shrank from the light of day and abstained from coming forward and telling everything they knew'. There were eleven petitioners, and now Sir Hugh focused on four of them: Mrs Cecilia Ann Baring was Windham's aunt and had sworn an affidavit about him - but they had never even heard her name mentioned in the case so far. Why not? And what about Captain Henry Windham, 'who must know a great deal about Felbrigg', as he knew his nephew well, and had also acted as receiver of the estate's rents.

Sir Hugh then turned his considerable firepower on the banker Hook, another one of Windham's guardians. Why did he not appear to explain why his young charge was brought to London from the country to 'pass a season of dissipation in London and drink champagne'?

When had he decided Windham was of unsound mind - and why had he allowed him to 'choose his own lodgings and make his own bargains'? Did he, as Windham's guardian, 'interfere, advise him, rebuke him, restrain him, and, if necessary, remove him to some place where he would have been free from temptation'? No, he had not.

Finally, why had he not stepped in last July to stop communication between Windham still a ward of court - and Miss Willoughby? 'Nothing could have been easier'.

It was a damning list, but compared to his next target it was mild stuff indeed. Sir Hugh now turned to the General, 'the coryphaeus [leader of the chorus] of the petitioners'. The present case had only finally gone ahead when the General had made his four affidavits to the Lord Justices. No-one was better placed to tell everything that could be told about young Windham, but he had not put himself in the witness box. The General had attended every day of the hearing, 'instructing counsel and arranging the order of witnesses'.

Every day, that is, except this one.

'General Windham,' Sir Hugh thundered, 'does not dare to appear in the open light of day before an English jury; he does not dare to repeat in that court what he dared to say on oath in four affidavits before the Lords Justices.'

The General, he continued, had made much of the sacrifice he had made in coming home from India the previous year to attend to his nephew's affairs - but exactly what was the 'sacrifice' involved? There was no way of finding out as the General could not be cross-examined.

There were other matters the court should have heard about, said Sir Hugh, such as the letters he had received from his nephew, and the full story behind that coming-of-age meeting in the library at Felbrigg.

FOR THE second time, Sir Hugh had turned the petitioners' strengths back on themselves. There had been many witnesses; but that was a sign of weakness in the case, not confidence. They were many petitioners; but only two had come forward to the witness box. What about the others - why had they not given evidence? The answer was simple: they were too frightened. It was a brilliant stroke.

But why *did* the General not give evidence? It was surely obvious that the defenders of Windham would use it against him, and indeed that thought may have motivated him being 'conspicuous by his absence' on that day. If he had been present in the court there can be little doubt that Sir Hugh would have challenged him to his face to go into the witness box.

By not appearing he had sidestepped the problem - but at considerable cost to his public standing. He must have known the opponents of the petition would personalise it as a plot orchestrated by him, indeed the Roberts placard all but said as much. Why did a man who defied the Russian bullets in the bloody battle of the Redan not go into the witness box? It may have been that he thought the sheer weight of evidence would, by itself, provide overwhelming. But the insider gossip had a rather different explanation.

One of the racy letters of barrister and journalist Sir William Hardman, published as A Mid-Victorian Pepys in 1923, states: 'The present enquiry is chiefly got up at the instigation of the notorious General Windham of Crimean pseudo-fame, and Indian disgrace.... the General refuses to enter the witness box from a dread of having his foul practices exposed.

'He was once accused of indecent exposure in Hyde Park, and was got off by his counsel on the plea of insanity.' Thanks to his dual role, Sir William would have been doubly well-placed to know the inside story. Put the General in the witness box with that sort of background, and Sir Hugh and Karslake would have ripped his claim to be on the moral high ground to shreds within minutes.

Sir Hugh branded all the evidence given about Windham's early years as 'flimsy', 'trivial' or 'unintentionally exaggerated'. He read aloud several of Windham's letters from 1859, remarking on their powers of description and reasoning. Sir Hugh had taken the whole of the day to make his speech but it had been time well spent. It had been a masterly performance, probing and undermining the petitioners' evidence and focusing a highly-effective attack on their leader. It had been a most satisfactory day - and the next could promise yet more of the same.

DAY FOURTEEN of the inquiry, Friday 3 January, saw Sir Hugh once again taking each witness' statements apart with forensic ease. He dealt first with the only two petitioners who had appeared - Lord Alfred and the Marquis. Both had based their opinions on what they had read, not what they had seen. In passing he mentioned that Lady Sophia 'lies on a bed of sickness, and I fear of death'.

Turning to the various post-1854 tutors, he said their evidence had been contradictory. Yes, Windham had been called 'Mad' Windham while at Eton, but that was of no practical consequence. Many former - and distinguished pupils - had been branded 'mad' in their day too. There was a break in the evidence from summer 1857 to May 1859, but Sir Hugh promised he would fill that gap.

Col Bathurst had admitted to only one 'injudicious purchase' (a suit) by Windham in their time together, while there had been a 'standing feud' between his successor Horrocks and Windham. Horrocks' evidence, too, was full of inconsistencies. 'He threatened his pupil that if he did not behave better, his uncle would come home from India and take all his property away from him,' Sir Hugh said. 'Nobody could believe that Mr Horrocks was ever a good tutor, but all must admit that he had proved himself a very good prophet.'

As for the next tutor, Peatfield, 'his whole statement was blown to the winds by an admission [that] Mr Windham had plenty of brains if he chose to apply them.' One by one Sir Hugh assessed the witnesses, and found them wanting. Dr Dalrymple had 'completely failed' to back his statements, so all were worth 'nil'; Dr Johnson's evidence was 'perfectly childish', while Mr Scott's theories were 'utterly unworthy of any attention'. And Farrow's and Wilkinson's tales of the goings-on at Spa were 'flimsy and immaterial'.

Now Sir Hugh turned to two crucial witnesses: the Llewellyns. How, he asked, could Windham's guardians think of taking him away from the countryside to launch him on 'a season of London dissipation, uncared for and unchecked'? Despite that, Windham had made his own lodging arrangements, had made an agreement with his landlord about looking after his cash, and had opened an account with a distinguished wine merchant - all marks of a rational mind. 'Nothing was easier for a witness' than to describe shouting and howling and throwing-up of windows but, Sir Hugh asked, where was the proof? Not a single independent witness to any of this had been produced.

The Llewellyns had made much of Windham talking about his future wife and discussing her character. But what could be more natural for a man eager to marry? As for the tale of Windham running naked out of the bathroom: 'Mere rubbish' and 'the thing is grossly incredible and overthrows the credibility of the witness'. The talk of his being sick at table? 'Altogether unworthy of attention'. Mrs Llewellyn had claimed Windham 'exposed his person' to her on more than one occasion, Sir Hugh continued. 'Fancy a modest virtuous woman coming forward in open court and saying that such an offence was repeated once or twice in her own house by one of her own lodgers!... it was utterly beyond belief that a respectable woman would have permitted it to be repeated once or twice,' he added.

The QC was playing a clever 'heads I win, tails you lose' tactic: if she were lying, her evidence should be discounted, and if she were telling the truth, then clearly she was not a respectable woman - and so her evidence could be discounted again. The evidence of Augusta Llewellyn, he contended, had been full of 'contradictions and inconsistencies', and the couple had seemed in a hurry to tell an obviously pre-arranged story. Mrs Llewellyn's brother and sister would both be making statements about these which would be heard in open court, he added.

SIR HUGH then returned to the issue of that August meeting in Felbrigg library. The London lawyer Jackson was supposed to be Windham's attorney, but he was actually acting on behalf of the General. 'It was a proposal for and from General Windham and against his nephew.' The General had talked about 'sacrifice', but it was all just rank 'hypocrisy'. 'If the proposal had been carried out,' Sir Hugh insisted, 'they would never have heard of the current proceedings.' Indeed, 'if Mr Windham had accepted the disinterested offer of his affectionate relatives' - sarcasm on sarcasm - 'we should not have had them skulking in the seat beside their counsel, but we should have seen them rushing into the witness box, testifying their admiration of their young relative, and declaring him to be as sane as any man in England.' At this point, a correspondent for an Irish paper noted, 'General Windham grew very red, and looked very angry at this expression, especially as a subdued murmur of applause came from the spectators'.

The counsel took a softer, even bordering on sympathetic, line on his next subject: Agnes. He went through a summary of that first meeting at Ascot, courtship and marriage settlement, painting Windham's interest as purely romantic, and Agnes' acquiescence as stemming from a sincere desire to help her two young sisters. Of course, Sir Hugh was careful to add that 'such a marriage was no doubt much to be regretted; it was properly distasteful to society.'

At the same time, he added, 'nobody had suggested or could suggest that such a marriage was in the slightest degree evidence of insanity', except for one medical man. But the matter was only a 'matter of taste' and nothing more. The QC wisely kept his comments brief over the affair of the timber contract. He contended - as he had to - that the contract was a fair one, at a fair price. He was on firmer ground with claims about the nature of the questioning by Dr Winslow and Dr Mayo, saying it had been intended to 'drive Mr Windham into admissions of unsoundness'. Sir Hugh continued: 'Here was not an examination by medical men, but the torture and rack of the Inquisition.'

Sir Hugh concluded his lengthy address with a rousing plea for fair play for his client. It was an 'exquisite torture', he said, 'which would consign a warm and living soul... to the icy and corpse-like embrace of legal incapacity and lunatic restraint. Such, gentlemen, is the torture which his relatives have prepared for Mr Windham, and of that torture they ask you to be the ministrants and agents. I appeal to you, from who I can confidently expect justice. I implore of you, gentlemen, to sweep away the cobwebs which theory and prejudice, which partisanship and ignorance, which interest and falsehood, have woven round this case... It is at once the highest and most grateful duty of an English jury to detect deceit, and to defeat oppression.'

As he sat down to more rousing cheers and applause, even Sir Hugh's dry and disapproving features must surely have re-arranged themselves into a smile. It had been a tour-de-force performance, stretching over ten hours and blending rhetoric with shrewdness, bringing in at various times appeal to English fair play, patriotism and common justice. The Times and News of the World would both later single out the brilliance of Sir Hugh's oratory. Sir Hugh had expertly laid the foundations for victory; now it was time to build on them.

DR HARRINGTON TUKE, the first defence witness, was questioned by Karslake. He began by talking about the various interviews he had with Windham, including that of 12 November when he had told him he was confident of winning his case. Dr Tuke also said that Windham's father had 'saved General Windham from the consequences of some act which he had done years ago by pretending that he was insane' - an incident not amplified in court but which we now know as the alleged indecent exposure. He had gone with Windham to the Essex Street offices of his solicitor Coe while he prepared his defence, and took the opportunity of observing how Windham handled himself. The doctor was impressed: Windham 'perfectly understood' what was going on, showed 'great powers of memory and attention' and knowledge of his estate and the various financial outcomes.

Windham told him his debts were £25,000 to £30,000, mainly to Emmanuel the jeweller, but that he hoped to deal with them by 'living quietly at Felbrigg' and using his income from the timber. Dr Tuke took the jury through the various meetings he had had with Windham, the final one being on the evening of 11 December after his exhaustive session with Dr Winslow and Dr Mayo. 'I never,' said Dr Tuke, concluding the day's proceedings, 'during the whole of my interviews, saw the slightest indication of unsoundness of mind. I found no inconsequence, no incoherence, no want of attention.'

And so the careful dismantling of the petitioners' evidence had begun - step by careful step.

12

4-11 January 1862: 'Faults too common to mankind'

'The Alleged Lunacy of Mr Windham:
EXTRAORDINARY DISCLOSURES'
Headline in Reynold's Weekly News, 5 January 1862

DAY FIFTEEN - Saturday 4 January - saw Dr Tuke cross-examined by Chambers. He said he had had about '20 hours' of interviews with Windham after 5 November. He reiterated his evidence of the previous day, adding that Windham had told him it was the 'incident' involving the General which was the reason why his uncle would not go into the witness box. He had added that another uncle, whom he did not name, but subsequently claimed to be Captain Henry Windham, was also unlikely to testify as he was 'always drunk'.

Dr Tuke admitted that he told Windham during the course of another interview that he thought in four or five years he would be a lunatic or kill himself if he insisted on carrying on his drinking and dissipation. But throughout his cross-examination, the doctor kept to his consistent claim that Windham was not mad. Windham had frequently been accused in the affidavits of telling aimless lies, but Dr Tuke said he not seen any evidence of this during their conversations. 'Mr Windham is certainly not an idiot, not could it ever enter my mind that he is an imbecile,' he added. Being thousands in pounds in debt because he had given jewellery to his wife was not evidence of insanity, just of Windham being 'desperately in love with her'.

Another medical man - and former Commissioner in Lunacy - Dr E Seymour said he had interviewed Windham twice. His conclusion, like Dr Tuke, was that it was impossible for a jury to find him of unsound mind. One answer Windham had given him during their interviews was to become hugely significant later in the case. Windham said that the General had called on him after his marriage, had spoken to him very kindly, and wished to sell his nephew a small property. 'He then said,' reported Dr Seymour, 'and this remark struck me very much - "If my uncle thought me mad, why did he try to make a bargain with me?".' Dr Seymour thought the ordeal of the proceedings was actually having a salutary effect on Windham and would help by 'steadying' him. 'It will make him more like a man,' he added.

MONDAY 6 JANUARY - Day Sixteen - saw the first casualty of the already-marathon hearing, when one of the jurors was forced to step down on medical advice, leaving 22 jurors remaining. There were so many jurors (the Lunacy Act insisted on at least 13) because the Master had suspected the hearing would be a long one and he wanted to ensure there would be a quorum at the end. He was not the only one starting to feel the stress. Before the business of the day got under way another bitter exchange took place between Chambers and Karslake. The former, piqued by implied criticism of the petitioners in that day's papers, said he thought it was his 'duty' to ask the court whether it should not caution certain writers in the public press about making any comments on this case while it was proceeding.

Chambers said if persons were 'unwise and indiscreet enough' to approach the press it would ending up having a 'ruinous effect' on their own case. Such behaviour would create 'an amount of excitement... in the public mind, calculated to destroy the character and defeat the great objects of English justice.' He suggested that the court should consider issuing a 'caution' to the writers concerned. This was all too much for Karslake, who resented the obvious implication that it was Windham's side which had stirred up the publicity and said he hoped that 'nothing which had fallen from Mr Chambers' lips' would imply that.

'Oh, no, no, no,' Chambers replied, 'I did not intend anything of the kind.'

Karslake pressed his point. Chambers had used 'a significant gesture which might imply that some secret understanding existed between the advisors of Mr Windham and a certain portion of the newspaper press'. Agnes' counsel Coleridge then pitched in, saying he treated with 'scorn and indignation' any such suggestions. Chambers, having carefully laid the imputation, then said he had never had - but of course - 'the remotest intention' of implying that.

The Master optimistically (and naively) expressed the hope that the press would refrain from commenting because of their love for the 'pure administration of justice' - betraying his ignorance of the newspaper world too. One further matter to discuss was the need to move proceedings out of the Court of Exchequer from Thursday, possibly to the much smaller parliamentary committee rooms ('Heaven forbid!' the Master muttered).

WHAT HAD sparked this exchange was an item in one of the racier Sunday papers, Reynold's Weekly News. As well as summarising the previous week's evidence, the paper featured a column by its writer 'Gracchus', who took his pen-name from the populist and reforming brothers of classical Roman history. Unlike the rest of the press, which reported the evidence but - as yet - had kept a discreet editorial silence, Reynold's had decided to break from the pack. The column began with the portentous words 'The liberty of the subject in this country cannot be trifled with' and soon continued in even more outspoken vein. 'There is something very suspicious about the proceedings instituted against Mr Windham,' Gracchus alleged. 'It would really seem, judging by the manner in which the case was got up, that nothing less than his incarceration in a lunatic asylum... could have been contemplated by certain interested individuals.

'Although his [Windham's] actions are bestial, his manners offensive, his tastes depraved, and his mind debauched, yet no evidence of his having committed any act sufficient at once to stamp him a madman was adduced.' The 'unpleasant circumstance' of Windham 'having married a prostitute' was certainly not one, it argued, as 'some peers of the realm... must likewise be pronounced mad'. All the evidence against Windham had now been heard, and although the hearing was by no means concluded, Gracchus could not 'for one moment imagine that an English jury will be swayed by the very frivolous and suspicious testimony brought forward against young Windham so as to place any restraint either on his person, or his property.'

MEANWHILE, back in the Court of Exchequer, at last, the real business of the day could begin. Dr Seymour, cross-examined by Chambers, said Windham had told him he 'was in the habit of driving a railway engine and that... many young men did the same'. Chambers tried to draw him on the presents to Agnes, but he refused to be diverted from his conviction that it was mere youthful 'extravagance'. Dr Seymour said Windham had told him that he was in love with his wife, and he did not know that she had committed adultery and so a divorce was being planned. But that did not matter: 'I should have regarded his conduct as inconsistent... It would have been one of those inconsistencies which are too common to mankind.'

The next witness, Mr Hancock, Chief Surgeon of the Charing Cross Hospital, talked about Windham's 'peculiarly shaped' mouth, with an upper jaw drawn to a point so narrow there was room for only two teeth in front. This would explain perfectly the reports of slavering, noisy eating, his tone of voice, the famous laugh - and even the 'vacant look' which more than one witness had commented on. He said he had first met with Windham on 1 November. The young squire wanted to see him because of the rumours his uncle, General Windham, was spreading about his sanity. 'He told me that it was very foolish of the General to treat him so because he had over and over told him again that it would be the worse for him and his sons. But it was no use, he added, "and therefore as my father left me power by his will to cut off the entail, I have done so". Windham explained how Roberts had been 'a good friend' to him.

Hancock added: 'I then said, "As insanity has been alleged against you, have you been examined by any medical man on the part of General Windham?"

'He replied: "I don't know whether it was a medical man or no, but somebody called upon me a short time ago pretending that he came about a debt which he said was owing to him by my mother. I therefore began to suspect and very quietly bowed him out of the room, saying he must know as well as I did that I have nothing to do with my mother's debts."

Hancock then recommended to Windham's solicitor the names of various experts on mental health, including Dr Winslow - an idea which lasted only until the moment someone spotted the General sitting in his waiting room. He concluded: 'His [Windham's] demeanour was characterised by perfect self-possession, perfect calmness, and total absence of levity, especially when he referred to his father. I observed no signs of slavering. I should say that Mr Windham, as far as his physical appearance goes, is a well-developed young man. He seems to have plenty of animal spirits.' Finally, Hancock dismissed a suggestion by Chambers that the peculiar formation of Windham's mouth meant there was less room for his brain.

THE NEXT witness was another medical man - and one with a close Norfolk connection. George Frederick Gwyn practised in Hammersmith but was from the county and had known William Frederick as a child. He met Windham on 21 September 1861 and was invited to Felbrigg, where he arrived on 23 September. Windham was there, as were Agnes and Roberts.

'While I was at Felbrigg, Mr Windham consulted me professionally about his throat. He was suffering under syphilitic ulceration of the throat,' he said, baldly. This was the first time a name had been given to Windham's 'loathsome disease'. It is yet one more aspect of this remarkable case that the word was even uttered; not for nothing has the author Deborah Hayden pointed out that it was 'life's dark secret' and rarely mentioned directly.

Windham's disease at last had a name, and its implications must now be considered.

If we accept, as both Windham and his doctor did, that he was indeed suffering from the disease, then it does not necessarily follow that he passed it to Agnes. What is crucial is the timing of Windham's original infection. His throat condition could have been a manifestation of the mid-period of the disease known as 'hidden'. The fact that sufferers of this phase often complained of being poisoned - that is, exactly what Agnes suspected on September 22 - may also be significant. The implication is, therefore, that he became infected with syphilis, not in his summer of Haymarket debauchery, but much earlier - perhaps this was the infection (which he falsely believed to be healed) from 1857 or even earlier.

The initial highly infectious period of syphilis is the first two years, then declines sharply. So it is possible that the infectious stage may have been over by 1859 or 1860, before he had even set eyes on Agnes. True, Windham did have some sort of other infection that summer, as the notorious 'trouser chafing' incident shows, but was adamant that 'the character of the disease had been mistaken'. If this argument is correct then it was this, secondary, venereal infection which he, briefly, passed to Agnes. This supposition is supported strongly by the fact that nothing in her subsequent history hints at any of the manifestations of the dreaded illness.

With Windham, however, it is a different story. And it is a tantalising possibility that his syphilis actually caused much of his later behaviour. It is a well-known facet of the disease that in its later stages, known as general paresis, the sufferer can exhibit aberrant behaviour. In 1902 William Osler (quoted in Hayden) warned of a 'change in character... which may astonish' and lead to 'offences against decency'. And offending against decency was something Windham was all too good at.

Gwyn saw Windham several times over the next two days, and a further five times back in London. 'I have been Mr Windham's medical attendant ever since,' he said, adding that he had witnessed Windham being examined about his mind with no alteration in his opinion about his sanity. Gwyn returned to Felbrigg on 8 October to attend Agnes, and was next consulted by her on 18 or 20 November. He told how he had accompanied Windham on the fruitless quest to look for Agnes in Glasgow on 3 November - and how they had found her back in London. And with this cliff-hanging ending, the court duly adjourned.

DR GWYN returned to his story when the court resumed the next day, Day Seventeen, being quizzed by Chambers on the various well-established infidelities of Agnes with 'Mr ------, No 1' [Garton] and 'Mr --------, No 2' [Giuglini]. He also said that Agnes was still suffering - as of her consultation of Friday 3 January - from the same disease she had developed in early October. Windham had also spoken to her, politely and calmly, on that same day and they had travelled quietly together in Agnes' brougham for a short way.

There then followed a succession of witnesses drawn from current or former members of the Felbrigg household, whose testimony - unsurprisingly - ranged from forelock-tugging obsequiousness to non-insightful sentimentality. Ex-housekeeper Mrs Martin - a trusted family servant from 1832 to late 1861 - had more to say. Windham 'was, and is, very fond of me', she said, telling about his lonely childhood and friendships with the servants. She was, she admitted, 'a good deal distressed' at his marriage and told the court how she and her husband had travelled to London to try and stop it, but in vain. When the newly-weds had turned up at Felbrigg, Mrs Martin said she 'was not disposed to live in the house any longer' and went to Home Farm on the estate instead. Chambers then tried to get Mrs Martin to admit to witnessing all the bad habits the petitioners had made so much play of. But she would not be drawn.

DAY EIGHTEEN - Wednesday 8 January - saw one of Windham's former schoolmasters giving evidence. The Rev Frederick Askew Bickmore told how he had prepared Windham for Eton by teaching him from 1848-50. Windham was 'rude, boisterous, and not very tidy in his dress', but there was 'no mental incapacity whatsoever'. He had asked him to leave at Christmas 1850 because younger boys were coming into the school and Windham was in the habit of swearing.

The next witness was Norfolk gentility personified: Sir Edmund Lacon, Colonel of the East Norfolk Militia, Great Yarmouth MP and member of a Yarmouth brewing family. It was in connection with his military duties that he entered the witness box, saying that Windham had done 'nothing unbecoming a gentleman and an officer'. There then followed a succession of Felbrigg retainers who, again unsurprisingly, all testified to the stalwart qualities of their master.

Jane Morris, a chambermaid at the Victoria Hotel in London, was told the hearing Windham had acted like a gentlemen and never had - as Chambers tried to hint - any 'business' with him. When butler James Nolls came into the witness box, Chambers tried to wrong-foot him with claims about what Windham had done the previous Christmas Day when he gave a dinner for his tenants. No, his master did not come into the room with his face blacked up or like a clown, or fall on the ground pretending to swim. The accusations were bizarre, and also, naturally, implied that the petitioners had a spy in the heart of the Felbrigg household.

Decorum was restored with the next witness, Edward Smith, travelling salesman for the Burlington Street tailors Buckmasters. He had met Windham in May 1861 when he was 'reading for the army' and who had told him that he was hoping to get a commission with the 2nd Life Guards in May 1862. Windham had made a 'moderate' order, which had not yet been paid.

THURSDAY 9 JANUARY - Day Nineteen - began with the foreman of the jury, Sir George Armitage, handing the Master an anonymous letter which he had not opened. The master did so, said the first sentence was 'offensive' and tore it up. Anonymous letters were not the only thing on the jury's mind. Several asked when the evidence might be finished - Karslake thought 'Monday or Tuesday'. Lady Sophia was formally excused as a witness after her surgeon John Robinson said his patient, whom he had been attending for two years, had not left her house for two months and was unfit to be called to the hearing.

Windham's immediate superior in the militia, Captain Charles Ensor, agreed with his brother officers that Lieutenant Windham had been 'from first to last... like a gentleman'. The next witness, Norwich tailor Thomas Bingham, was destined to play an important part in Windham's life after the hearing. But, for now, he was mainly asked about his work for the squire. He first met Windham on 29 October 1859, and had made clothes for him at intervals ever since. He had been invited to Felbrigg on 10 October for a day's fishing. His bill for 1860 - £56 - had not been paid.

Another tradesman, Norwich ironmonger Charles Howlett, said Windham had dealt with him perfectly competently concerning some work on the stables in early 1861. Together with the other traders being called as witnesses, Windham was currently paying for their stay in London. He had treated them to a visit to Drury Lane to see a pantomime during Christmas week. Innocuous enough, but Chambers also wrung an admission from Howlett that he had twice seen Windham in a 'common public-house'.

H W Burr, who had helped teach Windham in preparation for the army in late 1858 to early 1859, talked about their studies together, but conceded that Windham had occasionally been 'in a passion' when he drank too much, and had left owing money. Oh, and he used to drive an engine on the South Western - or so he had been told. Windham's laugh, he added, was not an idiotic laugh, a comment which drew applause from the public gallery - and a stern reprimand from Master Warren. Other Wokingham acquaintances - the Rev William Hurst and a solicitor, Mr T W T Cooke, also testified to his 'sound' intellect. Elizabeth Crossley, chambermaid of the Duke's

Palace Hotel in Norwich, and Mrs Anne Warner, landlady of the Bedford Hotel, Covent Garden, both testified to Windham's gentlemanly qualities.

The evidence of the next witness, William Seeley, station master at Norwich's Victoria Station, prompted an exchange with Chambers born out of the latter's frustration at the defence's long stream of unimpeachable witnesses. After he had gone through the total sum of his evidence - which amounted to, yes, he had seen Windham, yes, he took his ticket in the ordinary way, and no, he didn't do anything out of the ordinary - Chambers asked him: 'How much did it cost to bring you from Norwich?'

'Well, I paid my fare,' Seeley replied.

Then the sooner you go back, the better.' After the laughter in the public gallery had subsided, he added: 'I have no question to put to the witness, who has cost us much and told us little.'

After a few more inconsequential witnesses, all testifying to Windham's business skills, the hearing was adjourned once again. It was to be the last time the Commission sat in the spacious Court of Exchequer. Now, added to the problems of the complications and sheer volume of the evidence was the ordeal of an venue which was plainly unsuited to stage it.

ON FRIDAY 10 January - the twentieth day of the hearing - the disadvantages of the Westminster Sessions House became immediately apparent. The Norwich Mercury's correspondent wrote: 'The jury were crowded upon the bench like herrings in a barrel; counsel were separated from their solicitors, and the public were virtually excluded altogether.' Ventilation, too, was abysmal, varying from oven-like heat in one part of the courtroom to wintry draughts in the other. Karslake, for one, was suffering badly from a cold, which threatened to get worse. One important development was an agreement on all sides that counsel should be present when Windham was interviewed by the Master and jury at the end of the case. But quite when the end of the case might be was still in the lap of the gods - or rather, the counsel.

Witnesses continued to be of the 'stout yeomanry' class - a deputy-lieutenant here, a militia officer there, all testifying to the gentlemanly qualities of the young squire. But Sir Henry Robinson, a near-neighbour of Windham's, raised unintentional laughter when he mentioned a rather underwhelming militia review near Cromer, at which the cavalry forces - which included Windham - numbered precisely ten.

'I believe the troops ultimately made a charge,' he added, to guffaws, local militia being a proverbial source of public amusement throughout the land. Mrs Voysey, who hosted Windham at her Eton boarding house from 1855-56, remembered him as a 'noisy' and 'peculiar' boy but one who was obedient and treated her with respect.

Mrs Sophia Gibson, one of the head boys' maids at the school, said Windham was 'rough and rude', but apart from an accident to his friend Lord Marsham, there had been no incidents. The young lord had fallen on a knife Windham had in his hand and cut himself. But it was always considered an accident, and a minor one at that.

Miss Kate Archer, the next - and 100th - witness, told how she had met Windham in early summer of 1860 in Hyde Park when he steadied her restless horse one morning. On 28 September 1861 General Windham called at her house and... but Chambers objected to any more being revealed, and the Master agreed that details of the conversation should stay secret. This was too much for Sir Hugh who, with his usual skill, managed to convey exactly what he would have questioned Miss Archer about. He would, he said, have tried to show that the General had 'actively interfered' in trying to manipulate the evidence, in order to gain control of the property. But the Master had made up his mind.

Lord Claude Hamilton, MP, who was next to speak, was Colonel for the Donegal Militia, which was quartered in Great Yarmouth in 1860. He met Windham on the train to Norwich and mentioned that he had been shooting at Felbrigg in 1856. They spoke in a 'most cordial, rational and gentlemanly way' for about an hour. He had been in Yarmouth once or twice more, and had met him at a ball in the town in September of that year at which Windham was 'decidedly intoxicated' and complaining that no young ladies wanted to dance with him. Lord Claude said he had advised him to go home.

Lord Claude did not consider Windham's passion for railway engines a sign of insanity. Quite the opposite, in fact, as he himself had attended several lectures on the subject and knew how much 'skill, self-possession, coolness of head and delicacy of touch' was needed to drive an engine. Railway matters also featured in the early part of the evidence of the final witness of the day, Windham's valet William Badcock. Originally a guard on the Eastern Counties line, he had received an engraved watch from Windham the previous August, a gift which had created so much 'difficulty' with his managers at the railway that he had left his job and entered Windham's service instead. Badcock was asked by Chambers about the Christmas Day dinner - and, at last, had some confirmation about Windham's behaviour. Yes, he had blacked his face to sing 'negro melodies', and appeared with a banjo. But he had gone to bed 'quite steadily' around 2am on Boxing Day, and had risen at 5am.

The final part of the day saw Sir Hugh make a surprise - at least to the jury and public gallery - announcement. He would avoid trying to prove Windham's claims about his uncles (the alleged drunkenness of Captain Windham and 'insanity' incident involving the General) if Chambers agreed not to allege that the claims were entirely without foundation. It would mean the court would avoid having to hear an 'irksome' amount of evidence. Chambers was happy to agree - much to the relief of the Master.

PAINFUL MATTERS, not in the evidence but in anonymous letters, concerned Master Warren at the start of the next day's hearing, Saturday 11 January, Day Twenty-One. More had been sent to him, and to the Foreman of the Jury. The letters were 'impudent in tone and scandalous in substance', and had been immediately destroyed.

After hearing briefly from pub landlord Mr H Drew, who had met Windham in March 1860 at Shorncliffe, it was the turn of Thomas Wyndham Cremer. His middle name was no coincidence - he was a descendant of a branch of the Windhams founded in the seventeenth century. Cremer lived about five miles from Felbrigg, and had known both Windham's father and the young heir. He had been to a dinner party there in 1860, had shot with Windham a few months earlier, and in August 1861 had walked round the stables with him. Windham, although a noisy boy, had been of perfectly sound mind.

There were more ripples from the Llewellyns' evidence next, with Mrs Brown, a laundress in the Vauxhall Road, saying how she had asked Mrs Llewellyn for an extra payment to wash Windham's things in view of their state. General Windham had come calling round to see her (on Christmas Day) to ask about her work. But Karslake was stopped from probing further when a triumphant Chambers rose to remind him of the Master's ruling the previous Thursday.

Mrs Pritchard, who had been a servant at Duke Street from 21 June to the middle of August, flatly denied that Augusta Llewellyn's tales of excessive egg consumption and bathtime misbehaviour had ever happened. There was more: Mrs Llewellyn had approached her in early November at her new position and put pressure on her to back her stories and said the General 'would do something good' for Mrs Pritchard and her husband in return. Mrs Llewellyn returned on a number of occasions, including with Colonel Broughton - whom she called her 'baby' - and told her: 'You must come to my house to see the General, for Mr Windham has been and married a bad woman, and squandered all his fortune, and we want to do what we can for the General.' Pritchard had flatly refused.

If that were not damning enough, she told the court she had heard Augusta Llewellyn talk to her husband in mid-July and say, 'It is a shame for you to encourage that boy to drink; you are old enough to be his father. You are sucking the poor boy dry, and while he has any money left you will stick to him.' Mrs Pritchard had indeed seen Windham 'tipsy' most evenings, having witnessed him, Llewellyn and others quaffing wine and champagne since lunch (and all at Windham's expense, naturally). She said Windham had even tried to kiss her once when under the influence of alcohol.

Another former Duke Street servant, Sarah Brown, was next. As cook from 24 June to 26 July she was in the perfect position to establish the truth or otherwise of the bizarre breakfasts. And the truth was: there were none. Brown had left the house after David Llewellyn had used 'most abusive and insulting' language. Catherine Babbage, who worked in the house from 1 April to the end of June had even more to impart: she had seen Augusta Llewellyn trying to be 'familiar' with Windham on several occasions. Windham had rejected her advances 'and therefore,' added Babbage, 'it is not surprising that she should always speak ill of him.' Mrs Llewellyn was in the habit of going for afternoon drives with Colonel Broughton, she added. The final witness on Day Twenty-One was another servant, the Frenchman Henry Shappis, who - once again - had left the Llewellyns' suddenly and - once again - had been approached to give evidence against Windham. Shappis had angrily refused. It was no wonder, as he had a court claim pending against David Llewellyn for assault.

The Llewellyns' sensational evidence was looking flimsier with every witness.

13

11-19 January 1862:
A Family at War

'Young men do strange things in love.'
Sir William Foster on Windham's behaviour, 14 January

'This young man is the victim of an abuse which is a scandal to the age in
which we live, and a dark spot upon the national reputation.'
Reynold's Weekly News, 19 January

THE SAME day - 11 January - also saw drama outside the courtroom when the Suffolk
Chronicle reported that a crisis meeting had been held by Eastern Counties Railways
managers following Joseph Ford's sensational 'locked carriage' evidence. The directors
had ordered all available staff to the Bishopsgate boardroom of the company, where
they had conducted 'a minute and searching investigation into ex-Guard Ford's claims'.
They concluded that his evidence had been 'greatly exaggerated'. But their complacent
verdict would be shaken within months.

Back in the Westminster Sessions House there was growing disquiet at the length of
the hearing. The Times' report on Day Twenty-Two of the hearing, Monday 13 January,
began with a searing editorial judgement about its labyrinthine nature. The paper
had heard, to its near-incredulity, that the hearing could go on for at least

another fortnight. 'Indeed, as matters are managed at present' - with a obvious dig at Master Warren - 'there is no earthly reason why the case should ever come to an end at all.'

The absurdity was this: the defence seemed to want to call anyone who had ever had a five-minute conversation with Windham, sold him anything, sat at a dinner table with him or heard him laugh. The number of potential witnesses would be 'immense'. Besides, what on earth was the relevance of the Llewellyns' 'obscure and uninteresting family squabbles', it asked. If things went on as at present, 'the Windham case may be prolonged until the alleged lunatic is cold in his grave and his property has passed into other hands.' And the 'other hands' in question would, in all probability, be the lawyers. 'Can it be absolutely necessary, in order to decide the question whether Mr Windham is a sane man or an idiot, that he should be stripped of his property and made a beggar?,' it asked. The comments, coming from the country's 'paper of record' carried a huge amount of weight. The real-life equivalent of Dickens' fictional Jarndyce vs Jarndyce looked all too likely.

The Times was perfectly correct about the inadequacy of the legal process, but its judgement that the 'family squabbles' were of no concern was wide of the mark. The credibility of the Llewellyns was at the heart of the petitioners' case. The wording of the petition specified it was concerned with Windham's competency at the beginning of August, ie when he was at Duke Street. If that evidence collapsed, the rest of the petitioners' case would surely follow.

First, however, the inquiry heard from two of Windham's former tutors, Mr G Yonge, his private tutor at Eton from January to March 1855, and Mr Ingram, the French and Mathematical master at Mr Westmacott's school in Feltham in the early 1850s. For both men Windham was an average pupil; not brilliant, not clever, but there were plenty worse.

So far, so mundane. But now the court atmosphere became tense with the evidence of two key witnesses - Augusta Llewellyn's sister Eliza Sophia Dignam, and brother Conway Dignam. They were present in court to back up suggestions first put to Mrs Llewellyn by Karslake during her evidence on Day Five - the now long-ago 20 December. Eliza said she stayed at the Duke Street premises between March and 4 June 1861 and occasionally after that. Windham had always been a 'most gentlemanly' guest, with a hearty but not excessive appetite. She had gone to the offices of Mr Field the solicitor in October with her sister. 'We were in Mr Field's office for an hour and a half or two hours. I heard the statement made by my sister and to the best of my belief it was entirely false,' she insisted. Eliza protested to her sister about the lies and told the court she had not slept in the house in Duke Street since then.

Under cross-examination by Chambers, she said she had met Roberts once in

Cremorne Gardens when he fell into conversation with her and flattered her with the comment 'Oh what pretty eyes you have, I can see them half a mile off.' He offered to take her home in his carriage, but Eliza refused and he left her alone after five minutes. 'I have no income of my own and I am supported by kind friends. I had a quarrel with the Llewellyns in 1860 about an IOU for £30. I sued them in the county court and got the money. Sometime after I wrote to Mr Llewellyn asking forgiveness. I was then living with my brother Conway in Fulham Fields and was very ill-off,' she added. He brother had come with her to the court, 'for I am too frightened to walk alone as the Llewellyns are always after me'.

Her brother Conway confirmed the claims Sir Hugh had put to Mrs Llewellyn on Day Twelve: that she had tried to get him to lie about Windham. Conway Dignam said he had angrily turned down her offer. 'I have seen Mr Windham walking, riding and driving but I do not think I have ever spoken to him in my life,' he insisted. 'My sister did not know whether I was acquainted with Mr Windham or not.'

Chambers tried to undermine the witness by portraying him as Augusta Llewellyn had done, a down-and-out. But Dignam preserved some of his dignity by pointing out he had volunteered to give evidence after 'a false statement made by Mrs Llewellyn about Eliza Sophia, who I know to be a good virtuous young woman', and was taking his brother-in-law to court. Dignam's claim that his brother-in-law had assaulted him and he was prosecuting him turned out to be no idle boast: a few days after the Windham case concluded magistrates heard how Llewellyn had 'laid hold' of Dignam in Burlington Arcade and used 'disgusting' language. The court bound Llewellyn to keep the peace, a ruling which was tested immediately when he 'entered into scandalous personal statements' until he was ordered to shut up.

BACK IN the Westminster Sessions House it was the turn of Windham's bank manager. Mr Hill, of the Crown Bank in Norwich, said Windham had opened an account the previous August with two cheques: £908 14s, and the second, and last, of £1,000. He talked 'rationally and sensibly' in his dealings with the bank. That deposit had now shrunk to just £17 because of a series of 24 cheques, the largest being £300 to Agnes Windham. Next came Jean Souney, a waiter at the Windhams' honeymoon hotel, the Hotel de Menrice in the Rue de Rivoli, who said there had been nothing unusual in the stay in early September, save the newly-married Mrs Windham's obvious lack of affection towards her husband. One final thing for the day: the jury had objected to suggestions that the QCs should be present at the end-of-case examination of Windham, but no final decision was made.

DAY TWENTY-THREE - 14 January - began with yet more pressure heaped on the

157

luckless Master Warren. Several jurymen had complained that they had struggled in from their sickbeds only through 'a strong sense of public duty' and wanted to know when the case was going to end. The Master said he could do nothing but rely - which he did implicitly - upon the discretion of the counsel and he 'would advise the jury to hear the case to the end with that tranquillity and patience which they had manifested hitherto. If he had endeavoured to interfere with the petitioners in any way they would have probably said that they are not allowed to lay their case fairly and fully before the jury. He had not so interfered, and it appeared to him that he would be acting most unjustly if he were to place any restrictions upon Mr Windham and his advisers, who had an equal right with the petitioners to a fair and ample hearing.'

Mr Millward, one of the legal team for the young squire, said that the whole of the remaining proof had been 'carefully sifted and weeded and that every piece of evidence that had been withdrawn had been omitted with justice to Mr Windham and that in future not a single moment of time would be wasted'. He added he was 'not without hopes' that in a day or two the advisers of Mr Windham could close their evidence. The unspoken thought running through the minds of most present must have been one of polite disbelief.

The first witness - via a translator - was the Windhams' former Torquay friend, Italian composer Signor Campana, who gave the lie to the slightly bizarre claim of whisker-tugging. Windham had only done it gently, and as a joke. Then Glaswegian ironmaster Mr Murray told of his encounter with Windham on his 1858 trip round the Highlands. The next witness' evidence was, in its own way, highly significant. Mr Andrews of Rimpton in Somerset met Windham in the summer of 1857 while he was a 17-year-old pupil with the village rector.

Andrews had got to know him well and they stayed friends until Windham left towards the end of the following year. Andrews admitted he had 'rather a prejudice against him from his appearance and manners but afterwards he had changed his opinion of him'. Windham, he said, was very open and unreserved and was affectionate to those who treated him with kindness. Andrews said that Windham had grown fond of Mrs Andrews and their daughters, and had proposed marriage to one of them in 1858. The only reason the proposal was rejected was because of the parties' youth. There were no personal reasons, intellectual or otherwise to reject the proposal.

Norwich solicitor Sir William Foster then told how he had talked to Windham and considered him of sound mind, although he 'wanted a good deal of assistance'. He said Windham knew nothing about his estate, but then again there were hundreds of young men in a similar position. Windham had not consulted him about the plan to remove the timber; in fact he doubted Windham even realised the value of his estate.

The solicitor had 'absolutely declined' to meet Windham's new wife, saying the marriage had offended the whole county. He went on to suggest that Windham's marriage 'had been his ruin', but the fact it had taken place, along with the marriage settlement and £30,000 of debts in four months was not evidence of insanity. 'Young men do strange things in love,' he observed.

Mr Bruce, who lived in Westbourne Terrace, said he had met Windham and Colonel Bathurst in Baden Baden in 1859 and travelled with them for up to a fortnight.

He had witnessed Windham's fight with Bathurst, who had 'knocked him down'. Windham was in the habit of using 'coarse and filthy language', but this did not mean he was of unsound mind.

The inquiry then turned to the key issue of the timber. This was always going to be the most difficult part of the defence's case, with Sir Hugh having to prove that, far from being cheated, Windham had negotiated a reasonable price and had handled the matter in a business-like way. The court heard first from Mr Lawrence, the timber merchant, one half of the brokers Lawrence and Fry which had been handling the Felbrigg account.

He had been introduced to Windham by Roberts, a person connected with the timber trade 'for many years', and visited the estate between 24-26 October. Lawrence admitted the contract had not been 'a particularly advantageous one' from Windham's point of view, but said that his firm had since become so 'disgusted' with the affair that he had taken up the General's offer of £1,000 to cover his costs and abandon it. 'Not a single stick has been felled,' he added.

Before calling the next witness, there was another discussion between the counsel, the Master and the jury about whether Windham should be examined in open court. Sir Hugh - and his client - wanted it conducted in public. But the Master said he had no desire to make Windham an 'exhibition' in open court, and even Sir Hugh's no-doubt accurate statement that 'everything which could cause pain had been placed before the public' did not change his mind.

THE FINAL witness of the day, Mr Freebridge - 'the 76th witness for the defence', the court reporter noted dryly - returned to the subject of the timber. He said he was called down to the Felbrigg estate on 17 November by Lawrence and Fry to look at the timber. Much of it, he said, was 'very inferior' and not worth the money. Resuming his evidence on Wednesday 15 January, Day Twenty-Four, he said the shallowness and unfavourable character of a large portion of the estate's soil meant much of the timber was 'shaky' - poor quality - and with 'incipient decay'. He agreed with Lawrence that the deal had been bad for Windham, adding that in his experience he had never before heard of a new young landowner parting with £5,000-worth of timber without taking professional advice.

Two more voices - this time Norfolk ones - were heard on the matter. Robert Leamon, a farmer 'and one of the largest timber buyers in the county', had bought timber from Felbrigg in 1857 and 1858 and paid no more than two shillings a foot. He insisted that the market for timber within the county was slight, and prices affected by such issues as the current 'panic in the leather trade' which used the oak bark to make tannin. Most of the Felbrigg timber was poor, an opinion supported by the next witness, Great Yarmouth mayor - and timber merchant - Robert Steward who said the oak timber of Felbrigg was the worst in the county. Perhaps Windham's deal to sell the timber had not been such a bad bargain after all. Or at least that was the spin that Sir Hugh put on the evidence. The fact that the stripping of timber, good quality or not, from the estate would ruin its appearance was neatly side-stepped.

The court heard from another medical man, William Charles Hood, physician superintendent of Bethlehem Hospital. He had interviewed Windham on 13 December and they talked about much of Windham's life over the next hour and a half. As Windham, now very tired, was putting on his coat, he turned to Hood and said, 'Will you help to prove me sane?'. Hood replied that Windham's fate was in his own hands: if he behaved with dignity and befitting his social position he might become a respectable man, but if not he would die a beggar, 'without the regret of anyone'. After he talked to him again on New Year's Eve, he came to the conclusion Windham was perfectly sane.

At the close of the day the Master said he had made a final decision about Windham's examination: it would be held in private, but with the counsel present.

DAY TWENTY-FIVE (Thursday 16 January) saw the inquiry enter its second month. It was the occasion for The Times to launch another salvo of disapproval. The inquiry 'still enjoys a vigorous existence,' it noted, 'and with so many and such careful nurses its life may be prolonged for a considerable time yet.' But the biggest problem, it claimed, was the 'alarming' effect on the health of the participants caused by the move to the draughty Westminster Sessions House. The frequent icy blasts had led most of the jurymen to wrap themselves 'in thick overcoats, with collars tucked up above their ears, and several, sacrificing dignity for comfort, have even gone to the length of wearing skull caps'.

Despite these efforts several members of the jury had already fallen sick, and the Master had even hinted that the case might have to be abandoned. It also took a swipe at Karslake for claiming he would close the evidence by the Friday 'which probably means, in non-legal language, the middle of next week'.

The day's evidence featured two key players in the affair of the already-notorious marriage settlement. Dr Whidbourne told how he had first seen Agnes on the hunting field in Hertfordshire on one occasion and had been called in by her in 1860 as a patient. He had reluctantly agreed to be a trustee for her marriage settlement in August 1861. He then took the court through the events of the wedding day, and mentioned his brief stay at Felbrigg in September. He said he had witnessed a discussion between the

The weak spot: Trying to justify the poor deal Windham had made over his timber was the most difficult part of the case for his legal team.

General and his nephew about a parcel of land during his visit.

Bowen May was next in the witness box. He began by saying how he, too, had first met Agnes then later helped her when she had had an accident out hunting with Her Majesty's Staghounds. Soon afterwards he had become her solicitor. He then explained the circumstances leading up to the marriage settlement, incidentally contradicting his claim in the December contempt hearing that he had not known Windham was under age. But Bowen May was careful to maintain his previous account by saying it was not until 20 August that the issue of marriage had been 'seriously discussed'. The solicitor then explained the various proposals and counter-proposals which led to the draft marriage settlement. Windham had always talked sensibly during the times they had discussed legal and estate matters, he added.

Bowen May repeated his claim made in the December proceedings that he was unaware of orders made by the Court of Chancery. He also defended the appointment of Roberts as a trustee, saying he was worth £5,000 and was a man of 'honour and talent'. The settlement was what Windham had wanted. After all, he told the court, had not the heir of Felbrigg told him unequivocally: 'I have no friends or relations on earth that I care for; all my property must go to my wife; why, therefore should I refuse her £1,500 a year?'.

Friday 17 January (Day Twenty-Six) started with the exasperated Master asking Karslake the question all present wanted to know: when, exactly, would he finish his case? Instead of giving him a straight answer, Karslake said he would not hazard a guess because 'the public journals' had implied he had deceived the court about the matter. The Times, in its report of that day's proceedings, was having none of that. Karslake, it said, had 'ludicrously misconstrued a very harmless and inoffensive, but at the same time, a very true remark'.

Could it be, the paper suggested, that it was down to his temper being 'chafed and irritated' by the conduct and interruptions of his fellow lawyers? Perhaps. But all parties to the proceedings - Master Warren, the jurymen, the defence and the petitioners' counsel and, yes, the court reporters - could be held to be equally short-tempered. Ironically, another interruption by one of those learned friends - the indomitable Sir Hugh - was exactly what happened next. He argued, again, for Windham to be examined in public. And again, he was refused.

It was time for the court to hear from another witness, Mr Martin, lately bailiff at Felbrigg and one of the estate's most loyal servants. Not surprisingly, his evidence echoed closely that of his wife on 7 January. Windham had treated him with 'great kindness' but that had not stopped Martin from chastising Windham for his interest in Agnes and attempting to dissuade him from marriage. Despite their disagreement, and the Martins' refusal to have anything to do with the new Mrs Windham, William himself had remained on cordial terms with his tenants. Then it was back to more bad-tempered exchanges between the counsel.

The spark was the examination of Theodore Giubilei, Lady Sophia's young husband, which began routinely enough but soon produced a startling revelation. Giubilei told the solicitor Milward that he had first met Windham in April 1858, and in his dealings with the young heir had found him a person of sound mind, if rather over-indulged by Lady Sophia. He produced several letters which Windham had written to his mother, and also said he had had many conversations with the General and fellow guardian Hook over Windham.

This prompted Milward to ask: 'What did General Windham and Mr Hook say to you about Mr Windham?'

Chambers, inevitably, rose to object, supported by the Master who said he had no wish to deal with 'collateral matters' such as this, otherwise the inquiry could go on for another 12 months. Chambers then cross-examined the witness, who repeated his belief that Windham was of sound mind. It was at this point that Chambers arguably blundered.

He asked: 'Are you aware that at one time Lady Sophia proposed to join in this petition?', with the clear inference that Windham's own mother was unsure of his competence. But Giubilei's reply must have startled him.

'No, but General Windham offered Lady Sophia and myself two bribes to -'

Chambers interrupted - but not quickly enough - and repeated the question. 'I ask you again, Mr Giubilei, did you know that Lady Sophia proposed to concur in the petition?'

Karslake rose to object, and once again protested when Chambers asked the witness if he knew his wife had made an affidavit. Karslake said: 'I must say that when I have formally objected to the question, it is neither fair nor courteous to go on repeating it, and at the same time throw a triumphant glance at the jury.'

Giubilei said he, too, had warned Windham about Agnes, saying she was 'extremely extravagant'. Lady Sophia's counsel, Charles Russell, stood to say that his client 'does not concur with the proceedings; on the contrary, she disapproves them *(sic).*'

On the sour note of yet another courtroom display of bad temper, the hearing was adjourned until the following Monday.

ON SUNDAY 19 January Reynolds's Weekly News returned to the fray, with a hard-hitting editorial entitled 'The Inquisition in England'. It compared the way the Commission was being run to the methods of the dreaded ultra-Catholic tribunal. 'Never was a more atrocious injustice perpetrated - never a more diabolical injury inflicted - never was the sacred name of justice more libelled and belied,' it thundered. Estimating the cost of the still-unfinished hearing at £20,000, it argued: 'This young man is the victim of an abuse which is a scandal to the age in which we live, and a dark spot upon the national reputation.' It would have only taken 'a few pounds' to deal with the issue had the case been heard in another country. But in England matters were very different, it said. 'Mr Windham's position may be likened to that of the schoolboys who have to pay for the rods that scourge them.'

There was worse to come: 'Lawyers and barristers have pounced like hawks on their prey. They, like the Haymarket ladies, have found in young Windham a mine of wealth - a fat pigeon to be plucked... So much for cheap law and ready justice in England.' The criticisms it outlined would only continue to grow over the coming weeks.

14

20-29 January 1862:
'Frightful vice and wickedness'

'There is treason at work against Mr Windham.'
Karslake's speech for the defence, 22 January 1862

'Cruelly treated and wickedly aspersed.'
Coleridge on Agnes, 23 January 1862

DAY TWENTY-SEVEN - Monday 20 January - opened with evidence from one of Windham's former travelling companions, the Rev Devere, who had journeyed with the Norfolkman through North Wales and northern Britain for five weeks in the summer of 1858. He had put Windham's occasional boisterousness down to a lack of education. Then it was time for another medical man: Dr Sutherland, called in by Dr Neale to examine Windham on 6 November 1861.

As with the other examinations, his questioning had ranged over the young heir's financial affairs, marriage to Agnes and the affair of the timber. His conclusions were that Windham was not a congenital imbecile or had displayed idiocy. To modern eyes, his closely-argued conclusions are undermined by a belief in the discredited pseudo-science of 'phrenology' - behaviour inferred by the shape of the head. 'Imbeciles and idiots,' he asserted, 'have generally small misshapen heads, and in idiots I have remarked thick knuckles.' Windham had a larger head than the average; the state of his knuckles was not revealed.

Dr Conolly, who had also interviewed Windham several times, had concluded that his manner was 'perfectly cheerful, frank and gentlemanly' throughout. There was no evidence of insanity in his conversation, although the doctor was struck by Windham's 'somewhat hasty and impulsive character'. There were no foolish or fatuous remarks at any time. Dr Conolly's verdict was clear: 'No medical man could sign a certificate of insanity in his case,' he said simply. What Windham really needed in his life, he continued sympathetically, was 'one good, kind, virtuous friend'. If that was the case, then he 'would get through the world very well'. The present case showed the 'ill-effects of improper treatment and neglect in youth'.

Bowen May was then recalled by Chambers to explain more about the other documents he had prepared for Windham - the disentailing deed and the terms of the (now-destroyed) will. The solicitor said he told Windham he had 'done perfectly right' to tear up the latter document when his wife had left him. There were two more items to note: Karslake at last indicated that the evidence for Windham would be concluded the following day, and also that Roberts had 'commenced proceedings' against a solicitor for the petitioners, Mr Field, for certain 'words spoken'.

DAY TWENTY-EIGHT - Tuesday 21 January - saw Karslake at last begin his closing speech. But first the court heard from Lady Sophia's representative, Russell. His client, he said, had no interest in the case 'apart from the interests of her son'. He repeated his statement of the previous day that Lady Sophia had not 'concurred' with proceedings. 'On the contrary, all her sympathies, interests and wishes were with her son. It would be unnatural indeed for a mother, except upon the clearest grounds, and for the most incontestable reasons, to assist in branding her own child with the stamp of mental incapacity,' he said.

Russell went on to say that perhaps the only gratifying feature in the case was the 'deep and earnest affection' which Windham has shown for his mother. Lady Sophia regretted and grieved over the faults which undoubtedly had 'stained his youth' - which was as close as she got to admitting she had brought him up badly - 'but those features of the case had been greatly softened by the evidence for the defence'. The jury had the chance to give the verdict to her son, which would 'give him an opportunity of retrieving the follies of his youth, the follies of a raw, riotous, unrestrained and untutored youth and of playing a part, although not conspicuous by great deeds, might not be altogether unworthy of the name which he bore and of the social position into which he was born'.

It was time for Karslake to speak. There was none of Russell's flowery style here; instead, there was what he did best - a sober dissection of the evidence. Whatever the verdict, he said, Windham would be saddled with a debt of between £15,000 to £20,000, 'and for that enormous burden he would have to thank the petitioners'. All they cared about was the property, and to deprive Windham of it. Of course, Windham had, he admitted, created his own problems through his own actions. Even in contracting his marriage, he said, Windham had done an act which was 'calculated to disgust society'. Despite all that, however, the key to the case was most of the petitioners' refusal to back up their claims in open court. With that, 'the case ought to at once have been brought to an end'.

Chief among them, of course, was the General. Karslake said that 'no doubt' he should hear some specious reasons from Chambers for not calling him and the other petitioners to the witness box. But there was no reason which could remove the impression that Windham's accusers had acted 'incautiously and unfairly'. The petitioners had the right to institute proceedings - despite the cost to Windham and the resulting exposure to 'the public gaze every folly and vice of his early years' - but they had not done so in a fair-minded way. They had been guilty of the 'deliberate concealment of evidence' which did not suit their purpose, such as the well-attested character of Windham's father, or the evidence of the Martins.

There were two pictures which had been drawn of Windham, but only one could be true, he said. Chambers' case was that Windham was a 'congenital imbecile, continually slavering at the mouth, talking incoherently and screeching and howling like a madman'. But two doctors and one of the petitioners (Lord Alfred) had 'utterly wiped that up', he said. The issue at hand was not whether Windham had 'done many foolish and objectionable things', but whether the acts and events which had been proved in evidence were the clear and indisputable result of insanity.

Karslake admitted Windham had clear faults of character, but they could be attributed to his upbringing. The much-quoted Eton nickname of 'Mad' could be completely explained by Windham's 'somewhat riotous and boisterous' manners. And if Windham had been such a 'wild beast' as was claimed, then would he have been allowed to stay on so long at Eton, or have 'gentlemen of education, ability and position to live and travel with him'? Other witnesses had testified to Windham's ability to handle business matters, show a reasonable level of intelligence, discharge responsibilities and even demonstrate a suitability as a prospective bridegroom. The way that Windham was treated by his gentleman neighbours should completely negate the 'flimsy and worthless' claims about him by people of lesser status, Karslake insisted.

He then turned to the Llewellyns. It had been 'an evil hour' when Windham went to lodge with them. The couple had painted a picture of Windham as being 'more like a wild beast than a human being'. But he added, 'could anyone doubt that the Llewellyns were mere creatures of General Windham?' The General, he added, was no more than a 'carpet knight' if he made affidavits behind closed doors but refused to repeat them in open court. It demonstrated nothing but 'a moral cowardice almost unexampled'. The General's witnesses were 'hired and perjured' while he 'meanly skulked and hid himself in the seat beside his counsel'. And this was the man, Karslake continued, who had treated his nephew as sane and competent enough to want to sell him a property and who later went out on Christmas morning to the house of a witness to try to bolster his flagging case. He had proved himself 'craven, recreant, and coward'. Karslake was warming to his subject when the inquiry was adjourned once more.

RESUMING THE following morning, Karslake returned immediately to the attack on the Llewellyns, the de facto chief witnesses for the petitioners. No reliance, he said, could be placed on what they said. Why had the petitioners not found the Llewellyns' former servants who could back their claims? The defence had found some easily enough - and quickly discovered how the Llewellyns had distorted the truth. Worse, Mrs Llewellyn had tried to suborn one of them (Mrs Pritchard) to support her 'disgusting' story. 'The greatest misfortune that had ever happened to young Mr Windham was having gone to live at the house of the Llewellyns,' he added. David Llewellyn, Karslake said, had shown himself 'coarse and brutal'.

As for the evidence, 'Gentlemen of the jury, you may believe Eliza Dignam, or you may not, but I maintain that she is a ten thousand times better witness than either her sister or her "respectable" brother-in-law, who tried to cheat her out of the miserable pittance of £30.' 'The acts of the Llewellyns,' he went on, 'are a complete answer to their words, whether true or untrue. Is it likely that the Llewellyns, having had experience of Mr Windham in their house for one month, believing him to be a noisy, filthy, howling lunatic and imbecile, would have disregarded their own interests... to let him keep apartments for a whole year?' Windham had been accused of keeping 'low company', Karslake added, and the greatest example of that was when he consorted with the 'respectable David Llewellyn'.

Next, the policemen's evidence. Karslake dismissed it as 'utterly trivial and unimportant', before returning to the second of his two main targets: the General. That meeting at Felbrigg Hall would, if Windham had accepted the 'bargain', have deprived the new master of the power of disposing of his property. 'Still later the same General Windham bargained and negotiated with his nephew for his own advantage, and yet he now alleges, and attempts with hired and prejudiced witnesses to prove, that from his infancy upwards his kinsman was a lunatic and an imbecile, incapable of managing himself or his own affairs,' he added.

It was now time to consider the 'unfortunate' marriage. 'If every man who made a similar marriage is to be placed in a lunatic asylum, then the sooner lunatic asylums are enlarged, the better,' he said. Was it any wonder, he asked, that Miss Willoughby and her 'great personal attractions' should have proved irresistible to a young man on whom his relations had turned their backs? The discussions about the marriage settlement showed Windham was 'enamoured' of Agnes but also that he could carry them out in a business-like way.

As for the charge of Windham having infected his wife with a 'particular disease', there were three points to be made. Firstly, 'many a married man' had done exactly the same thing; secondly, Windham had no evidence he was infected when he got married; and thirdly, it had led him to incur a 'heavy debt' with the jeweller and also to overlook much of Agnes' subsequent behaviour. Karslake's comments about married men and venereal disease appear startlingly casual, indeed outrageous, to modern eyes, but Karslake was pointing out a reality of Victorian life. Between 1858 and 1901 almost 20 per cent of divorce petitions were on these grounds. Blame for this state of affairs usually devolved entirely on females, leading to notorious social legislation such as the Contagious Diseases Acts from 1860s onwards, which rendered women - any women - in the neighbourhood of barracks or naval bases liable to be forcibly examined for infection.

MEANWHILE, Karslake turned to the character of Roberts. The jury should dismiss such discussions about the subject, the QC said, as until very recently Windham was unaware of the accusations being made about his associate. They should, however, take notice of the many tradesmen and servants who had testified to Windham's 'sense, prudence and intelligence' in his business affairs.

It was the affair of the timber contract which 'in all probability' finally induced his uncle to apply for a commission of lunacy. But Windham's circumstances were such that a supply of money was 'absolutely necessary', 'for it is a remarkable fact that he, the heir of a property which in 1869 would realise a rental of between £12,000 and £15,000, ended his minority without a single shilling of his own in his pocket'. There were only two ways of raising money: borrow against the estate, or sell the timber. Windham had chosen the latter, and the terms of the contract were 'fair and reasonable'.

The result of the contract was that the General had then begun to secretly gather information for his petition, 'concocting his scheme, and preparing those blunted weapons which he has not ventured to wield in open court'.

'Mr Windham thenceforth was followed by spies and informers, his every action was watched and scanned, and the grossest treason was practised on him by persons who pretended to be his friends,' he added. Dr Winslow's questioning of Windham had been objectionable, claimed Karslake, with the doctor dwelling on 'filthy and frivolous' claims and not talking to him as he would have done with any other gentleman.

Karslake the forensic questioner had by now been replaced by Karslake the passionate advocate against injustice. 'The doctrine of the petitioners was monstrous,' he raged - 'moral lunacy' was an utterly discredited concept. If Windham was a lunatic for being profligate, then what about a man who separated from his wife for the company of a 'rouged and shameless courtesan'? Or one who had sold his daughter to some 'hoary lecher'? 'If profligacy and vice is insanity, the Divorce Court ought to be abolished, and lunatic asylums built for adulterers and adulteresses,' he said.

'There is treason at work against Mr Windham. His steps have been dogged for months, his confidential agents have been canvassed, and everything filthy and foul has been raked up against him.' The jury should beware of Dr Winslow's 'bait' in which he suggested Windham should be placed under surveillance for several years. If they agreed to that, Karslake said, 'they may depend upon it that the object... is to immure Mr Windham in a madhouse for life. Let General Windham once get his nephew within his clutches, and he will take care that the estates are secured to his own family,' with the rest of the spoils divided up among the other petitioners.

The jury needed to reflect on their own youthful follies or even vices which they might have committed and which they now deplored. 'Is it not the part of a friend rather to cover with a veil the foibles of early life than to expose them to a curious and gaping public?,' he argued. 'I am certain that I shall not appeal to them [ie the jury] in vain to draw the line between folly and insanity, and between profligacy... and unsoundness of mind.

'On behalf of Mr Windham I have no necessity to appeal for mercy. I ask simply for justice; and, if I can judge of the effect which the evidence will produce upon you, I think I may safely predict that your unanimous verdict will be that Mr Windham is of sound mind, and ought not be to be deprived of his liberty, which is dearer to him than life itself,' he concluded.

And then Karslake sat down, the applause perhaps not as enthusiastic as it had been after Sir Hugh's speech - but encouraging enough.

THE THIRTIETH day of the inquiry (Thursday 23 January) was mostly taken up with the speech of Agnes' counsel Coleridge. Although in the eyes of polite mid-Victorian society he was attempting to defend the indefensible, he tried hard to do exactly that.

Over the previous month, he began, almost every day had seen 'obloquy and invective, insult and reproach... heaped upon Mrs Windham' by Chambers. It was time to redress the balance, and try to deal with the 'mountain of prejudice' against a woman who had been 'cruelly treated and wickedly aspersed'.

Mrs Windham was a vital part of the petitioners' case, which is why 'her character, her marriage, her settlement, her whole life' were under scrutiny. Coleridge stressed - and here was polite society quickly re-asserting itself - 'I can say with the utmost sincerity that I should be sorry if such a marriage could be regarded with favour or approval'. He had no time for 'sanctimonious hypocrites' who pretended to be horrified at the situation, but he was 'heart and soul' with those pure and moral people who detested 'impurity and vice'.

The counsel reminded the jury that he had expressed his determination to be present at every examination of Windham which might take place, to counter the 'disgusting and filthy stories' which had been told about the couple and ensure the inevitable 'strong feelings and almost horror' against them did not obscure the aims of justice. Windham, after all, remained 'deeply attached' to the woman who was still legally his wife. No, persons of 'common human feeling' should instead feel pity - 'or at least forbearance' - for the situation.

'Everything prized by Mrs Windham is at stake,' he said. 'Her marriage, her settlement, her position, her prospects in life, the welfare of those two sisters of which we have heard so much... all hang upon the verdict the jury may give.' Not directly, he admitted, but indirectly, as it would add huge weight to any subsequent case to have the marriage annulled.

The petitioners' aim had been to 'get rid' of the marriage, he said. Like Karslake, he claimed that if the 9 August meeting had been a success then the inquiry would never had happened. But it was Windham's marriage which ensured it would. 'The marriage, from the beginning to the end, has been treated as the crowning act of his insanity, and in consequence, no imputation has been too gross, no sneer has been too bitter, no story has been too filthy for Mr Chambers to bring forward in the hope of aspersing and crushing Mrs Windham, and with Mrs Windham her husband.'

Like Karslake, Coleridge took Windham's supposedly caring relations to task for his upbringing. 'From the cradle to the age of 21 years, utterly neglected by all his family, with a set of second-rate tutors about him who did not understand and were incapable of dealing with their pupil, allowed to come up to London and to run loose about the streets uncontrolled by those attached relatives who, when he went to the devil, flew at him and attacked him with a charge of insanity,' he said, 'Such was the position of this unhappy gentleman in the bosom of his affectionate family when he married Agnes Willoughby.'

Windham was 'a young man of affectionate disposition' who was ill-at-ease with young ladies of rank but who was keen to marry and retire to the country with his bride. Agnes, in contrast 'was not yet 22 years of age [in fact she was still 20 when she met Windham]; she was a very pretty and attractive person; she had ladylike manners; she was a celebrity in certain circles in London'. Windham was not the first ('or the last') person who had been 'fascinated' by Agnes Willoughby. Coleridge even compared Agnes' attractiveness with that of Helen of Troy. 'For the pleasure of making a beautiful woman his wife many a man would cheerfully sacrifice all his possessions, and brave the censures of his kind.' From classical whimsy he came back to the realities of the real world. Mrs Windham, it had been alleged, was 'not merely a beautiful woman; she was a shameless prostitute, a person common to the whole town'. This claim Coleridge 'utterly denied'.

Much had been made, he continued, of the 'mercantile and mercenary way' Agnes set about obtaining her marriage settlement. Some might see that as evidence of 'low morality' on her part, but the fact remained that by marrying Windham Agnes was, in fact, making a 'considerable sacrifice'. Her affection for him was 'not strong', she had her oft-quoted allowance of £2,000 a year, and 'occupied a high position in her own circle'. She had accepted Windham because she wanted 'an accredited position in society and to secure the interests of her sisters'.

It was 'ridiculous hypocrisy', Coleridge added, to damn the marriage for the way the settlement had been negotiated. 'Half the marriages of our aristocracy are made for no better motive,' he said. Besides, not a single Windham or Hervey family member had told Agnes that the young squire was 'utterly unfit' to contract marriage because of unsoundness of mind. Since the marriage there had been no sparing of breaches in professional confidences, abuse of hospitality or plain treachery in trying to gather evidence against the young couple, he said.

Coleridge then turned his attention to the General with phrases even more ringing than Karslake had managed. 'Oh, good, kind, considerate, generous General Windham, the gallant officer, high-minded gentleman, tender guardian, affectionate uncle! See him at Felbrigg, introduced to its charming mistress, sitting in a very cosy armchair at a warm October fire, sipping his wine and munching his biscuit, but all the while keeping both his eyes wide open for evidence against his nephew or his niece!' No jury, he continued, would commit such a 'black and base infamy' as to 'find a man mad in order to set aside a marriage which was disapproved, and to get rid of a settlement which was disliked.' The enormous cost of the inquiry was 'lesson enough for the sins' committed by the couple.

CHAMBERS' REPLY - reported approvingly and at length by the Norwich Mercury - began with almost a note of self-pity, as the counsel complained of his 'life of struggles' which now included the 'difficult, trying and fatiguing duty' of the current case. He had listened to the speeches of Sir Hugh, Karslake and Coleridge 'with admiration' but said they had tried to mislead the jury. Chambers said he had given a great deal of study to the legal background to the lunacy laws (with the clear implication that his 'learned friends' were perhaps not quite as 'learned' as they ought to be).

There was an important case in 1802, involving an epileptic who was found capable by a jury. An appeal was made to Lord Chancellor Eldon and, crucially, he held that the jury should not simply have looked at the narrow question of lunacy. That, said Chambers, was a doctrine that had 'never been shaken' since. It was not a question of medical lunacy, but the much wider issue of whether the person involved could take 'ordinary care' of himself and his property. 'In that large circle we may wander,' he said. Other cases since had been 'sound and clear' on the subject. Sir Hugh had claimed, said Chambers, that the Windham case was 'unparalleled and unprecedented'. But it was his contention that there were many features which had appeared in previous cases, especially that of Lord Portsmouth several decades earlier.

There was one more issue he wished to raise. Sir Hugh Cairns had painted a picture of the 'horrible' state of those found lunatic. But, said Chambers, 'we have done with the cell; we have done with the straw; we have done with the shackle; and we have done with the straight waistcoat.' Lord Portsmouth, for example, was 'placed in his own house with kind friends' who kept him away from the 'harpies' - pausing for the parallels with Agnes to sink in - which surrounded him. Chambers said he was speaking not just to the jury but to the public about these matters, as he was keen to rid them of the 'fallacies and misrepresentations' they had fallen prey to.

The counsel then took the court through a long account of various medical authorities who had agreed that a definition of lunacy could also apply to cases of incompetence. As well as the Portsmouth case, he said, there were also clear parallels with the Bagster case in which a newly-married heiress had been found to be of weak mind. And another thing: the other counsel had been most unfair, he added, in their treatment of those who had brought the case to court.

'I have not the slightest hesitation in telling you that three or four hours have been employed in vilifying, in the most virulent style, General Windham and the other petitioners.' Karslake, even though he was a 'young man' (he was 40) 'should have known better'. If the General - who had been branded a 'slink', 'moral coward' and 'carpet knight' - had been called, he said, he would have had to endure 'worry and torment' in the witness box designed to deflect the jury's attention from the real issues. And was that a fitting reward for a man who had won his fame on the battlefield and who had 'never shrunk in the hour of danger or of trial'?

After briefly considering the evidence of Windham's physical abnormality - his mouth - which Chambers considered linked to a weakness of mind, counsel turned to the claims that Windham's education and upbringing had been badly handled. 'Untrue' claimed Chambers: 'No young man ever had more care and anxiety bestowed upon him', he said, but Windham had been 'barren soil' for all attempts to cultivate his intelligence. All the accounts of his childhood had shown his mind was still 'infantile', even aged 19, and had the habits of a child 'even when arrived at man's estate'.

ON 24 JANUARY Roberts broke his silence with a letter to The Times. He complained that he had been 'fearfully calumniated' during the case. He had demanded to be called as a witness, but to no avail. 'I have done nothing but endeavour to aid Mr Windham,' he insisted. Roberts

Detailed: Montague Chambers relied heavily on arcane case law to back up his arguments, an approach which, though technically justified, did little to win public support for the petitioners' case. *(NRO ref: MC580/1, 780x1)*

claimed he had never wanted to be Agnes' trustee and had had his name 'blackened' because he dared to 'thwart' General Windham. 'Had it not been for me, young Windham would have been now safely locked up in an   asylum,' he added. As for the claim he had immoral sources of wealth, 'I pledge my sacred word that I have not only never been an owner of brothels, but that I have not entered one for many years'. The already-notorious locked carriage incident was not as it seemed: 'the state in which Mrs Windham was when I unfortunately accompanied her in a railway carriage with a locked door does away with any motive on my part, could I have been base enough to follow the course inferred'. It was not the most convincing of explanations.

CHAMBERS RESUMED his speech on Monday 27 January (Day Thirty-One) by quoting the medical experts. His conclusion was straightforward and 'there was no absolute contradiction or inconsistency' in it. 'Dr Tuke has admitted that if Mr Windham had settled the whole of his property upon his wife he would have regarded him as an imbecile,' Chambers told the jury. 'Why, Mr Windham has given away more than the whole of his property, and therefore, according to his own scientific witness, is incompetent to manage himself and his own affairs.'

He turned to the notorious placard, describing it as an 'outrageous document' which showed Windham was acting under the 'control and dominion' of Roberts, and therefore needed protection. Dr Sutherland's evidence, he continued, ignored the 'middle ground' between idiocy and lunacy, and therefore should be ignored in turn. Windham had told Dr Winslow he knew that on the eve of his marriage his wife-to-be - 'the immaculate Miss Willoughby' - had slept in the same house as a former paramour. 'Such was his inexpressible idiocy that he led his bride to the altar hot from a bed of lewdness and vice,' he said. Dr Winslow's evidence established beyond doubt that Windham was incapable, he said, in fact most of the evidence given by witnesses on behalf of Windham actually corroborated the petitioners' claims.

Howlett the ironmonger had revealed that Windham had frequently visited the Haymarket since the start of the inquiry, showing he was 'utterly unconscious of the pinch of the case and the lamentable position in which he is placed'. With an accuracy he was as yet unaware, the QC said the absence of Lady Sophia and her solicitor indicated 'pretty clearly' what their true feelings were about her son's mental state. The evidence of the petitioners, Chambers insisted, had been 'credible, consistent and conclusive' throughout. 'The witnesses for the petition have been subjected to every species of vituperation, but I cannot help thinking that the case which requires to be supported by such language as that used by Sir Hugh Cairns, Mr Coleridge, and Mr Karslake, must be a desperate and hopeless one,' he said. Coleridge, especially, had spoken of the aristocracy as if they were 'the most despicable race in England'.

Chambers' feelings had been clearly hurt by the criticism directed his way, as he concluded his speech for the day by referring to its 'unsparing and virulent language'. 'A great equity lawyer has accused me of conducting this inquiry as if it were a case of petty larceny; but I can bear such twits [taunts] as these, because I attend here as an independent man, owing nothing to favour, and because, although I have been engaged in [such] cases... I have never been driven in pure desperation to make an unwarrantable attack upon those opposed to me,' he said.

THAT THE pressure was beginning to tell on Chambers was shown by a bizarreincident at the start of Day Thirty-Two (Tuesday 28 January) when, in the

Daily News' words, 'an exciting scene occurred in court'. Chambers, 'with a face flushed in anger and with a very energetic action, exclaimed: "I would rather the gentleman opposite to me should be removed. He has been grinning from ear to ear at me with a sort of contemptuous discredit. His time will come - his time will come when I speak of the marriage."' Dr Gwyn, the subject of Chambers' anger 'appeared petrified' by the outburst. The Master said a member of the jury had also raised the matter of Gwyn laughing during Chambers' speech, and he ordered him to move seats.

Chambers began by defending the doctors Nichol and Dalrymple. 'To assail such men with scorn and ridicule may be very clever, but it is an unmistakeable symptom of a desperate and hopeless case,' he claimed. He reviewed the evidence for the   petitioners, speaking for example of the 'careful and measured' answers of Colonel Bathurst in describing Windham's 'sudden and violent' behaviour, while Karslake had made an 'inhuman attack' on Mrs Wilkinson ('a lady of education and elegant manners') by implying she was trying to secure Windham for her daughter Clara while at Spa.

The meeting at Felbrigg had been 'twisted' into an attempt by General Windham and the rest of the family to benefit themselves at the expense of an idiot. 'Nothing of the kind,' Chambers insisted. The General had in fact tried to 'keep him in the right path and protect his property' at the meeting. 'It was true, then, that General Windham tried to treat his nephew as a rational agent... but it was equally true that he might as well have hammered at the head of a rhinoceros as attempted to make the plainest matter intelligible to his unfortunate and afflicted nephew,' he said. General Windham's sole interest, he added, was in making sure the estate would continue in the family in the event of his nephew dying without issue.

Windham - 'who, since he came of age has enjoyed the services of no fewer than seven attorneys, itself a proof of weakness of mind' - had now disentailed Felbrigg, which 'at any moment might fall into the clutches of the bad persons by whom he is surrounded'.

The evidence of the Llewellyns, he contended, was 'substantially true', despite the efforts of the other side to discredit them, while 'only a born idiot' would have allowed Roberts to travel with his wife in a locked carriage. In fact, the whole of his conduct on the railways was 'utterly inconsistent' with soundness of mind, and had endangered the lives of hundreds of passengers.

WEDNESDAY 29 JANUARY (Day Thirty-Three) saw the final part of Chambers' speech. He had saved the greatest expression of umbrage until last: the subject of the marriage. 'A marriage,' he said, 'in which a bridegroom was not taken to the altar, but a victim led to the slaughter'. Agnes had treated him like a child 'and the poor idiot had believed every word' she told him. The marriage settlement had seen Windham - 'this poor half-witted child' - settle on her 'an amount of money so extravagantly large... that no reasonable being could ever have dreamt of entering into such an engagement'.

Chambers attacked the conduct of Bowen May, and maintained that Agnes was fully aware of Windham's medical state before they married. In any case, 'the poor child was persuaded that he had inflicted a severe injury upon his wife,' buying her thousands of pounds of jewellery to compensate. But, Chambers inferred, it was all a lie: 'I doubt whether she had ever sustained such an injury.'

The marriage ceremony itself had been a 'desecration' of the institution, and Chambers poured scorn on the events that followed. By October, Windham had managed to get through all but £17 of a bank account which had stood at £1,098 only a few weeks earlier. Windham, he declared, 'was chained to corruption of the vilest kind, and would continue in that condition unless they declared him to be entitled to the protection of the law'.

If Windham were to be declared sane, then Felbrigg Hall would 'speedily pass from his possession. The ugly birds would fly into the portals of the ancient mansion, and Mr Windham would be turned adrift, a beggar and an outcast'. He reminded the jury of Dr Tuke's prediction that if Windham did not change his ways he would either end up in a lunatic asylum or would kill himself within five years.

'Mr Windham, therefore, must be saved, and saved, too, from ruin of health and character, from disease, from wretchedness of life, from disgrace, from scorn, from repulsion from the doors of his own wife living in luxury upon her £800 or £1,500 a year,' he concluded. 'From evils worse than death itself he can be saved only through the intervention of those relatives who have come forward, in spite of evil report and gross abuse, for the purpose of discharging a disagreeable duty, by the interposition of the law of the land, and by the verdict of a jury of his countrymen.' And with that, Chambers sat down.

Although the Norwich Mercury, inevitably, approved of Chambers' words, quoting them at vast length, the fact was that it was a weak speech. Wandering in delivery, it was high on rhetoric and medical jurisprudence and low on cohesive argument or passion. Chambers' avowed aim had been to speak beyond the courtroom, out to the opinion-formers in the wider public. But there were no ringing phrases about injustice or liberty to fire the consciences of his audience.

And there was nothing in return: when Chambers sat down, it was to silence.

THEN CAME the moment Master Warren must have willed to happen over many long winter's days: the summing-up. He was brief, and to the point. The case, he said, had been 'important, difficult and unprecedented'. It was the jury's duty to deal with it 'calmly and dispassionately'. If the public had felt 'irritable and impatient' with the daily reports, and shocked by their contents, then they should spare a thought for the jury and himself who had been forced to sit and hear them every day. Warren - with a clear dig at those who had complained at the slow progress of the inquiry - insisted it had been conducted with 'exemplary regularity and with a rigorous adherence to the law of the land'. The only question the jury had to consider was whether, according to the Lunacy Regulation Act, Windham satisfied its definition of a person who was found to be an idiot, a lunatic or of unsound mind.

The inquiry had begun with a 'mass of facts of a very grave nature' from Mr Chambers, and if the defence had applied for an interview to be made with Mr Windham there and then, he would have given 'very serious consideration' to the request. Sir Hugh had made no such request but instead had made a 'speech of uncommon brilliancy' and then called a 'great mass' of evidence. The inquiry had now extended over 33 days; 50 witnesses had been called for the petitioners, and 90 against them.

'I have taken 600 pages of closely-written notes, which I will go over, if you request,' he said, the papers reporting, with delicious understatement, that 'several of the jury intimated that this lengthy proceeding on the part of the learned master was quite unnecessary'.

The jury, he said, should not concern themselves with the validity of any of the acts of Windham - the marriage settlement, the timber contract, or anything else - or the motives and conduct of the petitioners, for that matter. The conduct of General Windham had been subjected to 'severe censure', but the Master would be excluding all evidence about it. The jury had to satisfy itself that Windham was incapable of governing himself because of unsoundness of mind; weakness of character, vice, extravagance, eccentricity and the like would not prove that by themselves.

The medical evidence had been conflicting - not unusual in lunacy cases - and members of the jury should make their own judgements. The jury should not apply 'too high a standard' to Windham. If he were deemed able to take care of himself and his property, that would be enough. Windham's letters, he added - and what they revealed about the young squire's competence - were deserving of the 'most serious attention'. The evidence of the Llewellyns had been largely corroborated by other witnesses, but it was the jury's decision to judge if perjury had been committed.

The jury was not considering the validity of the 'imprudent' marriage, so there was no need for it to dwell on the 'unutterably disgusting evidence' which had been laid before them. They were not there to read moral lessons to Windham, or anyone else, although there had clearly been 'frightful vice and wickedness' involved. The timber contract, too, was only relevant if the jury thought it so absurd and destructive that no man in his right senses could have entered into it.

He concluded by repeating his instruction to the jury to look at the case 'broadly and steadily', to discard 'incredible or irrelevant' evidence, and to give their verdict 'firmly and conscientiously'. And with those words, Master Warren declared the day's proceedings adjourned. Tomorrow would see, at long last, the dénouement of the astonishing inquiry.

15

1862:
A Hollow Victory

'If he had been a poor man, would there have been
such difficulty in this case?'
News of the World, 2 February 1862

AT LAST, on its 34th day, after numerous witnesses and hundreds of thousands of
words of evidence, the final hours of the Windham lunacy drama were played out in the
cramped Westminster Sessions House. The proceedings were scheduled to begin - in
private - at 11am. Chambers arrived in his everyday clothes, but Sir Hugh and Karslake
maintained court decorum to the last by appearing in their robes. Even now there was
one final display of the long series of bad-tempered objections and protests by counsel.
Sir Hugh rose to ask, for the last time, that Windham's examination should be carried
out in public. He was overruled by Master Warren, who 'recorded his protest' and told
him he was merely following legal precedent. Sir Hugh, temporarily nonplussed (or
with the show of it), sat down, muttering curtly that precedent had nothing to do with
the current case.

Soon after 11am the public and press were ordered to leave the court, while the jury,
at last, had the chance to quiz the young man whose fate had sparked this bizarre

inquiry. After the questioning, which took place under the watchful eyes of the counsel for both sides, the jury retired to consider its verdict. Windham, meanwhile, seemed utterly relaxed, laughing and chatting with Sir Hugh and his solicitors 'as if he had no concern in the result'. The jury had only been away for just over half an hour before sending a message to Warren that it had reached a verdict.

After the jurors had filed back into the room around 3.25pm, before a crowded yet hushed court, the coup-de-grace to the Commission in Lunacy upon Mr W F Windham was made.

'Are there twelve of you, gentlemen, agreed upon a verdict?' the Master asked, in time-honoured form.

There was, foreman Sir George Armitage replied - Lloyd's Weekly London Newspaper reporting, 'Every word of the verdict as it dropped slowly from the lips of the foreman of the jury was listened to with breathless attention by a fascinated crowd.

'It is,' he continued, 'that the said Mr W F Windham, at the time of taking this inquisition, was a person of sound mind, so as to be sufficient for the government of himself, his manors, his messuages, his tenements, his lands, his goods and his chattels.'

As soon as the final words had been uttered, the public gallery erupted into wild and loud cheering, 'the like of which has seldom been heard in a court of justice'. Master Warren in his final and, as with most of the others, utterly futile attempt to restore order was met with a final cheer 'louder and more deafening than any that had preceded it [making] the Westminster Sessions House ring like an alehouse'.

Suddenly everyone wanted to shake Windham's hand and congratulate him. As he took their good wishes, his face glowed with pleasure. After Windham had thanked Sir George and his fellow jury members for their verdict, he was swept along with the crowd outside the Sessions House. There, an even larger gathering waited to cheer him, and he was almost carried bodily to his cab, 'in which he drove away amid a thundering cheer'.

Meanwhile, back in the almost empty courtroom, Master Warren formally thanked the jury for the 'admirable manner' they had discharged their duties. Then he rose, and collecting his notes, walked from the courtroom, ignored and unnoticed, at the end of a hearing stranger than anything he could possibly have imagined in his fiction.

THE DAILY NEWS greeted the verdict on 31 January with relief. 'The Windham case,' it said, 'has died of sheer exhaustion.' It had little sympathy for either side, the "friends" [its quotation marks] of Windham, who 'shrank from appearing in the witness box', and as for Windham himself, as 'the evidence of the first few days showed [him] as little better than a gorilla.'

'Young Windham,' it said, 'was a striking, but unhappily by no means rare example of the results of neglected education. Not that his parents and friends thought education a thing of no consequence' - he had had private tutors and a place at Eton - 'but the education which is of biggest value - the early influence of a well-ordered home, of parental example and authority, and of suitable companionship, advantages which children of the provident and conscientious artisan may have, he never enjoyed.' Instead, it said, 'his father seems to have treated him like a toy' and he eventually ended up 'buying the transitory compliance of a notorious woman'. All told, it had been a 'nauseating story'.

The Daily Telegraph, too, described the case as 'nauseating'. Windham was a 'fool, liar, brute and prodigal', but just as bad was the behaviour of the petitioners who decided to 'ravage stable and slum' for their evidence. 'Thank Heaven the miserable business is ended, and to the discomfiture of these unnatural accusers. We rejoice at their defeat, not, indeed, because we have any spark of sympathy for the depraved profligate whom they have persecuted, but because a sacred principle of English law has been asserted.' It concluded: 'Folly is bad, but it is not mad.'

It was a sentiment heartily agreed with by the Evening Standard, which too praised the verdict: 'The glorious right of every Englishman to fool himself to the top of his bent has been vindicated.' Windham had shown himself to be an 'ill-bred and extravagant young sinner', but - again echoing the Daily Telegraph - there was no sympathy for the petitioners. Their behaviour in trying to bring the 'spendthrift young rogue' to heel had had exactly the opposite effect to one they had intended, with the public detecting 'an apparently nefarious attempt to pervert the arm of the law into an instrument for furthering private interests'. This had created an 'unworthy feeling for the parties most responsible for Mr Windham's present degradation'.

Which led the paper to consider the role of Agnes. Even a country grown 'hardened to the disgusting details of the immorality of England in the nineteenth century' was shocked by Windham's marriage to 'this dashing young person, who - disinterested and self-sacrificing creature - immolates herself on the altar of matrimony to provide for her two sisters, obscures in the depths of infamy, in which it shows every agent in the vile transaction, even the darkest pictures of the Divorce Court.'

The News of the World ended its account of the hearing on 2 February with a pithy summing-up: 'So ended an inquiry unprecedented for its duration, for the scandalous waste of money which it has occasioned, and for the inexpressible filthiness of some of its details... the bill of costs must be something frightful.'

These were observations which the paper expanded in its editorial in the same issue.

The Windham case, which so largely occupied the public mind for upwards of a month, is at last concluded, and the verdict is returned which everybody anticipated long ago. Young Windham is found to be in a sane condition, and capable of managing his affairs; but the expense of finding this out has been terrific. If he had been a poor man, would there have been such difficulty in the case?'

The paper, passing over the 'sickening details of folly and vice' (having, naturally, spent most of the past few weeks reporting them), praised the dedication of the jury. The case, it continued, had exposed to public view an aspect of the higher echelons of society which was disturbing. 'The curtain has been roughly drawn aside from a part of society in high places, and the disclosure is so disgusting that we have a sense of relief that it is now dropped. There can be no sympathy for any of the parties.'

Fellow Sunday paper Reynold's Weekly Newspaper had no sympathy for the victor of the case, noting that 'his profligacy, his vulgarity, and his coarseness [and] the circumstances of his having married a dissolute prostitute have [not] created an impression in his favour.'

THE Penny Illustrated Paper spoke for many in its report on the verdict on 8 February: 'The decision of the jury excited great enthusiasm among the people in court and will unquestionably meet with the approval of the entire country'. Many, but not all. The case might have ended, but the recriminations began almost as the cheers died away.

The bad-tempered exchanges between the counsel who had 'abused and vilified one another in language rarely heard in courts of justice', as the Norwich Mercury had it, set the tone.

The much-maligned General fired the first shot in this particular campaign, publishing a letter he had sent to Vice-Chancellor Wood. The General wrote to the vice-chancellor for Sir William's opinion on the claims made in the inquiry about his conduct as Windham's uncle and guardian. 'When a man's personal honour is assailed, it becomes a duty, no less to himself than to his friends, to meet and repel the attack as publicly as it has been made,' he fumed. In his letter to the Vice-Chancellor, the General asked for his honest opinion on his conduct.

The General said he had had 'no desire to bandy words with professional gentlemen who have permitted themselves to be the instruments of calumniating me'; instead, he was asking Wood whether there was really any more he could have done to protect his nephew from 'the consequences of his fatal weakness' and any more urging, too, than he had already made for Windham to listen to the Vice-Chancellor's advice. Had he not, he asked, introduced his nephew to a 'most respectable London solicitor', John Jackson - 'a man wholly unconnected with myself' - that he might protect Windham's interests? Or that he had sought, with a sense of 'anxious forebodings', urgent advice from the Vice-Chancellor on what to do next?

Vice-Chancellor Wood had replied the next day. He had, he said, 'no hesitation' in answering the General's questions. On the issue of whether he done his duty as a guardian, Wood said that in this 'the most difficult case which I have ever met with of the numerous wards of Court', he said the General's solicitor had been extremely helpful while the General was in India in adding to the list of guardians. Lady Sophia, the other guardian appointed by the court, had agreed to the addition of Lord Alfred Hervey and Hook.

Everyone involved, he continued, had tried their utmost to help Windham. Sir William he recalled how the General had sent him letters from India asking for his help in securing an army commission for his nephew. A plan, alas, in vain 'owing to [Windham's] weakness of mind'. The General, on his return to England, and his fellow other guardians had shown a 'lively interest' in Windham's well-being. 'I can most conscientiously say that, in every respect, you evinced the highest interest in your ward's welfare,' the Vice-Chancellor added.

Turning to the question of what lay behind the General's actions, the Vice-Chancellor said that although, of course, he could not 'fathom any man's motives' and would be offering no opinion on the conduct of the inquiry itself, he had always regarded the inquiry as the 'natural sequel' of all the efforts made by Windham's guardians as a 'last attempt to save him from the result of his disastrous marriage'. In publishing the exchange of letters, the General told The Times and the Daily News that he had done so because his motives had been 'somewhat roughly handled' in the inquiry. And finally, he wanted to point out that the matter of the £1,000 land sale and his approach to Windham about it - something, of course, which the defence had made great play of - had been made 'as the best proof that I was not inclined to be unreasonably angry with his conduct'.

The Norwich Mercury had already rallied to his defence. In a wide-ranging editorial, it castigated Karslake for his attacks on the General, and said that the business of the land sale had clearly been 'an act of kindness' out of the highest motives, and should have been accepted as such by all sides. Unfortunately, 'in cases where an attack is carried beyond the limits of truth, rectitude, and justice, its power for evil is lost, except that it returns to plague the inventor; and the vehement malevolence which counsel has been instructed to pour on all will be, a few hours after it was spoken, if not forgotten, at least more cautiously weighed in the scales of justice, and found wanting.'

The newspaper continued at length in similar vein, but buried among the rhetoric were some telling points. It was all for the freedom of the press and open courts of justice, it said, but this inquiry showed there was a case for some closed hearings, particularly in this case, where 'nothing could be a greater outrage on the feelings and decency of society than this inquiry has offered, without conferring one atom of good.'

As for the victor of the case, 'Mr Windham is merely a puppet in the hands of others, who have struggled that they may secure, through a verdict, the payment of the debts he has contracted, and the engagements he has undertaken, and the property he has been induced to transfer.'

There was further support for the General over the land sale issue from one of the witnesses in the inquiry, Norfolk solicitor W Henry Scott, who wrote that he had been the one who advised Captain Windham (while his brother was still in India) that he ought to buy the land as it was so close to Felbrigg. Everything had been done with the soundest of motives and did not justify this 'heaviest of the wicked and unjust imputations on General Windham'. The Norfolk News, meanwhile, branded the commission 'a most painful, and in some respects, disgraceful trial' which had caused 'indignation and disgust in the public mind'. It continued: 'Everywhere the impression prevails that Windham is a foolish, reckless, abandoned, youth', and 'young Windham, his counsel tells us, is very much what "Old Windham" made him'.

This initial flurry of letters concluded with one from Windham's solicitors, Gregory and Co. They countered the General's claims with a line familiar from the inquiry: if he was so sure of the honour of his actions then why had he not allowed himself to be cross-examined in the witness box? And as for the affair of the land sale, well, that simply showed the double-standards inherent in the General's behaviour.

BUT FOR all this harrumphing about 'reputation', 'honour' and the 'scales of justice', the real issue to be settled was far more important: just who on earth was going to *pay* for it all?

For several weeks the issue of Windham's capability and incapability had become overtaken in more thoughtful quarters by concerns over the startling cost of the hearing. Estimates varied from £10,000, through Punch's claim in its issue of 1 February, in an item headed 'Diamonds from the Windham Mine', that it would reach £50,000, to The Times' estimate on 14 January ('on the most moderate computations') of an astonishing £60,000 - or almost £2.5 million in today's money. This was against an estimate made during the hearing that the whole of the Felbrigg estate was worth an absolute maximum of £90,000. And all this, of course, took no account of any subsequent court action.

The Norfolk News reported on 18 January that it was common knowledge in London about the huge fees being charged by the lawyers: both Chambers and Sir Hugh were on a case fee of 500 guineas, plus a 'refresher' of 50 guineas a day - and a ten-guinea 'consultation fee' each evening. Karslake was claiming a fee of 150 guineas, while it had been worked out that the cost of each witness was £110. The Penny Illustrated Paper of the same day had similar figures, and estimated the cost at £1,000 per day. An aside in the proceedings of Great Yarmouth Council on 28 January illustrated tellingly the public's perception of the escalating costs of the inquiry - and its inherent absurdity. A debate over how much to give to a national appeal for £2,000 for the families of Hartley Colliery disaster victims led to an aside from the mayor Robert Steward (himself a witness in the case) - to guffaws - that the cost of just 'two days on the Windham case' would settle the whole appeal.

PUNCH, in its first full comments on the verdict in its 8 February issue, went straight to the heart of the issue:

'A LUNATIC PROCEEDING.

'GENTLEMEN of the long robe, Punch will put a case.

'Supposing it be questioned (by an interested relative) if A. B. be mentally unfit to manage his own property what, then, is the proper cause to be pursued? Clearly, is it not to take away his property? And what so sure a way to do this as a law-suit, the costs thereof are so enormous that the property is certain to be swallowed up by them?

This is the course prescribed by the Wisdom of the Law, and no one but a lunatic would ever doubt its efficacy.'

Even more biting, in the same issue, was a spoof letter from an anonymous lawyer on the case. The correspondent had taken a 'great delight' that no pains had been spared in the making the trial 'as expensive as [it] possibly could be'. The calling of vast numbers of witnesses where one would have sufficed and the 'utter recklessness' of cost has 'afforded me the greatest satisfaction and delight'. It concluded: 'A man who spends his income chiefly on his lawyers is a wise, judicious, noble benefactor of the species, and could not possibly employ it to a better end.' Had he been one of Windham's many lawyers, he would have written a letter of thanks to the 'fat young bluebottle'.

Its final word was the following pithy epigram under the heading 'The Double Verdict':

'WINDHAM is sane; but England must be cracked/
To bear such process as hath fixed the fact.'

No wonder it also added, as a one-liner on another page, punning on London's clubs: 'The LAW'S NEXT MOVE. - (It is hoped.) - from the WINDHAM to the REFORM.' In early February, The Lancet revealed that the jury had been split-to-one over the verdict

- a fact which was made great play of in the subsequent appeal. Fortunately for Windham, according to the Norfolk News, the General and the other petitioners had by now decided to absorb their own costs. But that still left Windham's defence costs, estimated at £15,000, to be dealt with.

WHAT NOW for Windham? The News of the World, in its 2 February editorial, had concluded: 'Whether young Windham takes warning by the past, or heedlessly runs on in his old courses, involving himself thereby in utter ruin, is no concern of ours... it was his misfortune to be born with a silver spoon in his mouth; for if his lot had been cast in a humble station, he might have become a respected and respectable engine-driver or policeman.' The Daily News, too, had hopes Windham would learn from the inquiry: 'Mr Windham has been very unfortunate; he has committed some terrible mistakes and terribly has he been punished.' And the Daily Telegraph wondered: 'Does he drive off to spend more ancestral oaks upon harlots who loathe him - to confide again in the "tender mercies" of men who fleece and flout him?'

And while these weighty issues were being debated, what then of the victor of the inquiry? Windham proved to be the toast of the town, feted and - at least for a while - cheered wherever he went, his 'Dutch-cheese head and united eyebrows' making him easily recognisable. But after a few days he returned to Norfolk, where he resumed his penchant for driving recklessly. At 6pm on 9 February he caused consternation in Norwich's busy Magdalen Street by crashing his coach-and-four into a donkey cart belonging to one Robert Coggle and knocking off a cartwheel. Fortunately, that was the limit of the damage to either life or property.

Reynold's Weekly News reported approvingly on 16 February how Windham handled more weighty, estate matters. It told how Windham had given a 'handsome dinner' for his tenantry, with his witty speech of around 20 minutes showing once again how the inquiry verdict had been the correct one. 'Every effort is being made to induce Mr Windham to live more quietly for the future,' it continued. 'He was announced to patronise an entertainment at a circus, and also at the Theatre Royal, Norwich, but he was prevailed upon not to attend.'

Windham's relationship with Agnes, too, was apparently back on a steadier path than his coach-driving. She had refused to stay with him at his temporary base in Piccadilly, preferring 34 Clarendon Gardens, Paddington, while still living in adultery with Giuglini. Until 8 February, her daily routine was to go shopping, but sometimes visiting solicitors and other times to Westminster Hall 'to hear how the inquiry was going on'. On 8 February she was 'driven about town all day', then on to the Eastern Counties Railway station for travel to Norwich.

Agnes arrived around 8.45pm, when she was taken to Felbrigg. During the trial Windham had seen very little of her, save for two or three days in the early part of the hearing when she attended.

During the case he had met her once - with a chaperone - at Fendall's Hotel. She was interested only in how the inquiry was proceeding. When Windham was interviewed on the last day of the hearing, he told the Master he had no idea where she was living. He was being, at the least, disingenuous. In fact - as Windham himself was to confirm later - Agnes had promised outside the courtroom that she would return to him when the hearing was over. Now, at last, she had done so.

Windham's victory had changed matters, at least for the present. Agnes stayed at Felbrigg for most of February, although the Penny Illustrated Paper reported on 22 February that 'she is said to have been rather indisposed during the past week', a delightfully ambiguous statement which its readers must have enjoyed decoding. Windham, ever contradictory, took out advertisements in national newspapers, including the Daily News and Reynold's Weekly Newspaper, which read:

'MRS WINDHAM

Caution - I hereby give notice that my wife has not, and has not since the month of September 1861, authority to pledge my credit, and that I am NOT RESPONSIBLE for any DEBTS she has contracted since that time, or may contract.

WILLIAM FREDERICK WINDHAM

Felbrigg hall, Cromer 8th February 1862'

And this at a time when they were both - ostensibly at least - reunited and staying at Felbrigg. The Norfolk News spoke for many when it observed: 'It seems difficult to reconcile this notification with the fact of Mrs Windham having rejoined her husband.'

IN THE EVENT, Punch did not have to wait long for the reform process to begin. On 27 February, less than a month after the verdict, the Lord Chancellor introduced a bill to amend the Law of Lunacy, an extremely fast reaction to the case by governmental standards and testament to the widespread public concern over it. He began by saying there were some 'defects in the procedure' which needed change. 'It continually happens in this country,' he observed, 'that we go on with a bad system until some event occurs which places its defects so flagrantly before us that we set ourselves at once to the duty of remedying them.'

The Lord Chancellor was careful to say it was the rules which required attention, and not the conduct of the Master in Lunacy or any of the counsel.

The vice lies in the system,' he said. 'It is wholly cumbersome, expensive and ill-adapted to the exigencies of public justice.' He proposed some sweeping changes: evidence was to be treated exactly the same as any other criminal case or question of fact; the alleged lunatic would be interviewed by the jury before the case and not after; no evidence was to be accepted which was more than two years old; medical evidence would be judged judicially, that is, dealing in facts, not theories; and if the estate involved were less than £1,000 the Lord Chancellor could make an order directly, without a commission becoming involved.

As it stood, the present system meant that even an unopposed order would cost £60 - a sizeable portion of the estate of an average person. The last two cases before Windham's (Sir H Meux and Mrs Cummings) had been far more straightforward, but they had still cost £6,941 and £2,500 respectively. 'It is impossible that there was anything so objectionable as affecting both parties than the present system,' he added.

Lord St Leonard's, in reply, said: 'A case like that of Mr Windham, where the young man had many vicious habits and was addicted to low society... was obviously a case which would lead to an enormously costly contest, a vast waste of public time, and a great deal of public scandal.' There were points to be argued about - some peers want the medical evidence to be safeguarded, for example - but all were agreed: there would - could - never be another case like Windham's.

As Lloyd's Weekly London Newspaper pointed out, all the expense could have been avoided by having the jury interview Windham on Day One - not Day 34: 'Had the final proceedings of that trial taken place at first a hundred-pound note would have settled the bill.'

But it did not mean the end of the Commissions of Lunacy. In one notorious case eight years later, Sir Charles Morduant was persuaded to try to have his wife Harriett declared insane after she confessed to a string of lovers. In Westminster Hall, the jury heard from a succession of professional men and her amours (including the Prince of Wales). The jury, as with Windham, took only a few minutes to deliver its verdict.

Unlike Windham, the verdict was to declare her insane.

Harriett was to spend 33 years in a lunatic asylum.

A FEW DAYS after their Lordships' debate, at 3.40pm on Friday 7 March, the Court of Appeal began hearing the claims by Windham's counsel Sir Hugh that the petitioners should be made to pay for the whole proceedings. As well as Windham's legal team and those of the petitioners, Agnes and Lady Sophia were both careful to engage counsel to keep a watching brief. Sir Hugh's plan of attack was to prove to the Lords Justices that the petitioners' claims were contradictory, confused and unfair.

'I can prove,' said Sir Hugh, 'that the facts of this case had not been so faithfully and fairly stated by the petitioners.'

Lord Alfred Hervey, it would be recalled, had argued in his original affidavit that Windham was so incapable of managing his own affairs that his life could be in danger. But, Sir Hugh said, it had been a very different Lord Alfred who appeared in the witness box. He had told the court that he had received 'perfectly rational' letters from his nephew, who might converse with him for 'hours together and detect nothing irrational'.

Resuming the following day, Sir Hugh argued that a similar contradiction could be detected in the evidence of the marquis. A claim, for example, that he had seen Windham riding in Rotten Row with 'an expression of folly bordering on idiocy' was amended

Lord Westbury, the Lord Chancellor: The Windham scandal - and the scathing newspaper coverage it produced - forced the Government to take immediate action to reform the process of establishing lunacy. *(NRO ref: MC580/1, 780x1)*

in the witness box to Windham having 'a mingled appearance of fun and frolic' on his face. And this contradictory evidence had come from the only two petitioners who had been prepared to go in to the witness box. What value, then, on the affidavits of the rest of them? The QC then re-examined the 'three subjects which had been much discussed' - the marriage, the jewels, and the timber, and claimed that, far from being gullible, Windham had shown the 'greatest deal of acuteness' over the latter.

He returned to the evidence of the marquis and Lord Alfred on the Monday, reading out a letter from Windham to his uncle which showed that he been perfectly lucid. Sir Hugh told the court he would be telling the Lords Justices of several matters which the petitioners 'in a spirit of candour and fairness' should have disclosed to the commission. He reserved his greatest condemnation for the evidence which had probably been the most significant of the hearing - the Llewellyns'. He demolished their claims item by item - one had been 'a mere fiction, a deliberate untruth', another 'an entire fabrication', he said.

And so, he concluded, the petitioners had not carried out their duties to the court to gather valid and proper evidence. 'Instead of performing that duty,' he concluded, 'they recklessly and most improperly did not do so.' The Lords Justices should therefore order the petitioners to pay the full costs because they did not act in good faith to the court - or to Windham. As Sir Hugh sat down, Lord Justice Knight Bruce said that the original hearing had lasted 34 days, and this appeal looked as if it was heading in the same direction. 'But,' he added significantly, 'this case cannot be allowed to absorb all our time'. Three counsel (Messrs Milward, Rowcliffe and Karslake) then followed, backing up Sir Hugh's contentions. The Norwich Mercury continued, pointedly, 'The learned counsel [Karslake] proceeded at great length to examine the evidence in much the same manner as it had already been done by Sir Hugh Cairns.'

Leading the case for the petitioners, Bacon, after a side-swipe at the four days spent already, said the case was unlike any that had ever been heard since the law of lunacy was passed. There was no denying, he said, that Windham was 'if not of deficient intellect, his conduct, at least from his childhood, has been marked by a certain eccentricity.' Since his 21st birthday his behaviour had got worse, particularly by 'contracting a marriage which was so imprudent as that it could hardly be said any sane man would have entered into it'.

Faced with all this, he said, there was only one thing his family could do, as 'remonstrance had been tried, and tried in vain; persuasions were of no use to him; he had fallen into hands of the very worst kind, the very worst of all descriptions, and he was certainly a doomed man unless there was some protection provided for him'. Of course it was said that the petitioners should have framed their evidence more carefully - that sort of thing was easy to say after the event - but the only things that really mattered were whether they had acted in good faith, and if their statements were substantially true.

Contrary to rumours, and statements made to the jury by Sir Hugh (and, it might have been added, by public opinion and bar-room whisper), there was 'not a trace' of any pecuniary interest in proceedings by any of the petitioners 'from one end of the case to the other'. While Lady Sophia was alive, none of the petitioners had any chance of 'profiting in the slightest degree'. Perhaps, he suggested mischievously, Sir Hugh might wish to correct that impression?

The next day was taken up with a review of the letters - made public at last - which the General had sent to Lady Sophia telling her of his decision over his charge, and her replies, the contents of which disgusted the Norwich Mercury. In an editorial in its 15 March issue it asked: 'What is to be said of the terms for which Lady Sophia

Giubelei offered, through her solicitor, to sell her consent to the petition?

'What is to be said of the mother, except that it would not be beyond belief, did not the *litera scripta* stand in judgement against her?' The appeal, then, had claimed its first victim: Lady Sophia's reputation as a mother.

Summing up his arguments, Bacon - with an eloquence which was to prove as effective as Sir Hugh's had been in the original hearing - said the petitioners had started the legal process knowing it might well cost them a great deal of money, but they had no alternative in discharging 'a distasteful and onerous duty' without any 'sordid personal consideration'. He now turned to - and on - Windham, berating his character as 'this associate of the lowest and dirtiest people that are to be found in society'. Windham, he concluded, had no right to object to the petitioners' actions.

Bacon was supported by another QC, Bedwell, who in an equally eloquent speech, turned his legal fire on Sir Hugh's conduct, successfully (according to an approving Norwich Mercury) 'annihilating [his] inferences, deductions, and assertions'. Concluding the six-day hearing, Sir Hugh's gift for oratory for once deserted him. In reply to the powerful arguments of Bacon and Bedwell, he concentrated on technicalities in the statements made by the solicitor Chappell and behind-the-scenes comments made by the General. It was unconvincing stuff, and the Lords Justices were duly unconvinced.

The petitioners must surely have anticipated the result. The marquis wrote to Hansell on 27 March, thanking him for sending the Norwich Mercury reports of the case and added 'the speech strikes me as very able & as re the motives... of the petitioners was forcible & satisfactory'.

16

1862:
Grounds for Divorce

'I should not have to go near her afterwards if she had not bothered
my life out.'
Windham on Agnes, 1 December 1862

'SATISFACTORY' was hardly a description that could fit Windham's financial or
marital status by now. In late March he was forced to pledge his greatest asset, Felbrigg
Hall itself, for £35,000 with Norfolk bankers Harvey and Hudson, the money 'wholly
absorbed' in paying the interest on the debts the young squire had incurred: the interest,
not the capital. Windham was in a state of near-collapse financially, and his marriage
had already collapsed. Windham had decided - again - to cut and run from his brief
dalliance with Agnes. The marriage settlement which had been so notorious had been
defended by Agnes on the grounds that she needed an annuity. Windham began
negotiations to buy her out of the marriage settlement for £20,000 to £25,000 (reports
varied), and £5,000 was lodged with a Norwich bank.

The arrangement was made public in July because of a dispute over the
refurbishing of Agnes' London house at 3ª Westbourne Terrace, Marylebone, on
which she had taken out a lease and which would be her base for several years. The

house, part of a handsome Grade II-listed white-stuccoed six-storied terrace now forms part of the elegant Royal Park hotel, whose website advertises it - with unconscious irony in view of its past lessee - as 'perfect for... romantic trysts'. Agnes had initially agreed to pay the supplier of £3,000 of furniture (William Aspinwall of Grosvenor Street) half the cost in cash, paying off the rest at £500 per year.

But Aspinwall had got wind of Windham's plans - and realised Agnes could now settle his bill immediately, as she had £5,000 lodged with her solicitor James Davis. Frustrated by Davis' refusal to release the money, Aspinwall had lost patience and taken court action against Agnes and the trustees of her marriage settlement - Roberts and Dr Whidbourne - to stop her receiving any payment from them until she paid up in full. The court of appeal made no decision, but agreed to an immediate injunction on Agnes. The fate of this £5,000 was to be a major concern for Agnes for another three years.

By late March, as Lloyd's Weekly London Newspaper reported, Agnes was in Paris, her solicitor successfully resisting any more attempts to alter the terms of the marriage settlement. While Windham amused himself by 'tooling up to Norwich' in his coach, picking up stray passengers on the way, polite Norfolk society delivered another snub to the wayward young squire by rejecting him as a potential member of a local masonic lodge. His uncle, the General, was suffering too from the strain of the past few weeks. On 10 March it was revealed that he had resigned his Indian command because of ill-health.

On Wednesday 23 April, the Lords Justices delivered their verdict on the crucial matter of the costs. Lord Justice Knight Bruce began by saying that Windham's marriage with 'a person whom it is not necessary to describe' (or indeed, to name) had been followed by 'strange and startling' actions. These peculiar actions meant, he said, that a commission had been inevitable. As for Sir Hugh's claims about the petitioners, he continued, there was no evidence that there had been 'malice, bad faith, improper conduct, or bad motive' on their part. And so, 'the demand for costs is without foundation... and should not have been presented.' His view was supported by Lord Justice Turner, who pointed out that the strong views of the dissenting jurors was in itself a justification that the commission had been properly called into this 'very painful' case.

DISASTROUS as the appeal verdict was, it might have been even worse for Windham. The Lords Justices refused Bacon's call for the costs of the appeal to be awarded against Windham as well (in the event each side paid for its own). But the result meant that the Felbrigg estate was now piled high with even more insupportable debts.

Few commentators would have wagered that Felbrigg's 401-year tenure by the Windham family would - or could - last much longer.

Of course, the verdict delighted the General's allies. 'The judgement of the Lords Justice well confirms the view and the acts of the gallant General, and we are rejoiced that Justice has resumed her seat,' the Norwich Mercury wrote. 'Rectitude of object and an honest discharge of duty as a guardian, and a relative, have prevailed, and a discreditable attempt to tarnish the honour of a brave officer, and an honourable and determined desire "to do right and take the consequences," has ended, as it always does, in the long run, in the discomfiture and defeat of those who made the attempt.'

But if anyone felt that the complicated legal and personal affairs of the unfortunate William Frederick Windham were now at an end, they were mistaken. His remarkable and tangled life still had many more twists and turns in store.

In May, Windham's affairs were once more being examined in the Vice-Chancellor's court. The reason this time was the conclusion of legal proceedings between William and his mother which had been dragging on since 1857. Lady Sophia had argued that William could not be allowed to claim the 'furniture, plate, china, pictures & co' of Felbrigg as it was the 'clear intention' of William Howe Windham that they should pass to future generations as part of the estate. But this was one case that young Windham did win, with Vice Chancellor Wood deciding that existing property law was firmly on Windham's side.

During the month a rumour swept through legal circles, and was duly reported in Reynold's Weekly Newspaper, that another Commission of Lunacy into Windham was to be instituted - but this time by Lady Sophia. It claimed: 'His eccentricities are said to have developed themselves in so extraordinary a way as to render another enquiry probable. Amongst other strange things he has had an express mail-cart made, painted red, and having on the panel the royal arms with "William Frederick Windham" in small letters underneath. On this coach he starts from Felbrigg every morning to Norwich to fetch his letters and on receiving them he immediately returns to Felbrigg, thus every day accomplishing a distance a distance of 36 miles. Mrs Windham is not living with her husband.' The coach story was certainly true - but the commission story seems to have been mere wishful thinking on the part of some elements of the legal profession.

By this time Agnes was living in Brighton with her lover Giuglini. The impresario Colonel Mapleson does not name her in his memoirs, merely saying that his singer had caused him a great deal of difficulty around May after going down to the resort 'accompanied by a certain notorious lady'. The singer refused to return to London, pleading a 'migraine', but the wily impresario planted a story in a newspaper about a rival tenor being offered the plum role in Il Travatore.

On a stroll round Brighton he casually handed the paper to Agnes, telling her that her lover could now stay for as long as he liked. Giuglini was on his way to London within the hour, pleading desperately for the role. Even his passion for Agnes had crumbled, temporarily at least, in the face of his artistic ego. A formal separation between Agnes and Windham took place in June, months after she had left him. Under the terms of the agreement, Windham agreed 'not to molest her'. He complained later that year that 'I should not have to go near her afterwards if she had not bothered my life out *(sic)*'.

There was an insight into Agnes' world on 10 July, when Hammersmith court heard the case of Ann Connor, a 'genteel-looking young woman', charged with stealing a £10 note and other property from her. Giving evidence, Agnes told the court that Connor was her kitchen-

Appeal verdict: The General's actions were vindicated by the judgement of the Lords Justices. *(NRO ref: MC580/1, 780x1)*

maid. When Agnes had returned home from the opera on the night of 3 July she had missed the note. In a telling illustration of Agnes' predilection for portable wealth, she had a £300 banknote and four £10 notes under her pillow, and those were still safe. The servants denied any theft, but the missing note was traced to Connor via a washerwoman. When Connor's belongings were searched, Agnes found some of her stockings, collars, a handkerchief and a pencil case. Connor had since returned nine sovereigns and asked her employer to forgive her. And Agnes, belying her hard-hearted image, did exactly that.

By July the Windhams were having their third attempt at co-habitation. Windham said Agnes had 'kept on writing letters, begging and praying me to let her come back. At last I found it was impossible to bear with her any longer.' He lived with her at Westbourne Terrace in July and August, when he went with her on a yacht excursion to Boulogne - the latest of Windham's expensive passions. Then there was more servant trouble for the Windhams, with the Hammersmith court hearing on 26 August the case of 19-year-old Amelia Reeves, accused of stealing 12lb of sugar from Windham. Reeves denied the charge, saying she was so trusted by the couple that she had a set of duplicate keys.

She told the court if she really wanted to steal, she could have taken the valuables: Agnes never locked up anything, even leaving her jewel box unguarded when she went out to the opera. Mrs Windham had been kind to her, even giving her a gold watch which was very generous ('A bit too generous,' Windham was heard to mutter, seeing as he was paying for it).

THE VIEW of Agnes expounded by later writers Donald MacAndrew and Robert Ketton-Cremer that she was a hard-headed and hard-hearted schemer who associated with Windham merely to extract his fortune ignores the fact that she, too, paid a price. Most notoriously, and most humiliatingly, Windham had possibly passed his venereal disease to her, but there also was the indisputable fact that her husband could be a drunken and aggressive boor, and physically intimidating.

A perfect example of this was revealed, back in Hammersmith court, on 25 September, when Windham was in court once again. Not servant trouble this time: in the dock on this occasion was Windham himself, this time accused of threatening to cut Agnes' throat. Giving evidence, Agnes said that while Windham was at Boulogne in the summer he had met two men, William St Alban and Robert Burdett, whom he had invited back to stay at Upper Westbourne Terrace. On 23 September she had gone out with their guests for the evening 'with the consent of her husband'. They returned around 11.45pm, and shortly afterwards she went to her room. Within a few minutes she heard Windham shouting that he was going to 'shed the blood' of Agnes and the guests. 'He had a large sailor's clasp knife and said he would cut my throat,' she said. 'I go in fear of him. It is not the first time he has sworn to take my life.' Windham had thrown knives at her across the kitchen table from time to time as well, she added.

Windham said he was drunk and claimed, bizarrely, that Agnes or the two men had 'poured water into his ears' (they said they had lightly splashed his face). Agnes rejected the excuse that Windham was drunk, and said he knew exactly what he was doing. St Alban confirmed he had heard Windham threaten Agnes and telling her he would cut her throat 'from ear to ear that night'. Agnes' solicitor told the court that 'she did not want to hurt her husband; she simply wanted protection from his threats'. The court, wisely deciding it did not want to get involved in another intractable domestic dispute, ordered Windham bound over to keep the peace, or forfeit £500.

Her Majesty's Court for Divorce and Matrimonial Causes was, however, not quite so fortunate. The National Archives holds much of the material relating to the matter of Windham v Windham and Giuglini, mostly a series of affidavits between the parties. On 29 October Windham's solicitor filed his opening salvo: 'That on the twenty-ninth day of September 1862 and on other days between that day and the twenty-first day of October 1862 the said Agnes Ann Windham committed adultery with Antonio Giuglini'. There was more: on 'divers occasions' in September and October Agnes committed adultery 'with divers persons unknown to the petitioner' at 32 Oxendon Street (behind the Haymarket) and 23 Trevor Square in Knightsbridge. Two days later copies of the document were served on Agnes and Giuglini.

DESPITE MARRIAGE troubles, servant difficulties, estrangements and a succession of court appearances Windham was not distracted from another of his passions: the railways. Punch, in one of its more light-hearted comments on the Windham case back on 22 February, had combined his well-publicised liking for the railways with his strange upbringing.

With its habit of making heavy-handed puns, it headlined its piece 'How to Train up a Child', going on to explain that the 'best plan of training a child is to allow him to put on a railway guard's uniform, to jump up behind the engine, do stoker's work, slam the doors, call out the names of the stations, and to start the train by blowing the whistle, taking good care that he pays well for the latter. Such training may lead him eventually to a commission of lunacy, but that is no fault of his tutors, more especially as the charge is an even quicker method than the railway of allowing the young man to run through his property.'

But the public, having been given ample and startling evidence of Windham's railway antics during the inquiry, remained unconvinced - and alarmed - by further reports of his activities. Despite assurances from the highest level of management, the reality on the stations and on the trains themselves was that an appropriate bribe could still ensure railway workers looked the other way. A correspondent ('Viator') wrote to The Times on 5 December 1862 to say how he had been travelling on an Eastern Counties express train that morning when he was alarmed to see Windham dressed as a guard, complete with carriage door key and acting as if he were an employee.

It was only his 'uncertain mode of action' which led 'Viator' to query the guard's identity with a railway worker. 'Now, sir,' he wrote, 'I have no objection to young Windham travelling in any dress he may think appropriate, but I certainly, on the grounds of public safety, object to his being allowed a key to open and shut doors at his discretion, or perhaps, indiscretion. I consider it not unlikely, if he be allowed to follow his present amateur employment, that an accident may be brought about.'

Windham, stung, wrote to the railway's company secretary at Bishopsgate on 8 December, a letter duly passed to the paper for publication. 'Having seen a letter in The Times of Saturday, which is likely to do me a great deal of harm, as well as the Company's servants, I beg leave to inform you, on my word as a gentleman, that the statement of Mr 'Viator' is totally without foundation; therefore I hope that this explanation will be satisfactory to you and to Mr Love [the railway's chairman] also... All I did was lock my own door, as I had some game (and my portmanteau) in the carriage, in case any one might take it out. I write this as it appears to me there is some one who prides himself on writing malicious lies about me, and reporting untruths to you about me.' The company secretary, J B Owen, backed Windham's claim, calling Viator's comments 'foolish and unfounded'.

But Mr Owen was sadly deluded about Windham, as two more letters indicated. Viator replied on 9 December that the very fact that Windham had a key in the first place proved his point, and that the 'guard' had been in 'almost the daily habit' for months of travelling to London on the 7am express, and returning at night 'always dressed as a guard, key in hand'. He had seen 'guard' Windham in action at Ely as well as Cambridge. And 'JB' wrote from London on the same day that he had witnessed Windham at Thorpe Station in Norwich, walking up and down, locking and unlocking the carriages.

Not being able to open his carriage door, he was forced to ask Windham to unlock it, watching with disquiet when the 'guard' insisted on joining him there. 'I had him as my only companion as far as Wymondham [a few minutes from Norwich], where, to my great relief (as he rode with his body out of the window) he leaped out of the train as it was about to stop,' he added. Clearly Windham's 'word as a gentleman' could not be relied on. And just to make sure no-one missed the exchange of the correspondence, it was reprinted in the Norfolk papers.

There was one consolation for the long-suffering public: at least by turning his attention to his coach his reckless driving had less potential for disaster to life and limb.

ON 1 DECEMBER the Court of Exchequer heard the suit of livery stable keeper and job master Bramston Bateman against Windham. He claimed for £9 16s for hire of broughams and horses, but the real significance of the case lay in the insights it gave to the Windhams' continuing marital complications. Windham engaged the redoubtable Karslake to challenge the claim, which turned out to be a wise (although, no doubt, costly move). The gist of the case was this: Agnes had used the carriage between 31 January and 8 February, Bateman had duly sent in his bill but 'I never got the money'.

After hearing from a succession of tradesmen, Karslake got to the heart of the case: 'She lived in open adultery... and if she chose to leave her husband, and more especially, for the purpose of committing adultery with other men she could not legally pledge her husband's credit for debts contracted by her while living in that immoral state.' It was a view with which Mr Baron Martin agreed, directing the jury that by living apart from her husband and in adultery, Agnes 'had absolutely destroyed her agency' to claim her debts were her husband's - crucially - whether Windham had taken her back or not in the meantime.

There was more gossip on 6 December when the Penny Illustrated Paper reported that 'it was stated that Mr W F Windham has sold the Felbrigg Hall estate to a member of the peerage for £135,000. The incumbrances upon the property amount to £110,000.' The report was correct in that it mentioned a change of ownership, but it would not take place until the following year, and to a person far removed from the House of Lords.

Three days later Agnes was to be seen - scandalously - with her lover at the Italian Opera Company's visit to Edinburgh. The Stirling Observer branded her 'the very Queen of Spades', accusing Agnes of 'outraging the public sense of decency'. But it also took a side-swipe at the hypocrisy of the self-appointed moral judges of the city. Once again, Agnes' behaviour had prompted searching questions on wider issues of public morality.

On 17 December, two days before her 23rd birthday, Agnes finally responded to her husband's divorce petition. She flatly denied any impropriety, but adding that if she committed adultery then Windham had 'connived' in it, 'condoned' her actions and had often strayed himself during their marriage. Worse, he had shown 'cruelty, wilful neglect and misconduct' towards her. Giuglini's response, made the day before, took an almost identical line.

And so the year ended with the estranged Windhams firmly at war, but there was also further evidence that the ripple of publicity created by the sensational events of the winter of 1861-2 were still spreading outwards. The Straits Times reported in November how Windham had left Singapore in an American steamer, bound for China, 'accompanied by his favourite horse and £80,000 in sovereigns'. A few weeks earlier another foreign newspaper had reported how Windham was at the Cape of Good Hope in South Africa, where he could be seen with a monkey on his shoulder, and carrying a doll in his arms 'which he keeps from its likeness to his wife'. This travelling 'Windham' - if he existed at all - was, of course, an imposter. The Windham case had just added yet another bizarre layer to itself.

17

1863-1865:
Decline and Fall

'Saw Mr Windham in Norwich. He has degraded himself from a first-rate
position in the county to become the driver of a stagecoach.'
The Rev B J Armstrong, writing in his diary on 30 January 1864

ON 13 JANUARY 1863 the divorce petition was heard for the first time in open court.
Windham, inevitably, said he would be accusing Agnes of committing adultery with
Giuglini. For her part Agnes would be contesting the petition, citing 'adultery, cruelty
and wilful neglect'. She would also be alleging that Windham had condoned her
behaviour prior to 9 September 1862. On 3 February, Windham's advocate Dr
Wambey, who had been poised to add fresh charges to the ones Windham had compiled
against Agnes and her lover, said his client had decided to withdraw them to speed up
the case. Giuglini's representative immediately asked for costs. 'You must have them,'
said the judge Sir Cresswell Cresswell. Agnes' lawyer, Dr Spinks, then asked: 'The
respondent will have her costs, as a matter of course?' Sir Cresswell said simply: 'I say
nothing of that'. The petition may have been scaled-down, but the clear implication was
that Agnes had deserved all she got.

Windham, meanwhile, was seeking amusement in another popular pastime
followed by the 'man about town': the often brutal world of prize-fighting. In January
he was to be found in Bradford, spending money freely in support of the celebrated

English champion (and fellow Norfolkman) Jem Mace. That was nothing compared to the extravagance he demonstrated the following month, when, at the Criterion Music Hall in Leicester Square, Mace was presented with a gold cup which, of course, had been paid for by Windham. Mace told his cheering supporters that Windham (who was absent 'through illness') was a 'true supporter of the ring and a man of good heart'. Those supporters then gave Windham three cheers - as well they might: the trophy had cost a reported £525.

Windham was back in two courtrooms that month. On 13 February he was sued by the Llewellyns for the £109 14s rent he had agreed to pay in August 1861 before he had left suddenly to marry Agnes. Windham's counsel, the ever-dependable Karslake, was forced to concede the case when he was unable to put Windham in the witness box because his client was 'labouring under some excitement'.

And at the beginning of March, the Penny Illustrated Paper reported: 'Mr W F Windham made his appearance before the Norwich magistrates last Saturday on a summons charging him with using threatening language to Mr Sproul, station-master on the Great Eastern Railway at Thorpe [Norwich]. Windham, who it will be remembered, has started a coach, appears to have desired that all the parcels which were directed for along the route of his coach should be given to him to carry.' But Sproul told him - with a regard for company rules sadly lacking in many of his company colleagues over the years - that without an order from the directors, he would not let Windham touch the parcels. 'Upon this Windham used violent and blackguard language and threatened Sproul with bodily harm,' the paper continued. A cut-and-dried case, surely? Being Windham, however, nothing was ever as straightforward as that. The magistrates threw out the claim after Sproul refused to swear he was afraid of Windham. The squire-turned-coach proprietor 'left the court in high glee that the railway company was "floored this time".'

Earlier, The Times reported on 10 February, approvingly if sarcastically, 'MR WINDHAM WELL EMPLOYED', pointing out that he 'continued to work his coach very steadily' running services on Tuesdays to Fridays and keeping very good time - 'though he has not been overburdened by passengers'. Windham had even managed to keep getting up at 7am, it reported, clearly with some amazement.

OF MORE significance for posterity was the news on 26 March that Felbrigg had new owners: the Ketton family. The loss of the historic heart of the Windham family's North Norfolk estate had, of course, been widely predicted since autumn 1861. But John Ketton's purchase must still have come as a stunning blow. It was, after all, four centuries since the estate had passed from the Felbriggs to the Windhams. Ketton, who had changed his name from Kitton in 1853, was an enterprising merchant in cattle feedstuffs who had taken shrewd advantage of the business opportunities of the Crimean War to move into farming and stock-raising on a large scale.

His descendant Robert Wyndham Ketton-Cremer, a distinguished historian, former High Sheriff of Norfolk and as much the acme of a good landowner as Windham was a bad one, wrote in his 1962 history of the estate that posterity had reason to thank 'Mad' Windham, precisely because of his sudden fall from grace. He explained: 'It is seldom that a historic house with its entire contents - pictures, furniture, books, documents, everything - is transferred from one family to another... [Windham's sudden ruin] had proved the means of preserving the greater part of them intact to the present day.'

But, back in 1863, it was the here and now and not posterity which was exciting more comment. The behind the scenes tit-for-tat series of affidavits continued in the divorce case. On 6 March things became even more heated when Windham replied to Agnes' latest claims by contending that 'if the Petitioner [Windham] was infected with syphilis as alleged... the said Agnes Ann Windham had knowledge of the fact and consented to connubial intercourse with the Petitioner notwithstanding'. He denied cruelty and said if he had committed any acts it was 'in consequence of provocation'.

On 21 April Judge Cresswell ordered that the 'questions of fact' thrown up by the various affidavits should be tested by a special jury. The stage was set for a case to rival the commission of lunacy in its sensationalism. And with Agnes' affair with Giuglini continuing, Windham's decision to resume his divorce suit was seen as inevitable. Surely no gentlemen - albeit one with such a tarnished name as the former squire of Felbrigg - could countenance being cuckolded so publicly? So it was with a mixture of astonishment and disbelief that the public learned in the middle of May that the pair had been reconciled and the divorce case finally abandoned. True, there had been gossip about just why Agnes - according to the Norfolk Chronicle of 16 May - had been seen 'in Norwich and its immediate vicinity very frequently of late'. But, it added, 'the divorce proceedings so long pending seemed to preclude all notion of a reconciliation between the parties'.

Agnes had dispatched one of her circle, described by the Norwich Argus as 'a gallant officer' (not named but perhaps another lover, 'Captain' Steward), to Windham with a package, containing her photograph 'together with a letter announcing her readiness to disgorge cash received, jewels presented, opera box, town house, &c, &c, if her outraged husband would only consent in taking her back'. On receiving the package, Windham had kissed the photograph, studied the letter and had immediately, 'in a burst of tenderness', given way.

Beauty, preserved: The sudden transfer of Felbrigg from Windham to Norwich merchant John Ketton turned out, with the hindsight of posterity, to ensure the preservation of the historic house and contents largely intact.

On Tuesday 12 May Windham - 'fresh from the tailor's hands, ornamented with a bouquet, and accompanied by friends, bearing a reconciliation cake of 100lbs weight' - drove his coach from Norwich to a property near Cantley in the Broads, which was used as a fishing lodge by Agnes' gallant officer friend. The meeting was such a success that Windham immediately telegraphed his London solicitor Chappell with instructions to stay the proceedings. Word got out at once about the reconciliation, and by the time Mr and Mrs Windham set out in his coach from the Norfolk Hotel in St Giles' in Norwich the next day, a large and curious crowd had gathered to see if the stories could be true. They were; the Norfolk Chronicle setting the scene: 'And there, sure enough, mounted on the driver's box, sat Mr Windham, handling the whip and ribbons with his usual skill, his wife, apparently regardless of the gaze of the assembled hundreds, occupying an elevated position by his side.'

A SCANDAL AT FELBRIGG

The Argus took up the story: 'As the coach rolled on to Cromer, bearing on its knife-board, husband, wife, and friends, Mr Windham appeared bathed in a sunshine of perfect felicity. The slight domestic storm had passed, and the heart that had ached so long, and deserved to ache so little, was at last sorrowless. As the ex-Squire of Felbrigg cracked his whip, blew his whistle and coaxed his horses, we question if few crowned heads were ever more satisfied with having granted first an amnesty, and finally a pardon, than the driver of the Ocean [the name of Windham's coach] felt at first having melted towards, and finally forgiven, an erring wife'. The Chronicle added: 'On Thursday morning Mrs Windham was driven back to Norwich by her husband, and so far the reconciliation seems to be complete.'

There is no doubt the divorce proceedings, should they have happened, would have been a courtroom sensation. Windham's solicitors, Bugg and Chappell, the Argus revealed, had prepared a 'long array of unsavoury evidence' for the hearing. But all, now, would be shelved, much to the disappointment of the lawyers and the many witnesses.

The Argus' description of the reconciliation is a long one, going on for the best part of two columns, but it also contains two references which may cast a new light on Agnes' behaviour. The first is the role of Susannah Jeffey, who had reportedly masterminded the letter to Windham. The Argus described her variously as 'this choice attendant', 'with a countenance as keen and cutting as the east wind', 'spruce as a peacock and leering like a raven' and 'that image of touching frankness and affecting sincerity'. The innuendo seems clear: that Jeffey was fulfilling that time-honoured role of the courtesan's special servant, her procuress.

The second is mentioned during a description of Agnes herself by the Argus, a paper always far more daring about printing the latest gossip than its more staid county rivals. It calls her 'the Lucretia, who report would lead one to believe, ate up a young heir alive at night [ie Windham] and his guardian [ie the General] in the morning'. Remarkable, indeed sensational, if its hint at sexual entanglement is true - but what hard evidence is there? Circumstantially, the General was rumoured to be a man of passion in all things, so what could be more natural if he - like half of London - was intrigued by the fascinating and wilful pretty horse-breaker? But it is an implication we can quickly dismiss. The implacable and all-too-public opposition of the General to Agnes through the courts is one which is hard to gainsay. And, surely, any such relationship would have put Agnes in a strong position to, if not blackmail the General, at least put informal pressure on him. Besides, the General had been left £300 out of pocket by the collapse of the divorce suit, having, yet again, picked up the pieces left by his nephew's whims. And there were other matters to occupy his attention. During the year he was appointed a Lieutenant-Colonel of the Coldstream Guards, but the news was tempered by the shock of the death of his much-loved wife Marianne.

This time the Windhams' reconciliation was to have a more tangible outcome. Sometime in mid-July 1863 Agnes conceived a child. The identity of the father would occupy the gossips for some years to come. There were two more significant family events in this year: Agnes' sister Thirza marrying a Portuguese landowner, Signor La Fuente in Madrid in December, and the long-predicted death of Windham's mother Lady Sophia. The terms of her will gave Windham a welcome extra £1,500 a year, but it made little difference to his financial affairs.

THE NORFOLK vicar the Rev B J Armstrong wrote in his diary on 30 January 1864: 'Saw Mr Windham in Norwich. He has degraded himself from a first-rate position in the county to become the driver of a stagecoach. His magnificent Felbrigg Estate is sold to a mercantile man, one Kitton (sic), so that the saying is, "Windham has gone to the dogs, and Felbrigg to the kittens."'

Gone to the dogs he may have been, but he was also certainly gone - yet again - to the courtroom too. Arrested over an alleged debt for £417, he found himself in the Court of Common Pleas in Westminster on 8 February. The alleged debt had been incurred as part of the divorce debacle of the previous year. Mr Hewson, the former clerk of Windham's London solicitors Chappell, was suing for money still owing from a bill of £691 he had run up 'in frequenting night houses, getting up evidence in the defendant's divorce case, and expenses incurred in so doing'. His 198 days of work also included settling-up various accounts for Windham and 'squaring' a young woman named Cooper 'who alleged that he had committed an assault on her at Felbrigg Hall'. All his work had proven fruitless, of course, when Windham made up his quarrel with Agnes.

Hewson had sought a meeting with Windham to ask for the money he was owed. Hewson asked why he had gone back to Agnes. Windham's answer: 'Common sense'. The interview then took an even stranger turn with Hewson having an unexpected supporter: Agnes. She told her husband: 'The man has worked hard - he ought to have his money.'

Counsel for Windham, the inevitable Karslake, then tackled the issue head-on, challenging Hewson's legal team to produce 'one shred of evidence' that any such agreement had been made. For Hewson, his counsel Mr Powell went on the counter-attack, contrasting the distinguished former clerk's 20-year service for Chappell with the impression Windham had made when he had spoken earlier. 'Who,' he asked the jury, 'was the defendant? He was a young man who a few years ago might have been said to have the world at his feet - the descendant of an ancient and respected family, with an historic name, and possessed of a princely estate, and what was he now as they had seen him in the witness box?' Powell then turned on Windham's legal team. Karslake, he said, had spoken of the 'clouds of vultures' ready to pounce on Windham. 'Talk of "vultures",' he continued, 'And the plaintiff in his demand was a sparrow-hawk compared to the attorneys in whose hands he was.'

The jury, however, agreed with Windham, the judge, Mr Justice Byles, criticising the way Windham had been arrested as 'a kind of extortion'.

ON 19 APRIL 1864 Agnes gave birth to her son, the future Squire of Hanworth, Frederick William Howe Lindsay Bacon Windham. MacAndrew, writing in 1951, attributed, surely correctly, this extraordinarily elaborate series of Christian names to Agnes' desire to make utterly clear her position that this was Windham's legitimate son, and therefore a true offshoot of the ancient family. It was almost an act of defiance against polite society and the rest of the Windhams. The child's link to his mother was easy to see - he, too, sported a fine head of blond hair - but his links with Windham were not so obvious.

The birth, which took place at the Upper Westbourne Terrace house, was attended by doctors Farr, Priestley and Johnson; understandably, Agnes was taking no chances in what remained a hazardous time for women of all classes. It provided, too, a curious reminder of the close links between the story of the Windhams and that of the railways: Agnes insisted that to celebrate, £7 8s was spent on 587 pints of ale - one for each man - for workers at the Great Western Railway Terminus at Paddington on the day of the heir's birth. The bill for the beer, inevitably, was never settled.

But the celebrations were to be muted by another court appearance. A few days later the Court of Bankruptcy received a petition by 'Mr W F Windham, of 3ª Upper Westbourne-terrace, Marylebone, gentleman, lately also of Cromer and Norwich, stage-coach proprietor'. Felbrigg Hall, of course, was already lost; it had been assigned 'some time ago' for the benefit of his creditors, and the Bury Post reported that Windham's debts and liabilities 'are stated to be considerable'.

Windham appeared before the Court of Bankruptcy in Basinghall Street on 22 May. The public gallery was, naturally, crowded. A long succession of tradesmen and other creditors appeared, each staking their claim to a piece of Windham's assets. First was a Mr Richardson, owner of the Blue Anchor Tavern in Shoreditch, who had claimed £500, for two bills of exchange - promissory notes signed by Windham which could be sold on to third parties. Next up was the long-suffering Norwich solicitor Isaac Bugg, claiming £87 for services rendered and for cash lent to Windham. The court heard the firm had already received £1,930 from Windham, mostly due, it will be recalled, for the carefully-gathered and never-used evidence for the abortive divorce hearing.

Son and heir: Taken mid-1864, Agnes with her son, the elaborately-named Frederick William Howe Lindsay Bacon Windham in a photograph which also shows her famous striking blonde hair to good effect. *(NRO ref: MC580/1, 780x1)*

The hearing then entered the realms of the bizarre (as it usually did sooner or later with Windham) with William Howlett of the Norwich Music Hall claiming £115 for a 'grand American square pianoforte'. Windham had ordered the piano for an unnamed lady (clearly, then, not Agnes) who was 'resident in Claverton Street, St George's Road, Pimlico', but the instrument had never actually been delivered because Howlett could not find the address. Not surprisingly, laughter once more rang round the courtroom at yet another of Windham's expensive caprices. Norwich tailor Thomas Bingham was then called, and closely examined on his claim for a large number of clothes supplied for Windham and his friends. Bingham had appeared for Windham at the Commission of Lunacy during which he mentioned that Windham's tailoring bill for 1859 was £16 9s for the year. Since coming into his inheritance, Windham's sartorial tastes had clearly increased vastly; he now owed £214.

Around £2,000 in debts were admitted by the court for investigation, which included £44 for a stonemason. This would have been for the memorial to his father which Windham had by now had placed in Felbrigg church. The stonemason, incidentally, had managed to mis-spell Windham's second Christian name ('Frederic'). The court - and therefore the general public - heard that Agnes was making an annual allowance of £500 to her husband, in return for £3,000 insured with the Accidental. Once again, Agnes was in the position of financial control over her husband.

The reasons for Windham exposing himself to yet more public ridicule through the bankruptcy process were much debated at the time, especially as it would be made clear later that he still had - technically at least - assets running into tens of thousands. The timing of the declaration only days after the birth of an heir must, surely, be no coincidence. Agnes seems to have been seeking to draw a line under Windham's debts to ensure their son's inheritance, as the heir of Hanworth, would thus be completely protected.

That much is debatable. What is not in doubt is that Agnes had misunderstood the process as it related to the wives of bankrupts. She thought Windham's assets and debts would be the only ones exposed to public scrutiny; in this she was sadly mistaken. In late June the court ordered her to appear in person. But Agnes refused. She did not want to be even privately examined as part of her husband's bankruptcy process and had, the paper said, 'treated the matter in a very cavalier way, stating she would not attend the court unless taken there by force'. The court threatened to issue a warrant for her arrest unless she turned up. The Norwich Mercury observed, drily, 'Mrs Windham appeared to be under some misapprehension as to the power of the court not to compel her attendance.'

The bankruptcy proceedings led one of Windham's fiercest opponents, The Daily Telegraph, to write another ferocious editorial. Its comments began in uncompromising fashion: 'Long before this,' it wrote, 'we expected to see the last scene of this miserable Rake's Progress and the works of the sharpers and prostitutes consummated.' Windham, it continued, 'has deliberately prepared for himself the contempt and horror of decent people'. The paper went on to attack the 'conspirators' who had helped him fall, the 'group of human jackals' who had exploited the naive young heir. But it reserved its greatest scorn for the 'bloodsucking' lawyers who had exploited the family to grow rich by stripping away the estate's assets, piece by piece. They were, it said, 'worse than the Jezebels who led Windham through the path of misery'.

AMID ALL the court cases and newspaper reports, a remarkable book appeared on bookstalls across London during the year. Agnes Willoughby: A Tale of Love, Marriage and Adventure, by an anonymous author - but probably the colourful writer, gambler and former bankrupt William Stephen Hayward - was one of a series of similar books about celebrated courtesans of the era, including, inevitably, Agnes' rival Skittles. The book is now extremely scarce, but a copy survives in the British Library. Its plot weaves thinly-disguised echoes of the 1861 scandal with bizarre flights of fancy. In the book Agnes, aged 25, is living in a small but handsomely furnished house off the Finchley Road. Her associate Charles Dicks (clearly modelled on James Roberts) wants her to marry young heir Horace St John Warner (Windham), whose passions are steam engines, driving carriages and pulling pints. Agnes, meanwhile, is the amour of Lieutenant Graham 'of the ----- Rifles', with a further complication being a group of painters, the 'Blue Joneses', who want to kidnap her as an artist's model.

Dicks sets up the meeting between Agnes and Horace, the latter becoming instantly smitten. Agnes prefers her true love, an Italian operatic star who mistreats her. He refuses to marry her, so Agnes agrees to wed Horace instead. The young heir's step-father tries to buy her off, then bundles Horace away to Paris to thwart the marriage. Agnes and Dicks set off in pursuit, the marriage eventually taking place. On their return to London, complications ensue with the Italian singer trying to win Agnes back. Meanwhile, Horace's step-father has him committed to an asylum - but the young heir escapes, is reunited with Agnes and they live happily ever after.

Back in the real world 'living happily after' was hardly a likely option, with the reconciliation between the Windhams coming to an end by July. It is tempting to cite her anger at the court examination of her assets as one of the reasons which led to their final break. But more tempting still is the fact that she now had all she wanted: an heir to guarantee the eventual possession of Hanworth, and control of Windham's financial assets through life assurance policies - assets she had acquired, Ketton-Cremer was to complain in his history of Felbrigg, for 'a ludicrously small sum'

And surely it was only a matter of time before the dissolute Windham would provide a windfall on those.

Establishing the full extent of Windham's assets and debts was proving a complicated business. On 21 June there was a meeting for the examination of Windham and his possible discharge. 'The court was very crowded, a large number of persons being present merely from curiosity to see a person who has been so long before the public in various characters,' the Mercury reported. They were to be disappointed, however, and again in July when the hearing was put back to October.

WHAT HAD happened to Agnes' one-time great love, Giuglini, meanwhile? By the end of the London season in 1864, Giuglini accepted an engagement in St Petersburg, which ended in disaster when he threw his fee into a fire during a row. When Mapleson saw him on his return from Russia in 1865 he was shocked by the sight of Giuglini, distracted, sitting in his room without his trousers. The impresario checked Giuglini's possessions while the singer was asleep and found he had been meticulously robbed of all his jewellery, which would have probably included items which Agnes had bought him. Mapleson put him under the care of Dr Daniel Tuke, the famous specialist in psychological disorders who, it will be recalled, had given evidence in the Windham case. But it was to no avail. Giuglini was sent back to Italy, to his home town of Fano, for his final months. The Diritto reported on 25 August that the 'great tenor' had greeted his friends in his doctor's house by singing his role as Gennaro - then collapsed and 'fell flat like a man struck by lightning'. He died, insane, on 12 October 1865. By a cruel twist of fate his father, who also ended up insane, had died in the same room.

That Giuglini had an undeniably permanent place in Agnes' heart can be proved by the simple fact that among the mementoes she preserved until the end of her life - and one which is still in the possession of her family - is a framed caricature of the tenor sitting at a harpsichord. But that did not mean Agnes went without lovers: by 1865 her post-Giuglini amours included 'Captain' Steward, 'Captain' Marsden and Frederick Allen.

BY AUTUMN 1864 Windham was penniless, with the exception of a few pounds for expenses granted by the Court of Bankruptcy. The feeling of disgust about his conduct felt by the polite society of the county was still strong, if another diary entry by the Rev B J Armstrong is anything to go by. For his entry for September 2 1864 he wrote: 'Returned to Dereham making a detour through Felbrigg Park. Notwithstanding £20,000 worth of timber has lately been cut, you do not miss it, amid this mass of foliage, fern, heath, in hill and dell. As we drove through the park, we became more & more angry with the notorious Mr Windham, whose low & profligate tastes have caused the estate to be sold... There was the ancestral mansion surmounted by the motto in perforated stone GLORIA: IN: EXCELSIS: DEO - the pious feeling, doubtless, of the founder. What a parody this, upon the vulgar propensities of the degenerate heir, who married a prostitute.'

Armstrong has obviously half-remembered details of the original, unfulfilled timber contract here - a clear indicator, incidentally, that he must have avidly followed the reports of the lunacy inquiry. As, naturally, had his fellow 'disgusted' members of polite society.

Windham, meanwhile, went back to Norwich, and, yet again, to his long-suffering associate Thomas Bingham. The General was trying once more to help his nephew and, in the words of the Norwich Argus, 'was striving, through Mr Dolman, his solicitor, to scrape something out of the ruin'. The General and Bingham came up with a plan to keep Windham out of mischief - or as much mischief as they could prevent.

It was decided to go back to one of the few things Windham had achieved any sort of proficiency at: driving a coach. Bingham originally intended to fund the project for 14 weeks until a better plan presented itself. But a better plan never did, and the coach venture was to last almost a year and a half. The advertisements can still be seen in the yellowing back issues of the local papers: 'Express Coach. Leaves Norfolk Hotel, Norwich every morning at 7.45am, at Aylsham 9.05am, leaving 9.15am, arrives Cromer 10.30am. Returning at 5pm. Props. H Bingham & Co, Coachman W F Windham Esq,'.

It was during this period that many of the local legends about Windham grew up. The image of the Mad Squire hurtling round the Norfolk lanes, cracking his whip and swearing at those in his path, was the stuff of anecdotes galore swapped in the smoky alehouses of Cromer, Norwich, Aylsham and the villages in between. Nothing in Norfolk was to eclipse Mad Windham for notoriety until the bizarre case of the Rector of Stiffkey, 'Prostitutes' Padre' Harold Davidson, delighted the national newspapers in the 1930s. Windham's ability to slip easily into the Norfolk dialect added a further layer of strangeness for local gentry who found themselves being driven by someone who until recently was one of their own.

The Norwich Argus paints the picture: 'Seated on the box, Windham smacked his whip and blew his whistle, or, in the capacity of guard, got up a noise on his horn, or showed his danger and safety lights with extraordinary agility and discernment.' There was a distraction from the six-days-a-week Express coach service on 23 November when Windham found himself called down to London for the conclusion of the much-delayed bankruptcy hearing. Finally, almost six months after Windham had first applied for bankruptcy, the public's curiosity was satisfied at last as to the true extent of his finances.

The court heard that he had total debts of £4,612, made up of £3,187 of unsecured debts, £714 of secured debts, and another £711 which Agnes owed for which he accepted liability, despite their new estrangement. His assets totalled £33,364 'inclusive, however, of a life interest annuity of £3,000 and policies of insurance claimed by Messrs Edwin Fox and George Hooper, the trustees of Mrs Windham'. She was also trying to fight moves to have £566-worth of furniture at Upper Westbourne Terrace included in her husband's assets.

The Mercury reported: 'There was also jewellery in the possession of Mrs Windham, value £1,000, which she insisted also belonged to her, which, however the assignees did not agree.' If this was the sole extent of Agnes' jewellery, it meant that most of the £14,000 of jewellery which Windham had so famously bought her in 1861 had already been sold, and the proceeds spent. But Agnes, it would much later emerge, had been assiduous at keeping the true extent of her wealth hidden from the court. Included in the assets was an annuity granted by the Accidental Death Insurance Company, for which Windham said he had paid £16,000 and was now valued at the same amount. The bankrupt also had an interest in freehold estates (led, of course, by Hanworth) valued at £25,000. Mrs Windham's trustees claimed all property, together with policies of assurance said to be worth £41,000, the consideration [payment] for which was only £11,000, leaving a surplus value of £30,000. But the court disputed the transaction and already had filed a bill in Chancery to stop it. The court was told, in addition, that Windham had given up property worth £1,007 to pay his debts. A further complication was introduced by a solicitor, Mr Brough, who appeared for a Miss Laws. She had taken out an action against Windham for assault, and claimed £200. This, it subsequently transpired, was for an alleged rape and seduction.

But Bankruptcy Commissioner Winslow said it would be 'straining the statute to hold a man guilty of extravagant expenditure, when by his accounts - the correctness of which had not been questioned - he showed a surplus of £28,000'. His decision was inevitable: Windham was discharged. The irony was his 'paper wealth' depended almost entirely on those insurance policies and in fact Windham was still almost penniless. It was no good expecting the coach business to make money. The reality was that the venture, such as it was, hardly paid anything at all. And with Windham at the helm, it could surely have hardly been anything else. But it was better than nothing: the rationale of the General and Bingham was that 'the loss on the coach would be light in comparison with the loss arising from his accepting bills for anything he could get, and afterwards ridding himself of the proceeds with knaves and strumpets'. In an ironic twist, two of the customers who regularly entrusted their son to Windham's coach services were Mr and Mrs John Ketton - Felbrigg's new owners.

THERE WAS one loose end in Agnes' assured handling of Windham's finances: the fate of the £5,000, put aside in 1862 and kept out of her control ever since. Another cutting in the volume of Windham matters carefully compiled by Peter Hansell and now in Norfolk Record Office, and from an unnamed magazine report on 27 May 1865 gives a colourful and unashamedly biased account of an attempt by Agnes to get her hands on it.

In its report, headed 'NOT OVER YET', describing Agnes as 'that womanly constellation of delicacy, virtue, pride and honour... a life black with every species of wickedness and unilluminated by a single virtue', mentioned how she had rushed back from France because, she claimed, she had been told Windham was ill. Far from it - 'Mr Windham had, that very afternoon, mounted his coach, smacked his whip, blown his whistle, laughed his laugh and cracked his joke'. Windham had been told that Agnes was on her way (and after his money once again) and, this time, had refused to open his door in Cromer, despite her 'Willy, dear...' entreaties. He took his chance to later slip away back to Norwich, leaving Agnes in Cromer. 'Later in the day Mrs Windham got into the room,' the report claimed, 'and searched the drawers and read the letters of her husband,' before downing two or three brandies in her frustration at being thwarted. Vivid stuff, but it is hard to think how anyone could have witnessed all this actually taking place. The real point was its illustration of the hatred many felt for the estranged Mrs Windham.

But Agnes must have managed, finally, to overturn the 1862 injunction at some time over the following few weeks. There was a hearing on 20 July at which the Oxford Street store of Grant and Gask sought to get its hands on £1,136 for 'goods supplied previous to her reconciliation with her husband'. Windham may have managed to outwit Agnes in May, but his life continued its inevitable decline, as his absurd coaching business faltered, losing Bingham and the General a reported £1,040. He had fallen in love, yet again, this time with a local barmaid. She urged him to get rid of the coach and, infatuated, he even contemplated finally securing a divorce from Agnes. He failed to manage that - the reports were that he had been sent away in brusque manner by his uncle's solicitor who had refused to pay for yet another abortive divorce petition - but he did agree to sell his coach. Without the coach service in his life, everything fell apart.

ON 20 DECEMBER 1865 the Norwich Mercury provided some pre-Christmas amusement for its readers by relating the latest in a long line of 'Windham stories'. 'Mr William Frederick Windham,' the report began, 'appears to have become ambitious of military honours, for on Saturday last, having met Sergeant Bradford, of the 6th or Enniskillen Dragoons, with other recruiting sergeants, he persisted in bearing them company at several public-houses of the city, and taunted them that they dare not enlist him. He was quite sober at the time, and at last was taken at his word, the shilling was handed over, and Mr Windham found that his joke had cost him the usual guinea paid as smart money, which on after reflection *(sic)*, he deemed it wise to pay.'

Only a few months before a guinea would have been a matter of mere small change for Windham. Not any more. The public had been told on 22 May 1864, as part of his bankruptcy hearing, that Agnes was paying him an annual allowance of £500, her side of the bargain when she had taken out £41,000 of life assurance secured on Windham. That should have secured a comfortable living even for such a notorious rake as Windham, but in fact he was now in extreme poverty. The General had taken court action to force Agnes to pay the allowance, only for Windham to shoot himself in the foot yet again, by (also yet again) being persuaded - by Agnes, one can only assume - to change his solicitor. Agnes was later to claim that, despite the evidence of the May 1864 court report, she had not, in fact, bought Windham's life interest until February 1865. Whatever the truth, the reality was that Windham had never received the £500 at all.

When the coach venture crumbled, Windham and another man broke open the stables at Cromer and Aylsham, sold the horses for cash (£130) and then, in the words of the Argus, Windham 'went to a tavern in London, got tipsy and lost the whole of the proceeds save one five-pound note'.

Although the Windham case had never really faded from the public's imagination, by now it had been overtaken by another - that of society beauty Lady Florence Paget, nicknamed the 'Pocket Venus', who secretly married the notorious Marquis of Hastings days before she was supposed to wed Henry Chaplin. Even though it took place in far wealthier circles than even the once-wealthy Norfolk landowner Windham had moved in, there were curious parallels between the marquis and himself: both lost their fathers early (Harry Hastings when he was just 18 months), both associated freely with the 'lower orders', both spent only a short time at Eton, with Harry's upbringing - in words which exactly applied to Windham - described as 'far too much money, far too much freedom, and far too little discipline'. There was to be one more, grimmer, link: thanks to their lifestyles, both were to die at almost the same age.

And for 'Mad' Windham, his personal Nemesis was, at last, almost here.

18

1866:
'The Day of Retribution'

'Look at this unhappy wretch... Look at him, mark his history and his fall!'
Norwich Argus, 10 February 1866

'If you prefer low company, and idle pursuits and vice, you will certainly die
a beggar, and in all probability without the regret of any one.'
William Charles Hood, interviewing Windham on 13 December 1861

ALTHOUGH predictions of Windham's early death had been made for years, the end, when it came, still took many by surprise. 'The day of retribution has come when it was least expected,' wrote the Norwich Mercury, a view shared by many for whom the ex-Squire of Felbrigg's antics had now become merely part of an ever-present background of low-level local scandal.

From his base at the Norfolk Hotel in Norwich, Windham's days in 1865 and early 1866 were spent as they had been for years - in a continual haze of drinking with a merry-go-round of temporary boon companions, who usually lasted exactly as long as Windham's cash. His food intake, however, was now haphazard at best, and only the charity of his friend and fellow coach driver Tom Saul resulted in Windham being treated to his favourite meal (fried rabbit). The first hint that things were different came on Tuesday 30 January 1866 when Windham, now 25, complained of being unwell. It was dismissed as the inevitable result of too much alcoholic indulgence, but when he failed to improve the next day and said he was 'a little faintish', his medical attendant, F C Bailey, was sent for.

Bailey diagnosed him as having a 'slightly bilious derangement' - hardly surprising seeing as he had barely eaten for the previous fortnight - but by the Thursday Windham seemed better. Windham had in fact managed to get up after Bailey had left but could only stagger down to the hotel yard and quickly returned to his room, where he promptly retched for a period of twenty minutes. In the evening Saul called to see him and they talked about horses and coaches until 11pm, when he left the now 'drowsy' Windham. By the next day, when Bailey returned in the early morning to check on his patient, there was again talk of him getting out of bed. Bailey, reassured, went about his business in the city - but when he called in to the hotel at lunchtime he found the picture had changed utterly. Windham's symptoms had suddenly 'become so much worse and alarming' that Bailey immediately called in a doctor. What had happened was that around 8am the hotel waiter had taken a cup of coffee and some dry toast to Windham, but on returning twenty minutes later 'a fearful change' had taken place, with the patient's mouth open and his eyes looking up, blankly, at the ceiling.

Dr Bateman at once agreed with Bailey's conclusion that Windham was, in fact, dying, 'the symptoms being those of sudden collapse, either from an obstruction in, or from rupture of, one of the large vessels'. Windham's one-time business associate Thomas Bingham had heard about his condition by now and hurried to his side. The General was telegrammed with the news of Windham's condition, and yet another medical man, Dr Eade, was called in. Despite attempts to revive Windham with ammonia and brandy-and-egg, his condition grew worse. The drama in the room was played out in a 'dreadful silence' with only 'the ticking of their various watches sounding prenaturally loud'. Windham asked in a whisper if the General had been seen and then, spotting Bingham, said 'There's Tom!'.

They were the last words he ever said: an hour later, at 3.45pm on Friday 2 February, the last Windham of Felbrigg died, in the presence of the two doctors, Mr Bailey, Bingham and a clutch of curious hotel servants. The General, meanwhile, had caught the first available express from London but arrived too late, and returned to the capital on the Saturday. It was only at this point that Agnes, being still legally Windham's next-of-kin, was summoned. But she stayed on in London instead, being 'too ill' to leave her house. The Penny Illustrated Paper had another explanation, claiming that she was actually in Paris at the time. It was decided that the death had been so sudden that a post mortem was needed, and was duly carried out by the three medical men. They found a blood clot in the pulmonary artery, which quelled already-circulating rumours that Windham had been poisoned. They also, if the claims of the Norwich Argus are to be believed, took the opportunity to do rather more: 'Surgeons... were sawing off the top of his skull to take a survey of that brain which had played such games and caused so much perplexity and woe'. They removed the former squire's stomach and brain for later examination.

Ketton-Cremer blamed Windham's death on 'drink and nervous excitement', but his demise may have been caused by a more insidious underlying cause: his syphilis. It was not until nine years later that it was discovered that there was a direct link between syphilis and a large proportion of aortic failures. It is at least possible that this artery, rather than the pulmonary, was the real source of his heart failure. Significantly, too, behaviour frequently to be observed with the final onset of syphilis - violent mood swings, weight loss, tiredness, hesitant speech, inactivity - were all shown by Windham in his last few weeks.

If there had been little dignity in his death, and less still in the post-mortem, after his death things only became worse. Windham's shirts were so tattered that the undertaker had to use one from another corpse, to clothe the body, which was 'little better than a flesh shell carefully stuffed with straw'. An undertaker's foreman, sent by Agnes, arrived from London, measured the body, and returned to London again.

On the evening of Tuesday 7 February, the lead coffin arrived, followed the next day by the oak outer coffin. Agnes, meanwhile, had secured the agreement of the new owner of Felbrigg, John Ketton, that her husband could be interred in the family vault at the estate church. At 3pm on Wednesday Miss Harris, of the Norfolk Hotel, received a telegram instructing her to order a carriage to meet the London express train to take 'two ladies and two gentlemen' to Cromer. At 5pm the coffin, followed by a wagonette with Bingham, Saul, and just two others, began its journey to Cromer, where it would stay the night. 'And this was the end,' the Argus observed, 'of an individual who had possessed thousands upon thousands of pounds, as he was the possessor of hundreds upon hundreds of acres, and now he was hurrying "home" in another man's shirt, without a relative to accompany him.'

William Frederick Windham made his final journey to Felbrigg soon after nine the next morning. The cortege left the Belle Vue Hotel in Cromer for the short journey, arriving at around 10.30am at St Margaret's Church. The church is a few hundred yards from the hall, a typical handsome medieval church in a county where every vista seems to feature a church tower. The glory of St Margaret's is its brass to Sir Simon de Felbrigg, almost three metres long and one of the finest in England. But inevitably, of course, the eye is drawn to the various family monuments to the Windham family. It was a church which had seen many great family events in its long history. This was to be one of the last - and the least.

As well as the two Toms and their companions, the identity of the London party (in the event numbering only three) was revealed: Madama La Fuente - Agnes' sister Thirza - a Colonel White (described as 'a friend of Mrs Windham's and her family') and Agnes' physician Dr Gibson. They were joined by Windham's ex-solicitor Isaac Coaks, Felbrigg steward and stewardess and family friends Mr and Mrs Martin, and - the only one of his former tenant farmers to turn up - Mr Riches of Hanworth.

The service was taken by the Rev Mr Fitch from Cromer. It was all over by 11.10am. An anonymous correspondent wrote to the Argus on 10 February that 'There was no order or decorum - all confusion, and indeed any looker-on [implying, of course, that there were none] would have scarcely believed that there was a mourner present, unless detected by the manly emotion of his old chums. Hurrying to get the work done, the coffin was damaged putting it in its last resting place. The whole affair was a disgrace to the parties who conducted it. Poor fellow! We know he had his faults, but surely some one might have seen that he was placed in his last home in a decent and respectable manner.'

The Argus, in a searing editorial on 10 February, had little sympathy for Windham. 'It would be difficult to find a man so made up of absurdity as the one just passed away,' it wrote. 'He was born to do honour to his order; unquestionably he was its disgrace. He might have moved with the first people in the county; in place of which he preferred the carrion of the Haymarket and the boots and grooms of the sixth-rate "publics" in Norwich. From his marriage to his bankruptcy to his driving the "Express" for £1 a week, it was but one rapid decline, and his early descent to the grave has probably saved him from the further degradation of a cabmanship in the Strand, or the position of a pauper in the Erpingham hundred. He trailed his position in the mud and lost it; he associated with scoundrels and prostitutes, and squandered his patrimony.'

At the last his truest, his only friends, did not include the wife who had left him; nor those members of his family who had professed an interest in saving him from himself; nor the lawyers who grew rich on the pickings of his estate; nor his former tenants; nor the hundreds of drinking companions, whores and assorted hangers-on who had drunk to his health with Windham's own money. His only friends were his old coaching associates, 'the two Toms'. At the start of the funeral, Tom Saul turned to his companions and said - deliberately loud enough for the London visitors to hear - 'Fall in! We are the genuine people here.'

218

19

1866-1870:
Searching for Respectability

'The cries rang out:: "Long live the youthful heir!" '
The Leader, 30 October 1869

IT WAS not, of course, the end of the story.

'The public,' the Mercury suggested, 'will be naturally curious as to the position of the property.' Their curiosity was soon to be satisfied. But before that, Windham's death provided an excellent opportunity for newspapers and commentators to look back at why the young squire had fallen so fast and so quickly (and, no doubt, for plenty of clergy, too, seeking an example of moral turpitude for that week's sermons). It was one of these editorials, in the Daily Telegraph on 5 February, which was to spark off the next events in the affair. The paper's account piqued the General, once again, into writing his side of the story.

Although you have declared that you have done with my nephew,' he wrote on 8 February from his home at 60 St George's Square, 'I trust that you will publish these few remarks that I have to make on your article. You say that in young Windham's case "a weak brain and brutish temperament were left without education or care".

219

Was not he sent to a good private school at the age of eight, and afterwards to Eton? Did not the Vice-Chancellor, Sir W P Wood, take special interest in his case, and cause the best tutors he could find to be put about him? You say "that it was an honourable instinct that made the public denounce the relations who were anxious only about Windham's conduct when they saw it involved their reversionary interests". If that which is stated above be correct, how can this assertion be justified? All his relations could not be interested. The interests of the Bristol family [ie the Herveys] were directly the other way, and the greater part of my family had no interest in it whatever. I was, indeed, the chief person denounced, and the public were led to believe that Felbrigg, in the event of the young man being declared insane, would at his death come to me. This would not have been the case; it would have gone to my brother, who is a year older than I am.

'In another paragraph you say "it was painful to see the oaks falling at Felbrigg to pay for unbridled profligacy." No, Sir, the oaks at Felbrigg fell to pay robbery, not profligacy; and the great part of the money made away with during young Windham's life went the same way.

'You say of my nephew, "mad he never was" &c. May I ask which of his family ever said that he was mad? Did we not one and all declare that he had no delusions, and was not mad? Lord Eldon said that for a man to be legally of unsound mind it is not necessary that he should have delusions, provided he be so weak of intellect as easily to become the prey of evil and designing persons. It was their belief in the soundness of this opinion that induced Windham's family to try by law to save him. They did not succeed. Time has, I think, proved whether the jury formed a more correct estimate of the young man's mind than did his family.

'By the verdict of the jury he was left absolutely free, and, consequently, allowed to ruin his property and his health; to worry and annoy every one connected with him, and quickly to become a beggar and a bankrupt; and ultimately to die at the early age of twenty-five, leaving, as a climax, an infant son that he has solemnly sworn before the Court of Chancery is not his child, although the law gives it him.

'Surely, Sir, my family have had enough to bear through the imbecility of this young man, without your adding to the burthen by your unjust and charitable remarks.

'My nephew was not buried until to-day, or I should have written to you sooner.'

It was a powerful mixture of sympathy and rhetoric, complete with its coda, the apparently poignancy of which was only undermined by the undeniable fact that neither the General or the rest of the caring relatives had bothered to attend the funeral. But the public's attention would have been drawn to the reference to Windham apparently being about to repudiate his son and heir to the Hanworth estate.

The General's words were reported, approvingly, back in Norfolk by the Norwich Mercury and Argus, who had both supported his campaign from the outset. But the comments of the Daily Telegraph and the General had drawn a more intriguing commentator into the fray. For now Agnes, too, had broken her silence.

Writing on 10 February from Upper Westbourne Terrace, she wrote: 'My attention has been drawn to a paragraph which appeared in your paper to the effect that General Windham compelled me to grant my late husband an annuity. As that statement is not a correct representation of the facts, I trust, in common fairness, you will permit me to state what actually did occur. When I purchased my husband's life interest in February, 1865, which I was advised to do by my solicitors and the trustees to my marriage settlement, in order to save the property, I immediately settled upon him an annuity of £500 a year, to be increased to £1,000 a year in October, 1869, so that he might have a certain income for his life.

'This was an entirely voluntary act on my part, and entered into without any intervention, either direct or indirect, of General Windham. I take this opportunity of adding, with reference to the latter part of General Windham's letter to you of the 8th instant, that if my late husband falsely swore that my boy was not his son, it was by advice and at the instigation of members of the legal profession.'

This was too much for the Norwich Argus. On 17 February, in its second long editorial in as many weeks on Windham, it reported approvingly of the General's letter 'calling to account' the Daily Telegraph for 'his systematic annoyance to the Windham family' - but its real subject was Agnes' reply. Her letter, the paper waxed sarcastic, called on the public 'to believe that the exertions of this estimable lady have invariably been directed to the comfort and happiness of her poor passed away wretched husband'.

The Argus said it would not be commenting on the intriguing matter of the legitimacy of Windham's son - 'that important question must be settled at a higher tribunal than ours, and probably will cost many a thousand before it is finally disposed of' - but said the business of the annuity was something else, and 'respecting that, we do not intend to let the lady off so lightly'. They did not: Agnes, they said, was Windham's 'evil genius'. 'The settlement he made on her, the jewellery he bedizened her with, the sacrifices he made for her, all point to this.' The £500 annuity, they said, had been given by Agnes in exchange for a £3,000 life assurance policy on her husband. But the generosity was a sham, the paper alleged, as Agnes had carefully inserted a clause saying that if the rapidly-declining Windham went bankrupt, she would not be liable to pay it.

Just six weeks later, Windham had indeed been unable to fob off his creditors any longer and the 'expectant of Hanworth' was declared bankrupt. Since then, the paper claimed, 'all he had received from her has been a ten-pound note at Christmas, and a five-pound note since'. The paper's unnamed informant, but clearly Tom Saul or one of the Norfolk Hotel employees, went on to say how, after the final gift, Windham had 'got tipsy, slapped people on the back with his hard, strong hand; with a little cane he would switch them on the shoulders, he hit them with his hat, he punched them with his elbow, and when they turned he invited them "to a drain" at So-and-So's, as it was his missus's birthday [December 19], and she had sent him a "fiver". And when they hesitated, he shouted that they were "bound to go," and they went.'

If he had ever received this alleged £500, the Argus argued, then why were his bills at the Norfolk Hotel, lodgings in Cromer and innumerable Norwich pubs still unpaid? And why had he been destitute and, literally, 'without a shirt' at the end? The £500 had gone, it concluded, 'where all his other worldly hopes and prospects went - dashed on a reef called "Ann Agnes," which in place of forming a breakwater for him in the storm, drove him rudderless and compassless into a maelstrom of seething vice and unparalleled extravagance, without one attempt to soothe, one effort to recall, or half-struggle to restrain.

'And now that he is dead a letter creeps into the columns of the Telegraph which we hope this explanation will put to silence, and we trust, before many months are over, the "gentlemen of the long robe" will so arrange matters, that the dim eclipse and disastrous twilight under which the present "heir" exists, will be cleared away, and in the pure, unclouded rays of Justice, we shall be able to record the hands into which the Hanworth estate must eventually fall.'

If Agnes was left smarting at this latest editorial then this time, at least, she did not rise to the bait. She must have known that, with Windham dead, there could be no serious claim now as to the legitimacy of the son. Pure and unclouded the rays of Justice might be, but without any serious evidence to add weight to the widespread gossip they would not be shining anywhere. That did not stop the General from trying, but Agnes was able to prove that, contrary to his later repudiation, Windham had been on good terms with her at the time of the conception.

But Agnes did not have it all her own way. Sir William Page Wood made an order on 16 July 1866 that she must accept joint guardians for her son, Dr Septimus Gibbon - sometime Medical Officer of Holborn District and a Crimean veteran - and his wife Janet. Further, she was ordered to come up with a scheme for young Frederick's maintenance and education and - to her inevitable chagrin - allowed her only as much of £400 a year ('from certain trust funds') as she could prove was for her son's benefit.

The General, by now, was beginning to lose something of his stomach for another long and drawn-out fight. After the death of his beloved first wife in 1863, he married mutual friend, Charlotte des Voeux, in 1864 and - at last - was knighted in 1865.

A contemporary photograph shows him looking aged beyond his years, worn out by too many battles in war and peace. By 1866 his health was beginning to suffer. The following year he returned to Canada. Agnes had apparently outwitted the Hero of the Redan once again.

AND SO began the next stage in her life, that of the mother of the heir of Hanworth, a role to which she devoted the rest of her days.

Hanworth Hall, only a few miles from Felbrigg, is now only a couple of minutes' drive from the A140 along which the holiday traffic streams to Cromer and the north Norfolk coast. In Agnes' day it was reached via a maze of country lanes through gently rolling countryside, woods and meadows. To appreciate its setting, it is still best to do exactly the same. Although undeniably smaller than Felbrigg, it has some claims to be a more aesthetically satisfying house, being of classic - and elegant - William and Mary design.

Mortlock and Roberts wrote in 1981 how the approach to nearby St Bartholomew's Church, was 'a pleasing excursion into old England', and there is no denying that the view from the isolated building over to the hall (which, unlike Felbrigg, is a private house not open to the public) is a splendid one. Framed by the trees, the hall has a large ornamental lake in front (which did not exist in Agnes' day) from which two Elizabethan helmets were dredged up more than a century ago - or so the attractive story goes. Pevsner describes the building as a 'plain but very fine' two-storey house, while Kelly's Directory of 1908 was more fulsome, calling it 'a noble modern mansion of brick standing in a pleasant park of 160 acres'.

It was in this setting that the little Frederick William Howe Lindsay Bacon Windham was to inherit, the future possessor of the long-awaited £9,000 a year rental income. That his was a handsome estate can be seen by the fact it included lands in a seemingly endless list of Norfolk towns and villages, like Hanworth a litany of old England: Aldborough, Alby, Aylmerton, Aylsham, North Barningham, South Barningham, Baconsthorpe, Banningham, East Beckham, West Beckham, Bodham, Colby, Cromer, Dilham, Erpingham, Gresham, Ingworth, Metton, Roughton, Runton, Sheringham, Smallburgh, Sustead, Thurgarton, Thwaite, Tuttington, Honing and Worstead.

AGNES WAS determined that there should be no ambiguity about his status as a future country gentleman, and there is a tangible insight into her doting attentions with two items donated in the 1960s by an unnamed donor to the Norfolk Museums and Archaeology Service.

These are some of the day clothes, inspired by eastern designs, which were thought to have been Frederick's when he was aged perhaps five or six. Meant to be worn over shirts, they are made of taffeta, their most noticeable feature being their bold colours, electric blue and plum, using the latest and ultra-fashionable aniline dyes. Agnes had always been the acme of fashion; it was clear she wanted her son to follow suit. These were showy clothes, and meant to be: young Frederick, with his shock of brilliant blonde hair inherited from his mother, would have been a striking sight. The Penny Illustrated Paper, writing in 1869 described him as 'the youthful heir, a fine, handsome boy'.

Gradually she began to move away from her London past into that of respectable Norfolk country house life. The process was not a smooth one, however. In the autumn of 1868 there was a court hearing in which Agnes was sued to recover the cost of a telegraphic message sent to Cuba in April of that year to another lover, Silvio, saying 'he must come in a month, or give me up'.

Sometime over the summer of that year Agnes must have decided that her days of being a member of the London démi-monde were finally at an end, although she was to maintain her Upper Westbourne Terrace base for several years. There was no greater evidence for this than the news that she had married again, to George Walker, eight years her senior. Walker, whom she married in September in the village of Steyning in Sussex (they were staying at nearby Hove at the time), was the agent of the Hanworth estate. Significantly, Agnes intended to hold on to the Windham name for as long as possible - instead of becoming simply 'Mrs Walker', she persuaded George to join his name to hers and so the couple were styled 'Mrs and Mrs Windham-Walker'. Donald MacAndrew described the marriage as one of convenience - true enough - but described Walker as a 'block-like, God-fearing yeoman'. In this he, and Agnes, were to be sadly mistaken.

IN OCTOBER the following year the Court of Chancery considered Agnes' plea to have full custody of her son - and more money. Walker, she said, had 'no income or property of his own'. Vice Chancellor Wood agreed that Agnes and her son could move into Hanworth later that month, but Frederick still had the status of a 'Ward in Chancery' and was subject to the ultimate say of the courts. More inconvenient for Agnes, no doubt, was that fact that the guardians by now included her old enemy the General, as well as a court appointee (William Henry Griffin) and Frederick's second cousin, Charles, Lord Suffield. The truth was that Agnes had not been frank with the court. In her desperation to have full custody of Frederick she had concealed the true nature of her marriage, a fact which was only to emerge twelve years later.

That real story was that George Walker, far from being a docile and dull haven of respectability, was in fact a violent and grasping man who only married Agnes for her money, making this fact plain to her only a few weeks after their marriage. Agnes, so shrewd in her choice of rich lovers and husbands, had failed to see that as an extremely rich widow (she had inherited an estate of between £30,000-£40,000 on Windham's death, worth perhaps £1.7 million in today's money) she would herself be a target of sharpers. She was to conceal her unhappiness and the true state of the marriage for years.

FURTHER TO her quest for full respectability, Agnes was by now cultivating the local vicar, the Rev Veitch, on an avowedly spiritual quest. Was she sincere? It is hard to tell, but it is clear that even now she had not been entirely forgiven for

Frederick William Howe Lindsay Bacon Windham: Pictured aged five, in August 1869, a 'fine, handsome boy' in the words of one newspaper.
(NRO ref: MC580/1, 780x1)

her earlier misdemeanours. On 20 October 1869, there was a celebration fete to mark the final paying-off of the mortgage on Hanworth, raised by William Frederick Windham's father all those years ago from Hudson Gurney bank, and the consequent accession to his estate by the five-year-old Frederick.

The Norwich Argus reported, waspishly: 'Mrs Windham, who having remarried, is now Mrs Walker, appeared on the scene with her husband and some choice spirits from London, and, taken as a whole, despite the coldness of the weather, the rural sports may said to have been, in their way, a success. Most of the magnates of both county and city received invitations to the fete. The weather alone, we presume, prevented them personally doing honour to the young heir of Hanworth.'

But for those who had turned up, as The Leader of 30 October reported, it had been a splendid occasion. Despite being late in autumn, the weather was favourable with a clear blue sky over the two large tents which had been set up to house almost 900 cottagers in three sittings, plus 120 old folk in the hall itself. The guests managed to demolish a meal of heroic proportions, involving three sacks of flour, a bullock weighing 50 stone (carried in by eight men), six sacks of potatoes, 220st plums and currants, 40 brace of partridges, 20 brace of pheasants, 18 'hares, turkies (sic), geese & co', 40 gallons of soup, 150lbs or beef and mutton - plus 'bread, ale, champagne, sherry, butter, and game-pies in a species of titanic proportions'. The young squire was reported to be 'intelligent and winning in his manners, and declared refined in his appearance and conduct'. There was a procession, with the young squire 'lustily cheered'. The cries rang out: 'Long live the youthful heir!' and the health of Mr and Mrs Windham-Walker was drunk.

The Leader went on to say that Agnes then rose and was received with 'great cheering'. She told the gathering: 'Before returning to you my sincere and heartfelt thanks for the kind manner in which you have received the toast proposed by Mr Richardson, allow me to take this opportunity of thanking, and no one but myself knows how deep felt those thanks are, my kind friend, Mr Veitch, for the great honour he has done me and my child in being present on this occasion. From the moment that he planted the sign of the cross on the forehead of my baby and asked the blessing of God on his behalf, I have been under his ministration.

'I have appealed to him often for guidance and support. I have never appealed in vain. I am afraid I have sorely taxed his patience, but to him I owe the spirit of Christian humility and grace to which I was a stranger before I knew him. I am under the deepest obligations to him, more than I can express.

'I thank you sincerely, gentlemen, for your kindness in coming here today. My desire is to so educate my son that when he comes into man's estate he may prove a good landlord, and a sincere Christian - it was because I desired that your interest should ever be a consideration with him that I asked you to meet here this day, and I trust that the proceedings may be pressed upon his youthful mind. It is my desire that his interests shall be identified with yours, and no endeavour shall be wanting on my part, to educate him, in a manner that he may be worthy of the name he bears, and prove in after life a good landlord, and a Christian gentleman.'

That was the end of the speeches, with the company now adjourning to the lawn, where they were entertained with a 'fine display' of fireworks. Then it was time for dancing - which lasted until midnight - Mrs Windham leading off with the traditional

Sir Roger de Coverley. The Leader reported favourably on the 29-year-old Agnes: 'Mrs Windham was dressed in blue velvet, which favourably harmonised with her golden hair, and heightened the brilliancy of some splendid ornaments.' Even though Agnes was firmly on the path to matronly respectability, she had not lost her sense of style.

Perhaps it is from around this period, or within a few years of it, that the portrait of Agnes which is now at Felbrigg dates. It has nothing of the coquettish pretty horse-breaker about it, nothing of the bold, defiant stare straight to camera of her photographs. Agnes has become respectable, with only the star-like decorations in her still-richly blonde hair hinting at her earlier life.

Thirza de la Fuente: Agnes' sister, pictured here in June 1869, was, like Emma, the focus of Agnes' efforts to secure her family's financial future.

(Helen Denney)

The return of the young heir was a memorable occasion, then, and Agnes added one more extra to ensure it was not to be forgotten: commemorative coins - one of which is still in possession of the family - were struck, with the legend 'FREDERICK HOWE LINDSAY BACON WINDHAM OF HANWORTH HALL' and the Windham arms, and on the reverse 'TO HIS FRIENDS AND TENANTRY OF TAKING POSSESSION OF HIS ESTATES OCTOBER 11th 1869'. Agnes could afford to be generous: now the mortgage had at last been paid off, young Frederick had an income amounting to more than £5,000 a year. Joining the Windham Walkers and young Frederick at Hanworth were a governess and a tutor.

The satirical weekly Tomahawk could not resist sprinkling some sourness over the unbridled sweetness of the occasion. In its issue of 27 November it harrumphed over Agnes' mention of 'Christian humility'. It wrote: 'This profession of Christian humility is profoundly touching, and reminds us of the gentle spirit of Uriah Heep'. Clearly, Agnes' 'umble' protestations were too much, too soon, for many.

The Norfolk News was much more enthusiastic about Agnes' Christmas largesse the following month. It praised her 'kindness and generosity' unreservedly, saying her gifts to the poor might be 'truly described as lavish'. Agnes was also giving twice-weekly Bible classes, with soup provided for the poor every Saturday and Christmas gifts for the children. 'The Christmas of 1869 will long be remembered as one of the

Agnes Windham-Walker: The mother of the young squire of Hanworth was determinedly on the path - however rocky - towards respectability.

(© National Trust/ Sue James)

happiest ever recorded,' it concluded. The Christmas period also included an annual distribution of coal, carted in by local farmers for distribution to the needy. Agnes' generosity to her tenants helped create a deep affection for her among them. The appreciation was genuine: the life of the rural poor in Norfolk could be as grindingly bleak as anything in the stinking yards of the industrial cities, as the powerful writings of Victorian authors Mary Mann and the Rev Augustus Jessopp, among others, make clear.

And then in February 1870 came the closure of another chapter in the Windham story. Major-General Sir Charles Ashe Windham, KCB, 'Hero of the Redan', died. He had been in Canada since 1867, when he was appointed Commander of the Imperial Forces. While on a trip to Florida to inspect some land he had bought he suffered a series of heart attacks. And with his passing went Agnes' bitterest enemy. He was replaced as a guardian in July by Agnes' husband George, with a court order also increasing the allowance for Frederick from £400 to £1,200, half to cover essential running costs at Hanworth and the remainder for 'the maintenance and education of the infant'. The following month the Hon Arthur Fitzgerald Kinnaird was appointed Receiver of the rents of the Hanworth estates.

In the same year Agnes' sister Emma married Henry Denney, an auctioneer and land manager. It was not, perhaps, the brilliant aristocratic marriage Agnes had hoped for her French-educated sibling, but the Denneys' marriage proved to be a deep and loving union which lasted for 20 years and resulted in ten children. It also brought into Agnes' life Henry's best friend Rowland Jones Hughes - someone whom fate had determined was to play an important role in her own life.

20

1871-1896:
The Master of Hanworth

'Let us hope the troubles of the old house of Windham are over now,
and its lot is to be bright and happy.'
Norwich Argus, May 1885

IN 1871 Agnes was still living at 3ª Upper Westbourne Terrace, the census of that year giving a snapshot of her household. It consisted of herself and her husband George, then 38. At number four were her long-serving maid, 29-year-old Susannah Jeffey, an errand boy and a manservant - plus Agnes' 54-year-old mother Ann Burden (by now she had married Agnes' former 'butler' John Burden), and her two servants, Amelia Hobbes and Alice Lambert. On the same day, meanwhile, six-year-old Frederick was back in Norfolk in the village of Gresham, near Holt, visiting his aunt Emma.

Agnes' old enemy, the Norfolk News, left the Christmas festivities at Hanworth Hall unreported for several years. But its report of 1876 is notable both for its length and for the insight it gives into the Windham-Walker household. Its issue of 30 December reported two of the events at the hall. The first, on 19 December, was a concert to mark Agnes' 36th birthday.

Taking place in the large dining room 'tastefully arranged and decorated for the occasion', around 150 guests sat down for the soirée. The programme they witnessed was varied and 'excellently performed', according to the Mercury's correspondent.

After hearing from a chorus of a dozen of the local children - kitted out in 'neat and warm' frocks presented by Agnes - the hostess herself created a 'furore' (in the sense of widespread enthusiasm) with her 'charming and excellent voice' rendering Level's Angel's Whisper and Sullivan's Once Again. Then it was Frederick's turn. The 12-year-old young squire sang Dolores' Book to widespread appreciation. Now it was time to hear from Agnes' sisters, Emma and Thirza, who also 'sang very sweetly'. The other performers included Henry Denney's friend Rowland Hughes. The concert, which had begun at 7pm, drew to a close at 9.30pm, with young Frederick responding 'very neatly' to the vote of thanks. At 10pm, with the guests now dispersed, a select party of friends sat down to an excellent meal. It had been a most agreeable evening for all concerned.

As well as the birthday concert, there was a Christmas Day dinner for the villagers of Hanworth at the hall, so that 'a certain and attractive evening's amusement could be provided without resorting to the public house.' In the spirit of Saturnalia, Agnes and George and several guests served the 22 villagers at their 'capital' dinner, which took place in the servants' hall (the Saturnalian spirit only being permitted to extended so far). The villagers had subscribed money regularly towards the cost of the meal, which George now presented back to them in the form of vouchers redeemable for groceries or clothes - but not the demon drink, the point, of course, of the whole scheme. It continued: 'After dinner and dessert, an entertainment was given by Mr Windham Walker, who exhibited the magic lantern to the guests, schoolchildren and villagers.' Afterwards the room was cleared of furniture so everyone could enjoy country dances and songs, which all 'brought the evening to a most satisfactory conclusion'.

While her sister Emma settled down to a life of domestic rectitude in Norfolk, Agnes seems to have preferred a more peripatetic lifestyle, spending several months a year abroad in Boulogne, including at least part of the time at the Chateau Bedoêtre. There is a photograph of her, much faded, in traditional French country dress, taken at Quimper probably sometime in the late 1870s. She is pictured, rather unconvincingly, against a studio-created rustic fence. Another studio photograph, dated to between 1874-6, shows Agnes in more typical dress, with the distinctive double-skirt of the period and the gathering of the dress which was to evolve into the famous 'bustle' of the 1870s. Agnes, blonde hair still magnificent, has her favourite earrings - drop pearls - and a long rope of pearls around her waist.

But this apparent period of contentment was a sham. It was in fact a time of deep personal unhappiness for Agnes, the cause of which was her husband, whose grasping nature finally peaked in 1878 when their marriage collapsed. Walker took as much of her furniture and jewellery as possible and sold the lot, including jewels to the value of £15,000 - almost certainly the much-vaunted 'Windham jewels'. With this fortune he abandoned Agnes and set sail for Australia. All this only emerged two years later when a desperate Agnes applied for, and was granted, a protection order to save the rest of her property, pointing out to Bow Street Police Court that Walker had 'knocked her down' at times during their marriage as well as taking her money. Agnes was forced to go to court because she had heard that her estranged husband had made plans to return to England, and feared he would try to purloin even more of her property.

By now Rowland Hughes had become the new love in Agnes' life, one of the ties which bound them together being a deep mutual appreciation of music. Agnes had yearned to be a singer since her days with Giuglini, when she had taken professional lessons. She proved, indeed, to have talents in this direction both as a performer in public soirées (as shown by that 1876 birthday concert) but also as a songwriter. She had published at least two songs by 1883: What The Bells Are Saying and the patriotic Three Cheers For Old England.

The latter was performed by Hughes at the third of a series of annual charitable dinners given by Agnes each February for visiting British sailors in Boulogne. The Norwich Argus' report of this 1883 dinner reported that 400 guests had enjoyed Agnes' hospitality. A few days earlier, another 400 guests, members of the crew of a British steamer, were also given a dinner at the port's Salle Bouvier. The Argus described Agnes sarcastically as 'this pious lady', but also mentioned that every Saturday she paid for bread for a hundred of the local poor (with the addition of soup in winter). When it added the comment 'Truly, this is real charity,' it meant to do so with irony. But even Agnes' longest-running critics - and the Argus was certainly in that camp - would surely have had to concede that her largesse went beyond the mere socially-acceptable window-dressing of 'good works'.

An unattributed newspaper cutting from 1884 - collected by the ever-efficient Windham family solicitor Hansell - gives a few more hints of her life, albeit still rather acidly. It tells how 'Mrs Windham' appeared to be 'the patron saint of Boulogne' and was held in high esteem by the local people. The French journal La Colonne, it said, had reported further 'numerous' acts of charity on her behalf, including an annual fête for 105 of the area's poorest, with the 'charity shown not only to Protestants'. The French paper asked if Frederick was going to carry on with the good work done by his mother. The British paper had concluded, sarcastically: 'La Colonne is not a satirical journal.'

Rowland Hughes: Agnes' last love, a shared interest in music helping to bind them together and for Agnes to recover from her disastrous second marriage. *(Helen Denney)*

The Argus' 1883 report had mentioned that Walker himself was still 'touring in Australia' - clearly, Agnes' 1880 fears had not come to fruition - and the carefully-supervised 18-year-old Frederick (described as the 'wandering heir') was visiting India and China. Agreeable though it was to Agnes, the relationship with Hughes did not find favour with Frederick's guardians. The-now Lord Kinnaird, a guardian of Frederick as well as estate rents receiver, forced Agnes to agree to a Court of Chancery order on 1 August 1878 which made her 'undertake not to visit Eton [where Frederick was at school] or the neighbourhood thereof, nor to go into the county of Norfolk nor to have any personal communication with, or make any attempt to see, the infant Frederick Howe Windham without the consent of his Guardians or the consent of the court'.

Their reasoning behind such a draconian order has unfortunately not survived, but we do know that another order was made on 9 August 1879 to restrain Hughes from associating with the heir of Hanworth. Hughes continued to do so and was taken to court again on 23 November 1883. He only avoided jail for contempt of court by undertaking not to communicate with the 19-year-old Frederick, who was now at Magdalene College, Cambridge.

But in the High Court of Justice, Chancery Division in November 1884, Lord Kinnaird once again applied for Hughes to be committed for breaching the order. Far from avoiding Windham, he had in fact been with Agnes and her son in France from February to August of that year, later shooting with Windham in Dorset on a trip which the young heir had paid for.

By now Windham was living in London (with all its attendant temptations), but Lord Kinnaird insisted he wanted him to be at Hanworth, where it was felt a closer watch could be kept on him. Hughes' QC apologised, but Vice Chancellor Bacon said it was a matter of 'great importance', and an order was made to commit Hughes and order him to pay costs. Exactly what the nature of Hughes' unwelcome influence on Windham was not made clear, but from the hint given about the shooting party, perhaps it was felt that he was proving an unacceptable drain on the estate.

IN CONTRAST to his father's coming-of-age, which had been marked by an utter lack of celebration, Frederick's, on 20 April 1885, was an elaborate affair. The Norfolk News of five days later reported the event extensively: 'The home-coming of Mr Windham on Monday last was the occasion of great rejoicing'. It was all meticulously planned, even the fickle April weather behaving itself and delivering up a 'very fine' day. Nothing had been left to chance: the entrance to the park had been specially decorated with two arches, one reading 'WELCOME HOME', the other 'WELCOME TO OUR SQUIRE AND BENEFACTRESS'.

Young couple: Frederick and Catherine pictured at Gloucester. *(Helen Denney)*

The drive was adorned with Venetian masks and flags on either side, with the Union flag flying over the church and hall. Windham arrived at Aylsham station at precisely 2.15pm, to 'hearty cheers' from the assembled crowd, and he was met by his four oldest tenants. When his carriage arrived at the hall, the church bells rang out, which was the signal for the Band of North Walsham Volunteers, 'led by Mr Pigg', to strike up a lively tune on the hall lawn. When the carriage drew on to the drive way, it was stopped by the cottagers, who unhitched the horses and pulled the carriage themselves the rest of the way, with children scattering flowers in its path.

Frederick sat down to a celebration dinner with toast after toast proposed, seconded and drunk heartily. He made a short speech thanking everyone for the 'splendid time' he had had and saying he hoped 'he would shortly be able to become better known to them than he had been in the past'. Agnes, who was not mentioned in the Norfolk News report, must have looked on approvingly.

Even the once-churlish Norwich Argus had now, at last, finally softened its attitude. Its report of 23 April said: 'The Hanworth coming-of-age celebration Monday last seems to have been an exceedingly gay and festive affair....[his] family history has been a chequered one but let us hope the troubles of the old house of Windham are over now, and its lot is to be bright and happy.'

One of the young squire's first acts was to ensure his mother's financial security. Young Frederick gave his mother an annuity of £1,000 from April 1885 onwards, to be paid in three instalments, in October, June and April each year. Soon he had other financial commitments to think about: in June 1886 he married 21-year-old Katherine Eveleigh Batt, from Abergavenny in South Wales.

IF ALL this suggests that Frederick was about to settle down to a life of uneventful domestic rectitude, Fate - as so often in the Windham story - had other ideas. For, in an echo of the hedonistic excesses of his father, young Frederick found himself in court in early November. Like his father, it was a case which attracted a striking headline: 'Baccarat scandal'. It was a hearing which anticipated a much more sensational case from a few years later, one which was to embroil the Prince of Wales.

At the root of both scandals was the same allegation: cheating at cards. The Norwich Mercury - conduit of so much Windham family news over the decades - joined with several other provincial papers in giving the circumstances. It concerned an allegation for slander, and a demand for £1,000 in damages, made against Frederick by an army officer, Harold Alexander. The facts were these: in January 1885 Frederick had been introduced to the 'low London gambling club' known as the Road. Frederick had turned up one evening to take part in games of baccarat.

Soon he found himself playing against Alexander, who rapidly relieved Frederick of the '£20 or £30 in cash' he had in his pockets. Fatefully, Windham then began to sign IOU after IOU, eventually running up the enormous sum of £550. It was what happened next which was the cause of the court case. Frederick claimed he had seen Alexander palming a card, and so accused him of cheating. When the army officer had left the club, the young Norfolk heir quietly repeated his suspicions to several club members. For his part, Alexander told the court, it was a simple case of Windham being a bad loser - he was 'huffed', he said, at his refusal to play one more 'double or quits' game.

Who was telling the truth? The jury members could not decide. And so the case was adjourned, never to be resumed. Frederick had told the court that he had refused to pay the debt and in the absence of a verdict against him it must be assumed that the £20 or £30 in cash was the extent of his actual losses. One of the questions which had been raised at the hearing was why Frederick's complaints about being cheated had not been made more prominently. Alexander took this as evidence of Windham being a liar. But Frederick had another explanation: he had not made more of a fuss because, he told the court, 'he didn't want to get in trouble with his guardian'.

The ultimate truth behind what the judge called 'this low and dirty transaction' was never to be discovered. But, naturally, another story had been added to the Windham legend.

FREDERICK - who did not have children of his own - joined Agnes in being extremely supportive of his ten Denney cousins, never more so than when Henry Denney died in 1890 and Emma found herself obliged to leave their tied cottage in North Norfolk. Agnes paid for the family's move to Birdham in West Sussex, and also undertook to educate three of Emma's children in France. Frederick, for his part, helped out considerably with the costs involved when most of the children decided to move to Canada to seek a better life.

The date of George Walker's death and her remarriage remains elusive. There are no probate records listed, for example, for Walker's estate, which suggests that he may never have made the threatened return from Australia. There is another clue, from an unexpected source: her burial plot. She bought the plot, in the vast Kensal

Frederick Windham: An interest in country sports was matched in 1885 by a costly introduction to the gambling game known as baccarat. *(Helen Denney)*

Green Cemetery in London, in January 1883, when living at St Andrew's Hall, Regent's Park. Her name is given as 'Mrs Agnes Windham' on the deed of sale for the plot, even though it is clear from that February 1883 newspaper report that Walker was neither dead not divorced from her.

Where and when she married Rowland John Hughes (or, indeed, the possibility must be considered, if she ever legally married him) is equally hard to find, but the fact remains that he proved to be the most abiding of Agnes' loves - whatever the tenth Lord Kinnaird of Inchture might have thought of him.

Still elegant: From the family archives, two undated views of Agnes showing her flair for fashion and sense of style had not changed over the years. The left-hand picture was taken in Brighton, the right-hand picture at Boulogne. *(Helen Denney)*

THE WIDESPREAD agricultural depression which began in the 1870s affected the Hanworth estate as it did everywhere else. Cheap grain imports, poor harvests, the spread of cattle plague and other factors combined to depress Norfolk agriculture to such an extent that rental incomes plunged by up to a half. The solution for many local landowners, such as the Rolfes of Heacham (of Pocahontas fame) - and Frederick - was to let their property and live more cheaply abroad. Agnes, who ultimately relied for her income on the Hanworth rents as much as her son, was already living in France for much of the year by choice. Her son and his wife moved west instead. In the early 1890s Frederick and Katherine took out a lease on the Castle in the small Irish town of Castlerea, in Co. Roscommon. The town, the seat of Lord Mount-Sandford, was known for its distillery and little else, but it was the excellent shooting and fishing which attracted Frederick. Like his father, Frederick was a lover of all country sports but - unlike his father - his prowess was considerable.

The Windhams proved popular residents, playing an active part in town life, helping with a wide range of charities and - the Roscommon Herald reported with particular approval - the building costs of the town's new church, despite their being 'of the opposite creed'. In fact, Frederick's open-handed and open-hearted approach won him many friends across all shades of opinion and religion.

While living in Ireland, Frederick's allowance to his mother began to become sporadic fromaround 1894. From that date until early in 1896 Agnes - whose home was now at Gipsy Hill in South London - was due to have been paid £2,250, but from the start of 1895 the money was passed to Agnes in the form of a series of infrequent cheques, with sums ranging from £100 to just £5 4s.

BY 1895 thoughts of mortality had come to the forefront for Agnes. On 9 July she made her will, her decision to do so perhaps being coloured by her sister Thirza's failing health (she was to die in October that year). A few months later Agnes herself began to fade. Her husband Rowland penned a poignant farewell poem ('Goodbye') in a family commonplace book on 2 February. It is eloquent testimony to the depth of their love:

Goodbye! No words have I to wish thee well

No smile to speed thee on thy way, dear heart,

One kiss, one glance, my love and pain to tell, and so we part;

We part, and all the glad past fades and dies;

We part while yet the summer days are old

And other hearts will throb with passion's sighs, and lips will meet

But thou and I shall meet no more, no more.

Tho' woods and fields are lovely as of old

For us, love's golden summer is o'er -

Love's tale is told.

Good bye - oh, saddest words the lips may frame!

Good bye - oh, harshest fate the heart can know

For I do love thee darling still

The same come weal or woe!

No bright 'Good speed' have I to gladden thee

Mine eyes' tear wet yet make thee fond reply

My heart, dear love is crying bitterly, Good bye.

On 25 March Agnes died at Chalet Beau Sejour in Malo-les-Bains in northern France. The resort was then a couple of miles east of Dunkirk, although it has since been absorbed into the town, its surviving Art Nouveau villas along the promenade belying its bloody place in world history 44 years later. Had Hughes taken a dying Agnes to her beloved France for one last stay? We cannot say. Nor is it possible to identify the cause of death, as Agnes' death certificate, being an overseas notification via a consul, was limited to the fact of her passing. The nature of her last illness, like so many other secrets, she took with her to the grave.

Although she was only mistress of Felbrigg for a few months, it was clear that it marked the pinnacle of her life. That is why Rowland made sure her death notice included the phrase 'wife of Mr R J Hughes and widow of William F Windham of Fellbrigg (sic) Hall, Norfolk'. Walker was left out of the story. She was buried at Kensal Green six days later, joining such famous names as Wilkie Collins, Anthony Trollope and William Makepeace Thackeray and thousands of other Victorians in the 75-acre site, including, ironically, Sir Cresswell Cresswell, the disapproving judge who had heard the abortive Windham vs Windham and Giuglini divorce petition all those years before.

The plot also contains her mother Ann Burden (who died in January 1885) and her younger sister Thirza, who had reverted to her maiden name of Rogers. Agnes is buried close to a cross-section of the respectable middle (and upper-middle) classes: vicar's wives, Royal Navy captains, an envoy plenipotentiary of Her Majesty's Diplomatic Service, and General Richard Albert Bayly. The general has a handsome mausoleum but Agnes' memorial is altogether plainer, a simple though large black slab which is also inscribed to her mother and sister.

Agnes' inscription reads:

AGNES ANN HUGHES,
wife of R J Hughes
widow of William Frederick Windham of Felbrigg Hall, Norfolk
who died March 25th 1896 aged 56 [actually she was 55]
'Now we see through a glass darkly, but then face to face'

Her monument has fared better than some of the surrounding memorials. Only a small trail of ivy is beginning to creep over its corner, and the lichen and moss has yet to take a grip, even after the passage of more than a century. Around the grave is a smell of wild garlic, pungent even on a damp November day, while above, far more gaudy and exotic than her memorial, comes the discordant call and the occasionally-glimpsed green flashes of the wings of the cemetery's rose-ringed parakeets.

AGNES' FINANCIAL affairs were quickly dealt with, and within a month probate had been granted to her solicitor. Her estate totalled precisely £5,602 11s 7d. Her will is a long and detailed document, although not without some curious mistakes ('my sisters Mrs Denny (sic) and Emma Rogers' - one and the same person). It also made reference to her half-sister, Mrs Spencer, and made bequests to all her nieces and

WAIT FOR

ALSO OF

AGNES ANNE HUGHES,

WIFE OF R.J.HUGHES,

WIDOW OF W.F.WINDHAM,

OF FELBRICC HALL, NORFOLK,

WHO DIED 25TH MARCH 1896,

AGED 56 YEARS.

At rest: Agnes' grave in Kensal Green Cemetery, London, also contains the remains of her sister Thirza and their mother Ann.

nephews, underscoring yet again that there was nothing false about her love for her family. She directed 'my jewellery, plate, furs and lace' be sold at Christie's,with the proceeds paying off the bill of sale for the Gipsy Hill property. As for her famed jewellery there were bequests of a small diamond crescent brooch, diamond and sapphire ring and horseshoe-shaped diamond and sapphire brooch to various nieces - the 'Windham jewels' having long since been appropriated by George Walker. There were two more unusual bequests: £50 for a drinking fountain in Boulogne 'for wayfarers and cattle' in her memory - and the donation of all of Frederick's baby clothing to Madame Tussaud's.

Perhaps the most curious aspect of the will was not what was in it, but what was not. Nowhere was there any mention of a legacy to her son, or even a keepsake. Was the sudden infrequency of Frederick's allowance to his mother a result of this apparent estrangement - or its cause?

AGNES' Hanworth dynasty was destined to last only five more months. On 12 September, Frederick died suddenly at Gower House in Brighton Road in what is now the south London borough of Sutton. He had travelled from Ireland to visit his friends the Abrahams for some autumn shooting. He appeared to be 'in good health' when he left Ireland, but in fact he had been suffering from a severe illness since early 1894.

In contrast with his father's burial, Frederick's was an elaborate affair which gave ample evidence of his popularity in the area. The Cromer and North Walsham Post of 26 September summed it up thus: 'The large assembly gathered at the [Hanworth churchyard] graveside testified to the esteem and respect in which the deceased was held by his tenantry and others in the district.'

There was no room in the church for all the mourners, which were led by his widow Katherine and which included Samuel Hoare MP, representatives of leading local families, tenantry, estate workers and a representative of the Royal Irish Constabulary of Castlerea. The residents of the Irish town, too, were genuinely moved by Frederick's death: its court sessions were adjourned out of respect, and both the Roscommon Journal and Western Reporter and Roscommon Herald paid fulsome tribute.

In its report of the funeral, the Eastern Daily Press included another poignant observation, which once again highlighted the sharp contrasts in the funerals of father and son: 'The tear-stained faces of many of the villagers when the coffin arrived testified to their kindly remembrance of the "young squire" whose boyhood and youth had been spent among them and whose career had so prematurely been cut short.' And the Norwich Mercury added one final detail: 'The funeral car was drawn by four well-matched and magnificent black horses with well-appointed four-horse broughams'. Agnes, the pretty horsebreaker, would only have approved.

In their fulsome tributes none of the papers reported Frederick's involvement in a baccarat scandal. But there was something else they did not report on either: the cause of his death. For a young and active man of just 32 to die suddenly would seem to demand an explanation. And yet all of the papers, though reporting his funeral in full, kept a curious and discreet silence on this. His death certificate provides the reason: he had been suffering from a condition known as locomotor ataxia, now more commonly referred to as tabes dorsalis. The condition, affecting the spinal cord, causes progressive unsteadiness and lack of co-ordination, accompanied by sudden intense pain and stomach agonies, and would have been obvious to close family and friends. In the end it was vomiting and exhaustion which finally proved too much for him.

There was a terrible irony at work here: while Frederick had inherited his mother's blonde hair and open-hearted disposition, he had apparently something else in common, something terrible, with his father. For tabes dorsalis is a condition most commonly associated with the final emergence of latent syphilis, incurable before the development of penicillin G. One can only wonder how many other sons of landed estates have succumbed to similar, carefully unreported, causes over the years.

IT WAS not quite the end of the story. As befitting a son of the perpetually-litigant William Frederick Windham, the future of his estate - assessed at £10,756 in 1897 - was soon beset with legal claim and counter-claim. Among the complications was a bill for £312 from Frederick's estate by Agnes' executors. In 1898 speculation arose, and was just as quickly denied, that the Prince and Princess of Wales were interested in the estate as their second Norfolk home - testament to its attractiveness.

On 10 July 1900 Hanworth was offered, on the instructions of the Royal Court of Justice, at the Mart, Tokenhouse Yard, London - a well-known venue for the auctioning of fine property. It was described as an estate of almost 6,000 acres (four times its 1854 size), with the shooting 'among the best in the Eastern counties'. The rents were now down to £5,400 per annum, but that was offset by the excellent shooting bringing in £6,550.

'The estate is well-timbered, pleasing in contour, and is bounded and intersected by capital hard roads,' the auction particulars continued. In short, it concluded, it was the finest country estate to be offered for sale that year. But despite this effusive praise the property failed to reach its reserve. After a speculatively low bid of £40,000, the bidding rose to £116,000, but that did not reach their lordships' reserve price. Eventually, however, the estate was sold off, and ultimately passed into new hands. New owners the Barclays - of banking dynasty fame - were another of Norfolk's most famous families. Other branches of the Windham family were to survive - but the Windhams of Felbrigg, and then of Hanworth, had finally succumbed to history, within touching distance of a new century.

SO, in the end, what are we to make of Agnes? Our glimpses of her are coloured by being filtered through a sometimes astonishingly vituperative press. We have little in her own words - a published letter, some evidence in court cases, the speech at her son's homecoming. There was another letter, to be found in the Norfolk Record Office, but that is no longer available. But even through this filter of disapproval we can start to build a picture of her.

The widely-reported claims by Agnes (often with undisguised derision) that she wanted a generous settlement to provide for her sisters turned out to have been exactly that, with Agnes funding a good education and unstinting support for her extended family. Her unswerving and oft-demonstrated affection for her family is surely deserving of sympathy. Her determination to do the best for her son, even at the cost of enduring an unhappy and at times brutal second marriage is further proof. There are, naturally, many unanswered questions about Agnes. Paradoxes too: the quest for financial security matched with extravagant spending, the long list of admirers coupled with the decision to marry the unprepossessing Windham. Agnes wanted to lead as much of a respectable life as possible - and succeeded. For further confirmation one need look no further than the evidence of her own family: until 1951, when the writer Donald MacAndrew tracked down three surviving nieces of Agnes, the family insisted they were unaware of her racy past.

At the time of the Windham case, Agnes was branded a 'dissolute prostitute' by the press, but not by her admirers. To them she was an adornment, a trophy lover to show off at the races, at the opera or in her carriage. From Windham she received thousands of pounds of jewellery and a famous name. But he also brought her a torrent of moral revulsion from the nation's press and public humiliation. Above all else, to this writer at least, Agnes seems born out of her time. What would a 21st-century media have made of her? Condemned her - or fêted her?

Where Agnes had once helped set the fashion for the fashionable horse-breakers and worn the latest (and often absurdly impractical) crinolines, in the week of her death the papers were trumpeting the latest Cycling Dress (no bloomers required) - a 'perfect fit, perfect style, perfect comfort'. Where the columns of the papers had been full of tales of new-fangled ironclads, the bravery of Garibaldi and the American Civil War, now it was war in Rhodesia, a Fenian plot against the Czar, and the escape of Dreyfus from Devil's Isle. Dr Richat of Toulon had invented a machine which he was confident would fly, and Nikolai Tesla was telling anyone who would listen that electric waves would be able to travel between the planets.

And through all this change Agnes had lived and loved, a passionate woman - and a remarkable one.

Epilogue

FELBRIGG HALL survives and thrives thanks to the efforts of the remarkable Robert Wyndham Ketton-Cremer (1906-69), the acme of a thoroughly decent Norfolk landowner, who laboured long and hard to revive the fortunes of house and estate. When he died, with no heirs, he bequeathed the house to the National Trust on condition that nothing was to be taken away, and nothing added. And as Felbrigg Hall had passed into the hands of Ketton-Cremer's ancestors in almost exactly the same condition Windham had left it, and since the Trust has painstakingly carried out his conditions to the letter, what is left today is a living reminder of the follies - and wisdom - of two very different landowners.

It is a warm spring day when I visit. Sunglassed visitors sit in the courtyard of the carriage house in shirtsleeves, enjoying the first al fresco ice cream of the year to the soundtrack of a clattering of teacups. Inside, the quiet of the house is disturbed only by snatches of conversation, occasional footsteps and the heartbeat tick of its clocks.

It is not hard to picture the scene in the 1840s and 1850s, when it was oil-lit, gloomy and forbidding. No wonder the young Windham crept downstairs and to the kitchen for the company of the servants as often as he could. Here was bustle, warmth, noise, chatter, cooking smells, life; gleaming coppers to hover round and interesting cupboards to explore, a long stone-flagged corridor warmed by the sunshine flooding in through its south-facing windows.

Although the long shadows of his ancestors dominate what the visitor can see of Felbrigg, echoes of Agnes and William can still be found for those who seek them out. In the Morning Hall, looking back above the entrance doorway, there is an early 1840s portrait of young Windham, dressed in blue, with the conventional props of childhood - a playful puppy and a discarded toy. And flanking the fireplace, still watching over him, are two portraits of his father, bewhiskered and decisive, and one of his mother, demure, elegant-fingered, dressed in black velvet with a delicate red shawl over her shoulders.

Charles Ashe Windham, 'the General', is on display too. The Crimean War hero stares out of the foreground of a print in one of the corridors. It is an imagined panorama of the Crimea, in which the great and the good prance about on their steeds or confer in huddles, and there, in the left foreground, stands the General: bald, bearded, stout-hearted and decisive-looking. A man of purpose; a man of action. And, irony of ironies, alongside these reminders of the General is a portrait of Agnes, donated by her family.

And there is another reminder of her which is always on display. Not in the house, but a few hundred yards to the south-east in St Margaret's Church. There, high on a wall, is Agnes' parting shot to the family, a memorial to William Frederick Windham - 'by his affectionate wife Ann Agnes Windham'. Her amusement at the regular harrumphing of churchgoers as they glanced up at the lettering can only be imagined. It is her last trump card: a memorial to her husband in the ancient estate church which also, brilliantly, serves as a memorial to herself. Agnes had flitted across the pages of the Felbrigg story for only the length of time it took a gaudy butterfly to do so; she had left behind a permanent reminder of herself.

As I leave the church, glancing over at the old frontage of Felbrigg and making the short walk back to the car park, two thoughts come into my mind: a strange and lonely little boy dressed in blue running through the corridors of the house in search of companions. And a poor country girl whose eye-catching hair, figure, and steely determination allowed her to leapfrog class and convention to become, albeit briefly, the mistress of 10,000 English acres, and die as she wanted to be: utterly respectable, and no longer the notorious Miss Willoughby.

Sources and Bibliography

Original sources
Norfolk Record Office contains the 36 volumes of the official transcripts of the Commission de Lunatico Inquirendo into William Frederick Windham. The papers (WKC 4/29/1-43, 464) also contain seven volumes of transcripts of the subsequent appeal. Each contains up to 200 pages of immaculate copperplate, the slight differences in hand testifying to the use of a team of shorthand

Archive: Some of the 43 volumes of court transcripts relating to the Windham case which are in Norfolk Record Office.

writers to record the hundreds of thousands of words of evidence. I have used the 1862 account of the hearing, An Inquiry Into The State of Mind of W F Windham (W Oliver) extensively, with the original trial transcripts used to correct mishearings and amplify printed statements.

Among the other items held by the NRO is Windham family solicitor Peter Hansell's notebook about the case containing original letters and photographs, as well as newspaper and magazine cuttings about the case and its aftermath

(MC580/2/1,780X1). Records of the Court of Chancery (1857 W 164) and Her Majesty's Court for Divorce and Matrimonial Causes (518/128) in The National Archives have also proved invaluable.

Newspapers and Magazines
Accounts of the hearing, editorial comments, and reports of Agnes' and William F Windham's lives in the Belfast News Letter, The Cromer and North Walsham Post, Daily News, Daily Telegraph, Eastern Daily Press, Evening Standard, Freeman's Journal and Daily Commercial Advertiser (Dublin), The Leader, Lloyd's Weekly London Newspaper, The Morning Chronicle, Newcastle Courant, The Newfoundlander, News of the World, Reynold's Weekly News, The Times, Norfolk Chronicle, Norfolk Journal, Norfolk News, Norwich Argus, Norwich Mercury, various dates, The Penny Illustrated Paper, Punch, or The London Charivari (Vols XL, XLI, XLII); Suffolk Chronicle and Tomahawk, plus background material in The Economist and BBC History Magazine, Vol 2, No 1, 2001.

Books
Anderson, P, When Passion Reigned: Sex and the Victorians, BasicBooks, 1995
Armstrong, the Rev B J, A Norfolk Diary, Harrap, 1949
Armstrong, the Rev BJ (ed C Armstrong), Under The Parson's Nose, Larks Press 2012
Bailey, P, Popular Culture and Performance in the Victorian City, Cambridge UP, 1998
Barham, the Rev R. Harris, The Ingoldsby Legends, Richard Bently, 1847
Bédarida, F, A Social History of England 1851-1990, Routledge, 1991
Best, G, Mid-Victorian Britain 1851-75, Weidenfeld and Nicholson, 1971
Blyth, H, The Pocket Venus: A Victorian Scandal, Weidenfeld and Nicholson, 1966
Blyth, H, Skittles: The Last Victorian Courtesan, Rupert Hart-Davis, 1972
Buxton, M, Ladies of the Chase, The Sportman's Press, 1987
Collins, W, The Woman in White, 1860
Crow, D, The Victorian Woman, George Allen and Unwin, 1971
Denney, H, The Long Road: Pages of the Denney History, private family publication
De-la-Noy, M, The House of Hervey, Constable, 2001
Donaldson, W, Brewer's Rogues, Villains and Eccentrics, Cassell, 2002
Dymond, D, The Norfolk Landscape, The Alastair Press, 1990
Ellis, S M, ed, A Mid-Victorian Pepys - Letters and Memories of Sir William Hardman, Cecil Palmer, 1923
Frazier, M S and Drzymkowski, J W, Essentials of Human Diseases and Conditions, Saunders Elsevier, 2009

Gordon, D I, A Regional History of the Railways of Great Britain: The Eastern Counties, David and Charles, 1977

Hamilton, E, The Warwickshire Scandal, Michael Russell, 1999

Hayden, D, Pox: Genius, Madness, and the Mysteries of Syphilis, Basic, 2003

Hayward, W S (attributed), Agnes Willoughby: A Tale of Love, Marriage and Adventure, 1864

Hibbert, C, The English: A Social History 1066-1945, Grafton, 1987

Hickman, K, Courtesans, HarperCollins, 2003

Himmelfarb, G, Marriage and Morals Among The Victorians, Faber and Faber, 1986

Hoppen Theodore, K, The Mid-Victorian Generation 1846-1866, Oxford, 1998

Itzkowitz, D C, Peculiar Privilege: A Social History of English Foxhunting, 1753-1885, Harvester, 1977

Kelly's Directory of Cambridgeshire, Norfolk and Suffolk, 1892

Ketton-Cremer, R W, Felbrigg: The Story of a House, Rupert Hart-Davis, 1962

MacAndrew, D, Mr and Mrs Windham, from The Saturday Book 11, ed Russell L, Hutchinson, 1951

Maddison, J, Felbrigg Hall, The National Trust, 1995

Mansfield, H O, Charles Ashe Windham: A Norfolk Soldier (1810-1870), Terence Dalton, 1973

Mapleson, J H, The Mapleson Memoirs, Belford, Clarke and Co, 1888

Mason, M, The Making of Victorian Sexuality, OUP, 1994

Mills, A R, Two Victorian Ladies, Frederick Muller, 1969

Mingay, G E, Rural Life in Victorian England, Heinemann, 1977

Mortlock, D P, and Roberts, C V, A Popular Guide to Norfolk Churches, Acorn, 1981

Pearsall, R, Collapse of Stout Party, Weidenfeld and Nicholson, 1975

Pearsall, R, Public Purity, Private Shame, Weidenfeld and Nicholson, 1976

Pevsner N, and Wilson, B, The Buildings of England: Norfolk, Penguin, 1962 and 1992

Picard, L, Victorian London: The Life of a City 1840-1870, Weidenfeld and Nicholson, 2005

Porter, R, Madness: A Brief History, OUP, 2002

Royston Pike, E, Human Documents of the Victorian Golden Age, Allen and Unwin, 1967

Salzman, L F, ed, A History of the County of Warwickshire, Vol 5, Victoria County History, 1949

Saunders, H St G, Westminster Hall, Michael Joseph, 1951

Sichel, M, The Victorians, Batsford, 1978

Spence, J, Victorian and Edwardian Railway Travel, Batsford, 1971
Strachey, N, Ickworth, The National Trust, 1998-2005
Thompson, F M L, The Rise of Respectable Society, Fontana, 1988
Trudgill, Prof P, The Norfolk Dialect, Poppyland, 2003
Various, Oxford Dictionary of National Biography, Oxford University Press, 2008
Wade Martins, Dr S, Norfolk Origins: Changing Agriculture in Georgian and Victorian Norfolk, Poppyland, 2002
Walvin, J, Victorian Values, André Deutsch, 1987
Ward, S, et al, Seasons of Change: Rural Life in Victorian and Edwardian England, George Allen, 1982
Waterson, M, A Noble Thing: The National Trust and Its Benefactors, Scala, 2011
White, J, London in the Nineteenth Century, Random House, 2007
Wilson, A N, The Victorians, Hutchinson, 2002
Wilson, F M, Strange Island, Longmans, Green and Co, 1955